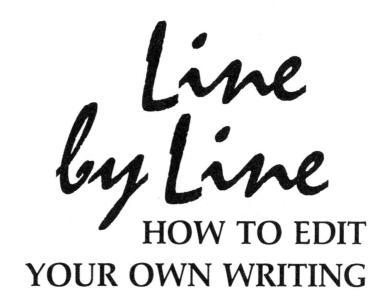

HOW TO EDIT
YOUR OWN WRITING

Claire Kehrwald Cook

Houghton Mifflin Company □ Boston

Requests for permission should be addressed in writing to
    Houghton Mifflin Company
    One Beacon Street
    Boston, MA 02108

Indexed by Philip James

Library of Congress Cataloging in Publication Data

Cook, Claire Kehrwald.
  The MLA's Line by line.

  Bibliography: p.
  Includes index.
  1. English language—Sentences. 2. Copy-reading.
I. Modern Language Association of America. II. Title.
III. Title: Line by line.
PE1441.C66 1985   808'.042   85-8346
ISBN 0-395-38944-5
ISBN 0-395-39391-4 (pbk.)

Manufactured in the United States of America

Contents

Preface

ike most copy editors, those of us who style manuscripts
for the Modern Language Association have had our share
of appreciative authors, and not uncommonly they claim
that we have taught them something. "I enjoyed being
edited by you," one said. "I hadn't learned anything about my writing
for years, but this year I did." Another said, "I feel I learned a bit
about good prose from comparing the original and improved versions
of certain sentences and I appreciate the pedagogic value of the process." Remarks like these ultimately led to this book, but at first they
puzzled us. In editing, we apply principles spelled out in many style
manuals—principles that our erudite authors, especially the English
teachers among them, would be likely to know. Even Homer can nod,
of course, and writers preoccupied with content naturally lack an
editor's focus of attention. Some of them, pressed for time, may even
rely on editors to smooth out the rough spots. But why had these
authors learned from us?

In discussing that question at lunch one day, my colleagues and I
came to realize what should have been obvious all along, that a
knowledge of principles does not necessarily confer the ability to put
them into practice. We began to see that our approach to sentence
repair involves specialized techniques that writers could profitably
train themselves to use. In revising their own writing, they would
have advantages denied the copy editor—an awareness of their aims
and the freedom to make substantive corrections. If professors of

literature had found our methods instructive, we reasoned, writers in fields less directly concerned with language stood to benefit even more. And so we conceived the notion of this book, a book that would show writers how to edit their own work. Its execution eventually fell to me.

In some seventeen years of editing, at the MLA and elsewhere, I have worked on a wide variety of manuscripts—not only scholarly essays, professional articles, reference guides, and research summaries but also press releases and promotional material, business articles, technical manuals, trade books, and textbooks in such diverse fields as mathematics, engineering, acting, broadcasting, and sociology. I have spent most of my working life rewriting writing, and some of it in training others to do so, and the techniques I describe here adapt to almost any sort of exposition. They should serve all writers, various creative authors aside, who care enough about their style to work at crafting clear, readable sentences—scholars and serious students, certainly, but also those in business, government, and the professions who have to prepare reports, proposals, or presentations. To anyone sufficiently motivated to polish a final draft this book offers ways and means.

Copy editors work line by line on finished manuscripts. They concern themselves with correcting sentences already written. Thus this guide deals not at all with the earlier and broader aspects of composition, such as gathering, ordering, and developing ideas or using examples and setting the tone. It focuses on eliminating the stylistic faults that most often impede reading and obscure meaning. These errors fall into five categories, corresponding to the chapters of this book: (1) needless words, (2) words in the wrong order, (3) equivalent but unbalanced sentence elements, (4) imprecise relations between subjects and verbs and between pronouns and antecedents, and (5) inappropriate punctuation. Punctuation merits inclusion here because it affects the clarity of sentences, but the other mechanics of writing—spelling, capitalization, abbreviations, and so on—lie outside the scope of this guide. However much these details concern professional copy editors, they have little bearing on how sentences work.

Two appendixes supplement the text. The first describes the parts of a sentence and the ways they fit together—the fundamentals of syntax. Those who have only an uneasy grasp of grammar should find this review helpful in following the explanations in the various chapters. Although I discuss grammar in the traditional terms that I am most comfortable with and that are still likely to be the most widely known, I do not mean to oppose or dismiss the newer systems. They simply seem less pertinent to my purpose.

The second appendix presents a glossary of questionable usage. While the dubious constructions it cites are only peripherally detrimental to good prose, writers who care enough about their work to do their own editing will probably want to avoid wording likely to provoke criticism. The concept of "correct English" is controversial, but no one denies the interest in the subject or the prevalence of language watchers ready to pounce on what they consider improprieties. Such flaws stand out like red flags to copy editors committed to upholding conventional standards. Violations can distract discriminating readers from a writer's ideas and may even diminish the writer's authority.

Editors apply their knowledge of syntax and disputed usage in routinely examining sentences for imperfections and making the required adjustments. Automatically checking for stylistic faults is what this book is all about. It is also, I understand, what some computer programs are all about. Colorado State University, for example, has been using such a program in English composition courses. Students type their themes into a word processor, which identifies various kinds of errors, and if they press the SUGGEST button, it offers possible remedies. This program obviously has a lot in common with a copy editor.

Although not many students, so far, have worked with these teaching aids, initial results indicate that those who have had this opportunity do better than control groups restricted to conventional instruction. Unquestionably the program owes its success in part to its one-on-one guidance. Students learn better by seeing their own mistakes highlighted than by doing textbook exercises that may or may not reflect the kinds of errors they are likely to make—just as authors who know the principles of good writing nonetheless learn from reviewing their copy-edited manuscripts. It's hard for writers to apply objective standards to their own work, especially when they are concerned with much more than style. The computer program or the copy editor makes the application for them.

Computerized teaching seems so promising that I naturally wondered whether this book would be obsolete before it got into print. From the practical point of view, of course, the day when every writer has the services of copy-editing software still seems far off. Moreover, impressive as the new word processors are, they must be less efficient than human beings who have absorbed more sophisticated programs. What this book tries to do is to program you to edit sentences, to train you to process your own words. Without buttons and display screens, without any cumbersome and expensive paraphernalia, and with far less chance of going "down," you can instantly react to flabby sentences, dangling modifiers, unbalanced constructions, and errors in subject-verb agreement.

And like a computer, even better than a computer, you will know how to go about eliminating the errors you detect. Neither you nor a computer, however, can be programmed to select the best remedy automatically. The choice here remains a matter of individual judgment based on your objectives and the context in which the error occurs. Thus far at least, there is no mechanized way to take context into account. If, for example, you discover *however* in consecutive sentences, you first have to decide which occurrence to eliminate. You can change one *however* to *but* or to *in contrast* or put the contrasting idea in an *even though* clause. What you do will depend on such considerations as the presence or absence of similar clauses nearby, the incidence of surrounding *buts*, and the structure of adjacent sentences. This book, like a computer's teaching program, can only suggest solutions. It presents revisions as possibilities and often offers alternatives.

Because the flawed sentences that serve as examples appear out of context, the discussions of possible solutions suffer somewhat from artificiality. The poor wording may seem perverse if a better version comes readily to mind, but considerations outside our view may have precluded what looks like the obvious revision. Isolating badly written sentences also compounds the difficulty of deciphering them. Several examples I chose were so muddy that I had to guess at the writers' intentions, and sometimes I could only infer the meaning from the context—a context impractical to reproduce. Thus some of the suggested revisions may appear to differ in sense from the examples. For our purposes, though, these apparent discrepancies do not greatly matter. Since we are concerned here with how writers can edit their own work, you should be looking at the examples as if you yourself had written them. Presumably you would know what you intended and could judge the validity of the changes you contemplate. Your revision might differ in nuance from your first version because you didn't initially succeed in saying precisely what you meant or because the slight change in meaning or emphasis makes no difference to you and permits a much improved sentence. Certainly as a copy editor I do not reword with the abandon I do here, and if I do suggest a major change, I ask the author's approval. But in the guise of a writer, I can obviously do as I please. And that, of course, is the guise you should assume in studying the examples and the revisions in this book.

Although I have copied most of the examples verbatim from printed or manuscript sources, I have doctored some to make them intelligible out of context. In these circumstances I have kept the structure that embodies the problem but changed the wording. I also admit to concocting a few examples of common errors when I grew frustrated in looking for suitable prototypes, but these, too, closely resemble real-life models. In the two appendixes, however, as well as in the Introduction and the chapter on punctuation, I have shamelessly fabricated illustrations to make my points as expeditiously as possible.

In likening this book to a computer program and stressing the semiautomatic aspects of revision, I do not mean to downplay the importance of the individual voice or to imply that edited manuscripts must sound as if they had been composed by machine. This book shows writers how to detect stylistic weaknesses and, without prescribing single remedies, suggests approaches to revision. It leaves ample room for choice and self-expression. Few, I think, would argue that their unique personal styles require leaving awkwardness and ambiguity intact. Those who know the rules but break them for deliberate effect are not the writers this book addresses.

Probably the best way to use this guide is to read through it first without attempting to study it—or even to argue with it along the way, since you may find objections answered later on. You will become familiar with the range of errors it covers and the editorial approach it advocates. If you are still shaky about some of the grammatical concepts, you should be comfortable with them by the time you finish and better equipped to benefit from the book when you take another look at it. You can then profitably return to the pertinent parts as the need arises.

When it comes to giving credit to those who have helped me with this book, I must begin by acknowledging my indebtedness to the authors of several style or usage guides: Jacques Barzun, Theodore M. Bernstein, Wilson Follett, H. W. Fowler, William Strunk, Jr., and E. B. White. When I mention these authors in the text, I am referring to the books that I list as primary references in the Selected Bibliography. These volumes are the most thumb-worn in my library, and the principles of style that I endorse are largely a distillation and synthesis of those they have taught me. In the ideological conflict between orthodox and permissive grammarians, all these authors clearly range on the side of the traditionalists, the side that it behooves an MLA copy editor to honor; but in the body of this book I have drawn on these writers not so much for their pronouncements on usage as for their advice on effective prose. In naming the books that have most influenced me, I am not necessarily recommending them over the competition. Readers who find no mention of their own favorite mentors should not take offense. The literature in this field is vast, and though I have sampled considerably more of it than my list of citations suggests, I am doubtless unfamiliar with many excellent contributions.

I am grateful, too, for the assistance of my family, my friends, and my colleagues at the MLA who furnished examples and acted as sounding boards for parts of the book during its preparation. Special thanks must go to Thomas Clayton and Walker Gibson, consultant readers for the MLA, who offered constructive advice on a preliminary draft; to Jenny Ruiz and her colleagues in secretarial services, who time and again converted heavily corrected manuscript pages into clean printouts; and to Walter Achtert, director of book publications and research programs at the MLA, who enthusiastically endorsed this project and brought it to the attention of Houghton Mifflin. But I am indebted most of all to Judy Goulding, the managing editor of MLA publications, for getting it under way. She and I planned the book as a joint endeavor, and though in the end the demands on her time prevented her from sharing in the writing, she cleared the way for me, freeing me from my ordinary responsibilities at no little inconvenience to herself. Moreover, she conferred with me at every stage, critically reviewed the entire manuscript, and contributed many useful suggestions. Her help and encouragement have been invaluable.

Finally, I wish to thank my collaborators at Houghton Mifflin not only for their skill and care in processing this book but for their unfailing consideration and tact in dealing with me. I must mention in particular Margery S. Berube, director of editorial operations, and Donna L. Muise, production assistant, who efficiently coordinated the editorial and production activities; editors Kaethe Ellis and David Jost, whose prodigious double-checking repeatedly saved me from myself; and Anne Soukhanov, senior editor, whose gracious and understanding support eased my transition from editor to author.

On Looking at Sentences

uthors whose writing has been professionally edited often marvel at the improvement, apparently regarding a blue pencil as some sort of magic wand. But those of us in the business of wielding that pencil know that most of the wonders we work are the routine adjustments of trained specialists. This book aims at demystifying the copy-editing process, at showing writers how to polish their own prose.

By the time a manuscript accepted for publication is ready for copy-editing, the consulting editor and the author have already attended to whatever major additions, deletions, rearrangements, or new approaches have seemed desirable. Charged with preparing the manuscript for conversion into print, the copy editor, sometimes called a line editor or subeditor, concentrates on the fine points, styling "mechanics" and revising sentences that are unclear, imprecise, awkward, or grammatically incorrect.

The mechanics of style are matters of form, such considerations as spelling, capitalization, treatment of numbers and abbreviations, types of headings, and systems of citation. In a first close reading of the manuscript the copy editor focuses full attention on these routine details and brings them into line with house standards. In addition to specifying the dictionaries and other reference works to follow for mechanics, publishers have guidelines governing the choices where these authorities allow options—between, for example, *adviser* and *advisor, the Third World* and *the third world, two and a half* and 2¹/₂. The point here is not so much correctness as consistency. Arbitrary variations can be distracting, since they would seem to indicate distinctions where none are intended. Even if house style does not prescribe one of two acceptable alternatives, the copy editor does not allow both to appear indiscriminately but settles on whichever predominates in the manuscript. Conscientious writers, especially if they do not expect the services of copy editors, should similarly verify questionable forms and strive for consistency, but they need no special knowledge to emulate editors in this respect.

Styling mechanics is a painstaking process that leaves little room for paying attention to entire sentences, no less to the argument of the text. Unless you blot out every other consideration, you can glide right over errors and discrepancies. Ideally, therefore, the copy editor devotes a separate close reading—or several readings if time allows—to removing any obstacles to the clarity and grace of sentences. With mechanics out of the way, the editor checks sentences for common structural weaknesses and applies the remedies indicated. It is this procedure that the following chapters describe, for it is here that pumpkins turn into coaches.

Although you can profitably learn to apply editorial techniques to your own writing, you will not be working in quite the same way that copy editors do. You will not have to worry about the author's intentions and sensibilities or about publishing costs and schedules. Copy editors have to guard against distorting the author's meaning or introducing changes that seem arbitrary or inconsistent with the author's tone. Often they cannot do as much as they would like, either because the publisher's budget precludes taking the necessary time or because the author's attitude discourages tampering with the text. Deciding what to alter and what to leave alone, when to revise and when to suggest a revision, involves considerable tact and judgment, and queries and explanations require sensitive wording. In correcting your own work, you have a free hand. You don't need editorial delicacy and diplomacy. You only need editorial skills that will enable you to look objectively at what you have written. If you can master them, you can do more to improve your writing than anyone else can.

To use an editor's techniques, you need, first of all, an editor's knowledge of sentence structure. The line-by-line editor looks at each sentence analytically, seeing its components and inner workings, using grammatical concepts as a set of tools for detecting and eliminating flaws. If you simply recognize that a sentence sounds bad, you can't necessarily pinpoint and correct what's wrong. Like the driver who knows that the car won't start but has no idea what to look for under the dutifully raised hood, you can only fiddle with this and that in hit-or-miss fashion.

Thus any manual of sentence repair must begin by naming parts and their functions. However much composition instructors would like to avoid jargon, they almost always end up using specialized terminology in training students to look at sentences with an eye to revision. In _Errors and Expectations,_ a breakthrough text for teachers of basic writing, Mina P. Shaughnessy says that explanations of what ails particular sentences "inevitably involve grammatical as well as semantic concepts and are much easier to give if the student has some knowledge of the parts and basic patterns of the sentence. . . . [A] rudimentary grasp of such grammatical concepts as subject, verb, object, indirect object, modifier, etc. is almost indispensable if _one intends to talk_ with students about their sentences."

This guide, of course, addresses writers far more sophisticated than the students in a remedial composition course, but many college graduates, including some English majors, claim not to know the language of grammar. If you are in this category, do not despair. The subject is much less forbidding than it may have seemed when you were a child, and even grammarphobes may readily learn as adults the battery of terms that made their eyes glaze over in junior high. Though the examples used throughout should clarify technical terms as you encounter them, you can profit most from the text if you start off knowing something about the anatomy of a sentence. Appendix A explains the parts of a sentence in considerable detail, and you may want to turn to it before you read the rest of the book. But this introduction, which provides a short preview of the appendix, may be all you need. Or it may be more than you need. If you're good at parsing sentences, you can stop right here and move on to chapter 1.

To look at a sentence analytically, you have to recognize (1) the units that fit together to compose the whole and (2) the types of words, called parts of speech, that make up the various units. Let's look first at the larger elements, the building blocks of the sentence.

A sentence is a group of words—or, occasionally, a single word—that readers recognize as a complete statement. The conventional type says that someone or something acts, experiences, or exists in a stated way (or did do so or will do so). Its two basic components are the subject, the someone or something, and the predicate, the statement about the subject's action, experience, or state of being.

The heart of the predicate, and sometimes the entire predicate, is the verb, a word that denotes mental or physical action or asserts existence and that can change in form to show the time of the action or existence as past, present, or future. Ordinarily, the subject comes first, as in _Children played, Glass breaks, Poltergeists exist._ It is the word or group of words that answers the question formed by putting _What_ or _Who_ before the verb. But though it governs the verb in the predicate, it does not necessarily dominate the sentence. Grammatically speaking, the subject of the sentence may not be the topic under discussion. If you say *I prefer vodka to gin*, the subject is *I*, but the subject matter is liquor.

Verb forms that consist of two or more words—for example, *were playing, will be broken*, and *have existed*—may be called verb phrases, since a phrase is any group of related words that functions as a unit but lacks a subject and a predicate. A clause, in contrast, is a group of related words that does contain a subject-verb combination. Not all clauses qualify as sentences. Though word groups like *while they were gone, after we had left, that you won*, and *as you believe* have subjects and predicates, they strike readers as incomplete. Unable to stand alone, these subordinate clauses must serve as adjuncts to independent clauses, which do seem complete in themselves.

A simple sentence contains only one clause. It is, of course, an independent clause, but that term comes into play only when sentences have more than one clause. Two or more attached independent clauses without a dependent clause make a compound sentence, and a single independent clause that incorporates at least one dependent clause constitutes a complex sentence. A compound-complex sentence, logically enough, has two or more attached independent clauses and at least one dependent clause.

Although, as we have seen, a conventional sentence can consist entirely of a subject and a verb, most statements need more words to express their meaning. The predicate may tell not only what the subject is doing but also what or whom the subject is doing it to, that is, who or what is receiving the action. In *Jones handles advertising*, for example, *advertising* undergoes the handling. Such a word is called a direct object. If you ask *What?* or *Whom?* after a verb denoting a mental or physical action performed by the subject, the answer will be the direct object. In each of the following sentences, the third word is the direct object: *I read stories, We made gifts, They gave advice.*

A sentence may also tell *who* or *what* receives the direct object; that is, it may state the indirect object of the action. This element goes between the verb and the direct object: *I read him stories, We made them gifts, They gave us advice.* When the same information follows the direct object, it appears as part of a phrase, after the word *to* or *for*, and the term *indirect object* no longer applies: *I read stories to him, We made gifts for them, They gave advice to us.*

Strictly speaking, direct and indirect objects occur only in sentences in which the subject performs the action that the verb describes. If the subject is not acting but acted on—as in *Stories were read, Gifts were made, Advice was given*—the subject receives the action, and there is no direct object. When the subject receives the action only indirectly, as in _Rookies were given advice by veterans_, the element that resembles a direct object (_advice_ in the example) is called a retained object. The subject of such a sentence would become an indirect object if you revised the structure to make the subject the acting element: _Veterans gave rookies advice_. A verb is in the active voice when it states what the subject does and in the passive voice when it tells what is done to or for the subject.

Some verbs convey no action but simply state existence and lead to words that say something about that existence. A verb like _be, become, seem, appear_, or _remain_ links its subject to a complement, a word or group of words that either describes the subject or serves as its synonym, thus completing the meaning of the sentence. Each of the following sentences ends with a complement: _She seems angry, You look ill, He remained silent, Running Water became chief, Cars can be lemons, We had been friends_. Some think of a complement as completing the meaning of the predicate and call it a predicate complement; others think of it as completing the meaning of the subject and call it a subjective complement. Those who prefer one of these terms may use the word _complement_ alone to designate either an object or a predicate complement; here, however, the term has only the narrower meaning given above—a word that follows a linking verb and defines or describes the subject.

The two basic parts of a sentence, then—or, for that matter, of any clause—are the subject and predicate, and the major components of the predicate are the verb and its objects or complements. Although the examples used so far include only single-word subjects, objects, indirect objects, and complements, these elements often comprise a group of related words that function as a unit; in other words, a phrase or a clause may serve as a subject, an object, or a complement. In _That he did not reply does not necessarily mean that he did not get your letter_, both the subject and the object are clauses; and in _She seems out of sorts_, the complement is a phrase.

Most sentences flesh out their skeletal parts with secondary components called modifiers—words, phrases, or clauses that describe or qualify other elements, either restricting their meaning or giving supplementary information about them. In _The man in the apartment downstairs is eighty-five years old_, the modifying _in_ phrase identifies the subject, narrowing the meaning of _man_ to a specific individual. Such a modifier is called restrictive or defining. In _My mother's father, who lives in the apartment downstairs, is eighty-five years old_, the modifying _who_ clause in no way limits or defines the meaning of _My mother's father_; it simply adds a detail. We would know the subject's identity even if the _who_ clause were omitted. Such a modifier is called nonrestrictive or nondefining.

Now let's look at the ingredients of the various sentence components: the types of words, or parts of speech, that serve as subjects, predicates, objects, complements, and modifiers. One of these, the verb, is the central element in the predicate of a clause. Since the term *verb* technically designates a part of speech, we should say *simple predicate* when we discuss the verb's function in a sentence, but since both terms designate the same word in a given context, the distinction becomes blurred.

Nouns denote persons, places, things, qualities, or feelings (*teacher, John Dewey, Chicago, cities, toys, beauty, grief*). They serve as subjects, objects, or complements (predicate nouns), and a group of related words that plays any of these roles is called a noun phrase or a noun clause (*Living on a poet's income* means *that you don't eat very well*).

Pronouns function exactly as nouns do, but without naming anything. Most of them stand for preceding nouns or pronouns and derive their meaning from the words they replace—their "antecedents" or "principals" or "head words." While such pronouns provide a useful means of avoiding repetition, they are clear only if they refer unambiguously to their antecedents. (In the last sentence *pronouns* is the antecedent of *they* and *their*.) Of the various types, those that come first to mind are probably the personal pronouns. These have the forms *I, we, you, he, she, it,* and *they* as subjects or complements and the forms *me, us, you, him, her, it,* and *them* as objects. Other important categories are the demonstrative pronouns—*this, that, these,* and *those* —which point to the words they replace (as *These* does in the preceding sentence), and the relative pronouns—principally *who, whom, which,* and *that*—which introduce clauses modifying the words they stand for. Indefinite pronouns—for example, *one, another, some, each,* and *everyone*—differ from the other types: although they qualify as pronouns (since they perform the functions of nouns but do not name anything), their identities do not depend on antecedents. Indefinite in meaning, words like *anyone, many,* and *few* do not refer to specific individuals and thus have no need for principals.

Two parts of speech serve as modifiers—adjectives and adverbs. Adjectives modify nouns or pronouns, indicating some quality of the words they describe (a *colorful* sunset, a *heavy* object, a *long* interval), showing degree, amount, or number (*slight* increases, *several* ideas, *two* signs), or singling out an individual from its category (*a* book, *my* report, the *third* quarter). A group of words that modifies a noun or a pronoun is called an adjective phrase or an adjective clause (the woman *in the gray flannel suit,* the man *who came to dinner*).

Adverbs qualify verbs, adjectives, or other adverbs. When modifying other modifiers, they usually indicate extent or degree (*extremely* happy, *somewhat* earlier, *quite* witty, *fairly* well, *partly* responsible).

Most adverbs answer the questions *How? Where? When?* or *Why?* about the verbs they qualify (danced *gracefully*, went *there*, arrives *early, sometimes* regrets, *therefore* declines). A group of words that modifies a verb or a modifier is called an adverbial phrase or an adverbial clause (went *to the bank*, refused *because I had an earlier engagement*).

The two remaining parts of speech that concern us, prepositions and conjunctions, are more functional than substantive: they show how the elements they precede fit into the context. A preposition—a word like *by, in, of, on, to,* or *with*—relates the noun or noun equivalent it introduces, the object of the preposition, to another word in the sentence. A preposition *by definition* is always part *of a phrase* that consists *of itself and its object or objects, along with any modifiers*. In the last sentence the prepositional phrases are italicized.

Conjunctions, the second category of connectives, come in two main varieties, coordinating and subordinating. The coordinating conjunctions—principally *and, but, for, nor,* and *or*—link elements equivalent in weight and function. In other words, they join compound elements: two subjects of the same verb, two verbs with the same subject, two objects, two complements, two modifiers, or two dependent or independent clauses. The subordinating conjunctions indicate the roles of modifying clauses, usually adverbial ones. Such clauses may, for example, state a condition (*if, unless*), a time (*when, before, after*), a contrast (*although, than*), or a cause (*since, because*). While a coordinating conjunction can connect parallel clauses, a subordinating conjunction is always part of a clause, just as a preposition is part of a phrase. In the last sentence, *while* and *as* are subordinating conjunctions.

As dictionary part-of-speech labels indicate, many words have fixed identities, but many others commonly function in two or more ways. Some words can be nouns or verbs (*love, hate, promise, race, effect, object*), others can be adverbs or adjectives (*fast, early, late*), and still others can be adverbs, conjunctions, or prepositions (*before, after, since*). *Like* can be a preposition (*You look like your sister*), a verb (*I like my work*), an adjective (*I am of like mind*), or a noun (*Likes repel*). *Near* can be a preposition (*I sat near the stove*), an adjective (*We had a near miss*), an adverb (*The hour draws near*), or a verb (*We are nearing our destination*).

Even words that are usually confined to single roles can sometimes function atypically. Thus, *horse* and *kitchen*, ordinarily identified as nouns, assume the guise of adjectives in the phrases *a horse race* and *the kitchen sink*; adjectives can turn into nouns, as in *the beautiful and the damned*; and parts of verbs regularly become nouns or adjectives, as in *I like dancing* and *a found object*. In general, we recognize a word as one part of speech or another by the way it functions in a given context.

Since nouns and pronouns function in the same ways, we obviously have to tell them apart by their inherent differences (fortunately, that's not difficult), but we identify most words as the parts of speech whose roles they are playing. In *Fish swim,* for example, we identify *Fish* as a noun because it is the subject of the sentence (subjects must be nouns or pronouns, and *fish* is clearly not a pronoun). In the sentence *They fish,* the same word is the predicate, and thus it has to be a verb. In *Don't tell fish stories,* where *fish* modifies the noun *stories,* we call it an adjective, the part of speech used to qualify a noun.

Parts of speech do have characteristics apart from the roles they play—adjectives have comparative forms, nouns can be singular or plural, verbs have many inflections, and so on. Some grammarians, in fact, would say that *fish* in the last example is an attributive noun, not an adjective, because it lacks the comparative forms intrinsic to descriptive adjectives (we can't say, for example, that her story is *fisher* than his, but yours is the *fishest* of all). Such niceties, however, are largely outside the concerns of this book.

Loose, Baggy Sentences

1 "Omit needless words," say Strunk and White, practicing what they preach. Their terse injunction sums up advice included in every contemporary style manual. Under a variety of headings—Officialese, Prolixity, Verbiage, Periphrasis, Windyfoggery, and Jargon—the experts agree that, when it comes to exposition, less is usually more. Surely most authors have read such advice or have heard similar strictures in composition classes, but economy and precision seem hard to come by.

Bad prose proliferates because writers model their style on what they read most, and their daily fare—whether textbooks, reports, memorandums, or newspapers—abounds in circumlocution. Educators, sociologists, scholars, lawyers, bureaucrats, technicians, and business executives are all notorious producers of gobbledygook. Here, for example, is a bank president addressing stockholders in a 1980 annual report:

> With the beginning of the new '80s, it is readily ascertainable that there has been little if any improvement in the overall national or general local economy. It is expected by some economists that a general upturn on the national level should come about sometime during mid-1981. However, with the increase in taxes starting in January, mainly an increase in social security, this will reduce the amount of free funds available for the stimulation of consumer spending.

Someone less given to beating around the bush might have written:

> In 1980 we saw little if any improvement in the economy, national or local, and although some economists expect an

upturn in mid-1981, the tax increases scheduled to begin in January, mainly for social security, will leave consumers with less money to spend.

A simple statement like this is usually harder to compose than a verbose one, but even if it came naturally, the banker might prefer the longer version. Straightforward sentences sound unimpressive to many writers, and officialese, creating tin ears, perpetuates itself. Unchecked by the efforts of learned and vocal opponents, logorrhea plagues the country. It's rather like smoking. This chapter can only warn of the dangers, describe the symptoms, and prescribe remedies, enabling writers who want to kick the habit to cure themselves.

Before we go on to examples and techniques, I should make clear that writing concisely doesn't mean composing sentences like "Me Tarzan, you Jane." It means omitting needless words, the deadwood that does nothing but detract from both substance and style. The pruned sentence must emerge not only leaner and clearer but also more graceful and more effective than it was, better able to do what you want it to do. Long sentences aren't necessarily wordy, not if every word counts. As good writers know, leisurely sentences have their purposes—to contrast with short ones, say, or to establish a desired tone. A sentence can be too tight. Sometimes you need a clause instead of a phrase, a phrase instead of a word. What you're after is a supple style; you don't want to compact your language, trading looseness for density. But you're not likely to run that risk unless you're a compulsive polisher. Condensing to a fault is so rare a failing that it needs only passing mention. Of course, if you'd like to change the last sentence to *The rarity of overtightness obviates elaboration,* you have something to worry about.

With these qualifications out of the way, we can turn to the problem of recognizing and excising verbiage. Certain telltale characteristics signal wordy sentences. As you read over your writing, watch for the symptoms described below, try eliminating them in the ways the discussion suggests, and see your style improve.

PROFILE OF A WORDY SENTENCE

You can almost detect a wordy sentence by looking at it—at least if you can recognize weak verbs, ponderous nouns, and strings of prepositional phrases. Each of these features typifies prolixity, and they often occur in combination.

Weak Verbs

A rambling, unwieldy sentence generally hangs from an inert verb—the verb *to be* (*am, are, is, was, were, being, been*), some other vague, actionless verb like *have* or *exist*, or a passive form (the verb *to be* plus a past participle; e.g., *is believed, was seen*). Pay attention to the verbs you use, and when you find a weak one, try substituting something more vigorous. Ask what happens in the sentence. If you haven't expressed the action as a verb, you've probably buried it in a verbal (the *to* or *ing* form of the verb), an adjective, a noun, or a subordinate clause, as the writers have done in the excerpts quoted below. Exhume the action, make it a verb, and you're almost certain to tighten and enliven the wording.

Consider this sentence, quoted from a computer company's promotional material. It appears in a paragraph explaining that the new technology, by enabling employees to work at home, will affect real estate values:

> More remote, less densely populated suburbs, whose lower values were often a function of how far they were from work centers, and small towns in rural locations, whose lower values were a reflection of the difficulty of earning a living, are likely to see considerable appreciation of their property values in the next two decades.

If you check the verbs in this long-winded sentence, you can readily spot the trouble. The verb *to be* occurs in the main clause as well as in the subordinate ones—four times in all—while nouns and verbals (*reflection, appreciation, earning, to see*) freeze all the action. A little analysis suggests that the "event" in the sentence is the appreciation of property values. When you make *appreciate* the principal verb, it attracts the proper subject, and everything else falls into place:

> Since many people will no longer have to commute to work centers to earn a living, property values in the more distant suburbs and rural areas should appreciate considerably in the next two decades.

Notice that the revision eliminates needless words as well as static verbs. While it may seem to leave out information included in the original, the omitted words tell readers nothing that they don't already know, nothing that isn't implicit in what's left. You could even tighten the wording a bit more:

> Rural and exurban property values should appreciate considerably in the next two decades as it becomes easier for people to earn a living in areas remote from work centers.

When you consider substitutes for weak and passive verbs, you may have several good options, and the choice will depend on exactly what you want to highlight.

In the following excerpt, from a newspaper article on a town's plans to build an animal shelter, the wordiness stems from the passive voice, the form a verb takes when its subject is not acting but acted on:

> The shelter will be owned by the town, but it will be run by members of the humane society and supported, in part, by funds raised by them. The bulk of the operating funds, however, will be supplied by the town.

When you make all the verbs active, other economies suggest themselves:

> Although the town will own the shelter and pay most of the operating expenses, members of the humane society will run the facility and provide additional support through fund raising.

The revision collapses two sentences into one. In the original the passive subjects *shelter* and *bulk of the operating funds* need verbs of their own, but when *town* becomes the acting subject, it can govern two verbs with different objects, thus enabling one clause to supply the same information that formerly required two.

The next example comes from a letter that the head of a college English department sends prospective majors:

> The English Department is unusually strong for a college of this size. It consists of twelve faculty members, whose fields of special interest cover the range of English and American literature. The diversity and educational background of this department is suggested by the fact that important work published by its members includes such subjects as Shakespeare, Milton, Jane Austen, Tennyson, Wordsworth, Pope, Melville, and Southern "agrarian" writers, T. S. Eliot and Katherine Anne Porter.

This excerpt has several problems, but notice particularly that the weak main verbs in the three sentences attract needless words, that the second sentence subordinates its primary information (the faculty members' range of interests), and that the third sentence repeats information given in the second. You might revise this way:

> The twelve faculty members who compose the English Department make it an unusually strong one for a college of this size. Their diverse special interests and educational

backgrounds cover the range of English and American
literature, and their publications include important works on
Shakespeare, Milton, Jane Austen, Tennyson, Wordsworth,
Pope, Melville, the Southern "agrarian" writers, T. S. Eliot,
and Katherine Anne Porter.

As you check your sentences for weak verbs, always consider
eliminating leisurely sentence openers like *There is* and *It is important
to note that.* You can usually cut them easily, and most sentences work
better if you go right to the point instead of sidling up to it. But
apparently not all experts agree. A composition manual provides this
example:

There is a hasty way of writing which is counterpart to the
hasty way of reading. It is becoming more common every
year and raises less and less protest.

Removing the weak verbs leaves:

A hasty way of writing, counterpart to the hasty way of
reading, grows more common every year and raises less and
less protest.

But you can condense even more:

Hasty writing, like hasty reading, grows. . . .

A financial columnist wrote the next example:

To make the most of your investments, it is essential that
you understand what your goals are and what your financial
temperament is.

As always, you can reduce *it is essential that* to *must* or *have to* and
eliminate the *what* clauses. Revised, the sentence reads:

To make the most of your investments, you have to
understand your goals and financial temperament.

The last two examples, unlike the earlier ones, may not strike you as
especially wordy, and perhaps the revised versions do sacrifice emphasis to brevity and directness. If you want that emphasis, if you
want to draw particular attention to a statement, you can justify slow-
ing the pace.

No one recommends that you banish the verb *to be* and all passive
forms from your writing. I wouldn't tamper, certainly, with "To be or
not to be, that is the question" or even with "She is more to be pitied
than censured." You may choose the passive, for example, because
you want to put its subject first in the sentence or because you do not
know, or do not want to reveal, who is performing the action. But

when you use extra words, make sure that you are doing so purpose-fully, that you are not just surrendering to laziness and poor crafts-manship. As you edit what you've written, always *consider* replacing static verbs. While you should keep those that provide the tone or emphasis or variety you want, you'll find that most sentences benefit when you shift to active verbs.

Ponderous Nouns

Wordy writing not only droops from weak verbs but sags under bulky nouns—especially long Latinate ones with endings like *tion* and *ment* and *ence*. The two characteristics complement each other. Con-sider this sentence from a letter to the *New York Times*:

> The inference that because high school graduates are more likely to be employed than dropouts, the differences may be attributed to the possession of a diploma is suspect since dropouts and graduates may differ in a variety of ways relevant to both graduation prospects and employment status.

Lifeless and noun-burdened, the sentence makes dull and difficult reading. You have to grope for the meaning. If you proceed mechani-cally, looking for verbs to replace and nouns to eliminate, you can eventually pare the sentence down:

> It is not necessarily the diploma that makes high school graduates more employable than dropouts; other differences may affect both their education and their job prospects.

Isn't the shorter version easier to understand? Does the original tell you anything more? Compare the number of nouns and the number of static verbs in the two sentences, and notice the economies achieved in the revision, despite that opening *It is*. Although the sen-tence could begin *The diploma does not necessarily make . . .* , the more emphatic lead, which adds only two words, stresses the statement as a counterargument.

The next example comes from an article on interdisciplinary col-lege courses. After pointing out that the instructors in such courses teach material in subject areas other than their own, the author goes on to say:

> One of the effects of this purposeful disengagement from expertise is that students are disabused of the notion that engagement in disciplinary material on a fairly elementary level requires mastery of that discipline.

If your ear doesn't tell you that this sentence needs work, the ratio of nouns to active verbs should (not to mention that string of prepositional phrases, the symptom of wordiness discussed in the next section). To revise, first choose an active verb for the main clause. Ask yourself what takes place in the sentence, and you'll find the event confined in a passive verb and tucked away in a subordinate clause—*students are disabused.* To make that idea active, you can either say that instructors, by teaching outside their disciplines, disabuse students of a false notion or that nonspecialist teachers enable students to discover something. Either way you automatically eliminate the limp opening—*One of the effects of.* A sentence can make clear that something is an effect without using the label, and there's no apparent need to specify that the effect is one of several. (If that information is pertinent, you can include it elsewhere; here it gets in the way.) You might then consider these alternatives:

> By venturing outside their specialties, teachers disabuse
> students of the notion that only those who have mastered a
> discipline can deal with its subject matter.

> When teachers venture outside their specialties, students
> discover that one need not have mastered a discipline to
> deal with its subject matter.

These versions do omit *on a fairly elementary level,* but why would students think that "engagement . . . on a fairly elementary level requires mastery"? Surely they wouldn't expect first-year French students to do without the translations in a Truffaut film. Nevertheless, the omission leaves something to be desired. The revisions almost imply the advisability of having know-nothings pontificate on a subject—an unlikely suggestion in an article favoring interdisciplinary courses. Presumably, then, the original sentence does not mean what it says. After explaining that instructors teach material outside their areas of expertise, the author probably intended to make this point:

> By venturing into another field, teachers demonstrate that
> nonspecialists can deal with the subject matter to some
> extent, thus disabusing students of the notion that any
> engagement in the discipline requires mastery.

Though not much shorter than the original, this version makes its words count.

Here's one more noun-heavy excerpt, this one from a manufacturer's annual report:

> The stability and quality of our financial performance will
> be developed through the profitable execution of our
> existing business, as well as the acquisition or development
> of new businesses.

Before you look at the revision below, try one yourself, following the steps used in the earlier examples. The verbiage should yield easily, but the muddy original—perhaps an example of intentional corporate obfuscation—makes more than one interpretation possible. You may prefer your condensation to this one:

> We will improve our financial performance not only by executing our existing business more profitably but by acquiring or developing new businesses.

Do you object to the omission of *stability and quality*? Would restoring these terms make the revision mean more? You would have a hard time justifying *quality*, but *stability* may be another matter. Although the idea of improved financial performance should encompass the idea of greater stability, readers don't necessarily think about stability when they see *improve our financial performance*, and they're not likely to stop to analyze the phrase. Undoubtedly the sentence concerns a company in which instability has been a problem, and the revision carries no such implication. If the idea is important, you might choose this wording:

> We will work toward a more stable and profitable financial performance not only by executing our existing business more efficiently but by acquiring or developing new businesses.

Strings of Prepositional Phrases

As you might expect, strings of prepositional phrases often keep company with weak verbs and ponderous nouns. Look closely at any sentence that depends heavily on prepositions, and if you count more than three phrases in a row, consider revising. The following examples exhibit all the symptoms of wordiness we have been discussing; again, even if you can't hear the problem, you can detect it mechanically. The first comes from a doctoral dissertation:

> The more reasoned analysis made by the Saint-Simonians of the nature of the new power situation in France and of the reasons the present government could not satisfy the needs of the people was confirmed by these developments.

This sentence features a passive main verb and seven prepositional phrases, four of them consecutive and all with nouns as objects. Changing to the active voice eliminates one phrase and gives you *These developments confirmed. . . .* (It also has the advantage, incidentally, of bringing subject and verb closer together, thus making the sentence easier to read.) As you look for expendable phrases, you should see that *of the nature of the new power situation* means no more than *of the new power situation* and that *of the reasons* can be left implicit; a *reasoned analysis* of the government's inability to satisfy would obviously give the underlying reasons. You can cut another phrase by using *the Saint-Simonians'* instead of *made by the Saint-Simonians.* (When an *of* or *by* phrase simply denotes possession or authorship, you can often substitute the possessive form of the noun. But be careful: not all *of* phrases translate into possessives. If, for example, you change *the assassination of the dictator* to *the dictator's assassination,* you risk turning the victim into a murderer.) With four phrases eliminated, the sentence reads:

> These developments confirmed the Saint-Simonians' more reasoned analysis of the new power situation in France and of the present government's inability to satisfy the people's needs.

In the next example, from a letter notifying stockholders of an annual meeting, only the first sentence has an objectionable string of prepositions, but the second plays a part in the revision:

> At the meeting there will be a report to the stockholders on the progress of the Company during the past year. A discussion period will also take place, during which the stockholders will have an opportunity to discuss matters of Company interest.

The two sentences convey information that, properly arranged, would fit in one. You don't need a knapsack and a briefcase to carry a book and a memo pad, and you don't need both *will be* and *will take place* to tell readers that two things will happen at the meeting. Then, too, the second sentence, in announcing that stockholders will discuss in a discussion period, gives readers the same information twice. Such repetition reflects sloppy sentence structure, and it should disappear when you tighten the wording. Finally, the phrase *matters of Company interest* tells readers something that can go without saying. Two or three short sentences in a row should trigger a check for wordiness just as a long rambling one does. Sentence-combining drills in rhetoric handbooks teach students how to subordinate some elements to others as a means of varying structure. The same technique often eliminates needless words. Doesn't this sentence say as much as the original two?

> At the meeting the president [or whoever] will report to stockholders on the Company's progress during the year and then invite questions and comments.

Now let's look at a literary example:

> How greatly Goethe was under the spell of the concept of the single ideal of beauty in his classicistic period is illustrated by the fact that he was pleased when readers could not distinguish between his and Schiller's anonymous publications.

Here five consecutive prepositional phrases limp up to the weak and wordy predicate *is illustrated by the fact that*. Structuring the sentence in this way relegates the dynamic content to a subordinate clause with another weak predicate—*How greatly Goethe was under the spell.* To avoid the passive voice, you might decide not to make Goethe the subject, since he is acted on, not acting. The action belongs to the concept that held Goethe under its spell—or that *captivated* him, a substitution that gets rid of one phrase. You're now down from three *of* phrases in a row to two. Can you do better? Probably not. You might be tempted to drop *concept of*, but the sentence would then suggest that Goethe endorsed a particular ideal beauty rather than the notion of a single ideal. And, of course, a *single ideal of beauty* differs from a *single ideal beauty*. Still, going from five consecutive phrases to two represents a considerable improvement:

> The concept of a single ideal of beauty so captivated Goethe
> in his classicistic period that he was pleased when. . . .

If you wanted more emphasis on Goethe, you might prefer to settle for the passive:

> In his classicistic period Goethe was so taken with the
> concept of a single ideal of beauty that. . . .

You might even think of a way to have your cake and eat it too:

> In his classicistic period Goethe believed so strongly in a
> single ideal of beauty that. . . .

The verb *believe* enables you to use *a single ideal of beauty* without a preceding *concept of*, but it lacks the force of the alternatives. You would have to decide whether you lose more than you gain. Each of these versions eliminates the prolixity of the original, and they do not exhaust the possibilities. In revising you usually have the leeway to do it your way.

When it comes to consecutive prepositional phrases, our final example, an obligatory statement in some financial reports, sets a record: it boasts a string of seven, not packed into the subject as in the Goethe sentence, but dragged along behind, like so many tin cans tied to the newlyweds' car:

> The financial statements and related data presented
> elsewhere in this report have been prepared in accordance
> with generally accepted accounting principles, which require
> the measurement of financial position and operating results
> in terms of historical dollars without regard to changes in
> the relative purchasing power of money over time.

If you look for the gist of this message, the sentence seems to be saying only that the report accords with generally accepted accounting principles in stating data in historical dollars. The long subject, *The financial statements and related data presented elsewhere in this report,* includes information too obvious to mention; the predicate, *have been prepared in accordance with,* says no more than *accord* or *follow;* and measuring financial data *in terms of historical dollars* makes no more sense than measuring a room in terms of square feet. Thus the statement boils down to:

> Following generally accepted accounting principles, this report states the Company's financial position, operating results, and related data in historical dollars, disregarding changes in purchasing power.

In fact, the last part, *disregarding changes in purchasing power,* translates into "disregarding inflationary changes"—since purchasing power has only declined in recent decades. But accountants accustomed to the original formula would probably agree to these revisions reluctantly if at all. Although a financial writer I consulted confirms that the condensed version neither alters the sense of the original nor omits anything that is not implicit, he also explains that *historical dollars* is a sacrosanct technical term designating sums not adjusted for current equivalents. But if *historical dollars* means "dollars unadjusted for changes in purchasing power," isn't that last phrase superfluous? "Not really," says my adviser. "It tells you that such changes have occurred." To the initiated, jargon apparently has its own clarity, and would-be reformers have an uphill battle.

SHORTCUTS

Routine Condensing

In addition to checking your writing for lifeless verbs, excessive nouns, and chains of prepositions, you should watch for specific constructions, stylistic mannerisms, and even words that almost always contribute only verbiage. With practice, you'll develop a conditioned response to these faults and learn to edit them out as soon as you spot them—and, eventually, even before you put them down.

Perhaps, as you've studied the examples and revisions, you've noticed that an active verb often replaces a noun or an adjective sandwiched between a weak verb and a preposition. Such a change eliminates two or three words: for example, *is indicative of* becomes *indicates; have an influence on* becomes *influence; gives consideration to, considers; make an assessment of, assess; is capable of, can; make use of, use; is of interest to, interests;* and *is a benefit to, benefits.* If you check your sentences for weak verbs and expendable prepositional phrases, you can't fail to notice such constructions; converting to an active verb is always easy and usually desirable. Similarly, when an *of* phrase follows a noun ending in *tion*, you can often economize by changing the noun to a gerund, the *ing* form of the verb used as a noun; thus, *by the implementation of the plan* becomes *by implementing the plan; in the creation of* becomes *in creating; in the discussion of, in discussing; through the examination of, through examining;* and *by the addition of, by adding.*

You should also always look critically at a relative clause—an adjective clause generally introduced by *who, which,* or *that* (understood or expressed). Sometimes you can simply delete the subject and verb. These sentences show the expendable words in brackets:

> There are at least two larger opportunities [that exist] in this area.
> (Or: At least two larger opportunities exist in this area.)
>
> The result is an organization [that is] uniquely tailored to its customer base.
>
> Those [who are] invited to participate on the panel pay their own travel expenses.
>
> Montaque, [which is located] in the far northwest corner of the state, is the best place for sighting blue herons.

Sometimes you have to substitute a word or two for the three or four you eliminate. For example:

>   *their*
> Poor households pay more for [the] food [that they buy] because local merchants exploit them.
>
>   *with indeterminate*
> This is a development [the] social consequences [of which are indeterminate].
> (Or: This development has indeterminate social consequences.)
>
>   *are our many community*
> Fundamental to our operation [is the variety of] services [that our company has to offer to the community].

Be alert, too, to the possibility of converting a prepositional phrase to an adjective or an adverb. *Of great complexity* can become *complex; at this point in time, now; of extreme importance, extremely important;* and *on many occasions, often.* Obviously you won't want to sacrifice every phrase that has a single-word equivalent. The phrases may provide the rhythm, variety, or emphasis you need. I would not say, for example, that the biblical merchant should have sold all that he had for an expensive pearl instead of a pearl of great price or that Macbeth should have referred to an idiot's noisy and furious tale instead of to a tale told by an idiot, full of sound and fury. (Writers like God and Shakespeare know when to break the rules.) I do suggest that you see what you gain—or lose—by substituting a word for a phrase. Sometimes tightening provides a way out of stylistic infelicities other than wordiness, and knowing the tricks of the trade gives you an advantage. Had you written _We will produce evidence at a later time that will prove us right,_ your readers wouldn't know whether the evidence or the time would prove you right. Changing _at a later time_ to _later_ would remove the ambiguity.

Also watch for common prepositional compounds that take two to five words to say what you could say in one word or could even leave unsaid. Here are some of the most common offenders:

He believes that [in order] to study efficiently you need. . . .

to explore
Research undertaken [for the purpose of exploring] the possibilities. . . .

The response [on the part] of top management to the proposal. . . .

about
She wanted to see me [in connection with] the new campaign.

The question [as to] whether it is safe to proceed needs an answer.

_If_
[In the eventuality that] the company goes bankrupt, its creditors. . . .

Since
[In view of the fact that] you are in the 50 per cent tax bracket, you should. . . .

In [the process of actually] doing the job, you learn. . . .

Finally, train yourself to recognize and remove empty prose additives like _case, character, degree, the fact that, factor, instance, level, nature,_ and _quality._ Almost always expendable, any of these terms should set off a reflex action like a flashing light at a railroad crossing. "Whenever . . . your pen betrays you to one or another of them," wrote Sir Arthur Quiller-Couch in his celebrated essay "On Jargon," "pull yourself up and take thought." Of course no one objects to these words in the senses in which they have content, such as _case_ referring to an argument or to an event like a fire or an emergency, _character_ as a figure in a novel, and *nature* as the Great Outdoors; but you should have no trouble distinguishing legitimate uses from the periphrastic expressions that clutter virtually all writing. For example:

> [In the case of] Layton Brothers[, the company] didn't adjust quickly enough to the changing market.
>
> The remark seemed hostile [in character] and offended the interviewer.
>
> They carried their complaint to [the level of] the top administration.
>
> Because [of the fact that] the development ran into delays. . . .
>
> The principal assets of the bank are monetary [in nature].
>
> The production was [of] inferior [quality].
>
> In [the instance of] our first production our mistake was faulty casting.
>
> We relied on [the factor of] surprise to give us an advantage.
>
> They showed a greater [degree of] interest in the outcome.

Eliminate all such circumlocutions—and I do mean practice total abstinence—at least until you break yourself of the habit; by then you should know when to break the rules.

Choosing Bargain Words

Every book on writing tells you to use vivid verbs and concrete nouns. If you don't, you'll probably find yourself trying to bolster lifeless verbs and vague nouns with modifiers, thus adding words only because you've settled for less than *les mots justes.* You might say, for example, *He walked wearily and laboriously* when you could convey the same image with *He trudged.* Precise words are bargains; by combining both general and specific meanings, they permit economies. You get more communication per word. *Trudge, amble, stroll, lumber, stride,* and *lope* all mean both walk and a particular way of walking; *coupe, sedan, convertible,* and *station wagon* all mean both car and a particular type of car. In some contexts, of course, *car* and *walk* provide all the information you want the reader to have—as in *A car usually travels fifteen times faster than a person walking.* More colorful wording of such a statement would only be silly and distracting, as in *A Mercedes travels twenty times faster than a strolling minstrel.* But when you want the reader to envision what you're writing about, as you usually do if you find yourself adding adjectives and adverbs, make sure to choose the most specific nouns and verbs you can. Surrender to modifiers only as a last resort.

You may detect a dependence on general and abstract words as you check for weak verbs and excessive nouns. But look at your modifiers, too, and ask yourself whether you would need them if you substituted stronger nouns and verbs. Often a sentence features a general noun or verb and then gives a supporting role to the specific word that should have had the lead. *The dog we owned was a beagle hound,* for example, doesn't say any more than *We owned a beagle.* The executive who reported that her company's new policy *resulted in increased morale among the employees* could simply have written that the policy *boosted employee morale;* and the agency that concluded an announcement with *For more information communicate with the director by writing him at . . .* could have communicated more directly with *For more information write the director at. . . .*

When you do choose a precise word, trust it to do its job without redundant modifiers—adjectives or adverbs that give the same information as the words they describe. If, in revising, you decided to change *In my final conclusion I stated that . . .* to *I finally concluded that . . . ,* you'd be on the right track, but you'd have retained a redundant *finally.* Here are some redundancies culled from manuscripts: *first introduced, final coup de grâce, a temporary sojourn, totally devoid of, flawless perfection, a small trifle, a new innovation, on first entering, straight linear movement,* and *general consensus.* You can save yourself from such solecisms if you watch for them and use a dictionary whenever you're a little hazy about the definition of a word you modify. The meaning may include the qualification contributed by the adjective or adverb. If you look up *consensus,* for example, you'll find that it means "general agreement in opinion."

Redundancy, of course, does not reside exclusively in modifiers. A banker with a decided flair for it refers to *unprecedented interest rates that set an all-time record,* thanks stockholders who have *generously assisted us with their help,* and reports that his institution has *continued to maintain success since the outset of our entry into the computer field.* Redundancy creeps into prose in such varied ways that there's no cut-and-dried method of avoiding it, but look for it. Qualifying *in* phrases, for example, always deserve a moment's thought. Writers commonly lapse into such obviously superfluous expressions as *green in color, larger in size, twenty-four in number, handsome in appearance,* and *rectangular in shape.*

You probably can't, and you undoubtedly shouldn't, eliminate all modifiers, but you probably should delete all intensive adverbs—*very, really, truly, actually,* and the like. If you've chosen the right word, adding a *very* defeats your purpose. If you haven't got the right word, the *very* offers poor compensation. Readers pay no attention to this overused word. If you want to put a *very* in front of a *large,* you should consider substituting *enormous, huge, gigantic,* or *massive.* Stressed when spoken, the intensive adverbs do accent the words they modify and sometimes attach themselves even to absolute words—like *complete, unique,* and *pure*—which, literally construed, have no degrees. In writing, however, they attenuate rather than strengthen. Consider *really terrific, absolutely stunning, truly sensational, extremely vital,* and *very devastating.* The adverbs reduce powerful adjectives to conversational gush, depriving them of their stark force. Almost all writers succumb to these trivializing intensives. Be on guard.

By the same token, don't use a strong word if you then feel compelled to pull its punch with a restricting modifier. If you write that someone was *rather furious,* you can't mean much more than *irritated* or at most *angered,* unless you're attempting humor; and something you describe as *fairly essential* can't be much more than *important.*

Leaving Unsaid

Sometimes wordiness comes from spelling out what can go without saying. For example, essays commonly begin something like *In this paper I will discuss three aspects of contemporary life that. . . .* If the writer omitted the first six words and led with *Three aspects of contemporary life that . . . ,* would the audience learn anything less? Wouldn't anyone reading such a topic sentence know that the paper discusses those aspects? A book review states, *The third chapter of the book deals with administrative problems and the solutions that have been proposed for these problems,* but *The third chapter deals with administrative problems and proposed solutions* would provide as much information. If a review refers to *the third chapter,* no one is going to wonder where that third chapter is, and if *solutions* appears soon after *problems* the reader can't fail to take "to these problems" for granted. Once you've described an idea—say, that human beings should seek harmony with nature—you can thereafter refer to it as "this theory" or "view" or "so-and-so's argument," without adding the defining *that* clause with every mention. And whenever you can use a pronoun to refer clearly to what you've already named, do so. If you find the same words and phrases recurring in a sentence or paragraph, ask yourself whether you're telling readers what they already know. In the following excerpt, from a bulletin for college teachers, the expendable words appear in brackets:

> [In the present paper I propose to deal with] one type of
> interdisciplinary curriculum [which] can be built upon
> material borrowed from related departments, whether or not

the specialists [in these related departments] choose to teach
the interdisciplinary offerings [so constructed. By this
remark I am recognizing the fact that] occasionally a
generalist who does not hold a Ph.D. in any of the
specialized fields [that have made a contribution to the
construction of such interdisciplinary course offerings] may
be the one to [take on the responsibility for] teach[ing] the
courses [so constructed, rather than a specialist from one of
the contributing areas].

If you remove the needless words and adjust what's left, you can get
something like this:

One type of interdisciplinary curriculum borrows material
from the related departments without necessarily borrowing
their faculty members. In other words, occasionally a
generalist, without a Ph.D. in a contributing field, may teach
a course.

Trim sentences, like trim bodies, usually require far more effort
than flabby ones. But though striving toward a lean and graceful style
involves hard work, it can also be fun—like swimming or running.
Shaping an attractive sentence from a formless mass of words is a
copy editor's high. One author sent back his edited manuscript with
the comment, "You seem to have chiseled out a fairly decent essay
from the pile of material I sent you." The metaphor is apt. An Eskimo
carver selects a promising stone, studies it to see what figure it suggests, then chips away at it to free the desired form; you can approach
your draft in much the same way. Or, if you don't fancy yourself a
sculptor, you can think of your draft as a puzzle; to solve it, you have
to find and eliminate the superfluities that obscure your meaning. The
object is to delete as many words as possible without sacrificing substance or nuance.

If you follow the steps recommended here—checking sentence
elements one by one, omitting the needless, replacing the weak—you
can't fail to improve your style. As you gain experience, the remedial
procedures will become largely routine. Moreover, your early drafts
will require fewer corrections. You'll be writing better sentences in
the first place. "Getting rid of superfluous words," Wilson Follett
says, "has an advantage commonly overlooked: the automatic sup-
pression of weaknesses that flourish in diffuse writing. . . . Anyone
who will struggle to reduce [a] hundred words to fifty without losing
meaning will see looseness, inconsistency, and aberration vanish."

Faulty
Connections

2 Sometimes a sentence fails to say what you mean because its elements don't make the proper connections. Then you have to revise by shuffling the components around, juxta-posing those that should link and separating those that should not. To get your meaning across, you not only have to choose the right words, you have to put them in the right order. Words in disarray produce only nonsense:

> Him stick with the before chased boy the that dog big had the attacked.

Ordered, the same words can make several coherent statements:

> The boy with the big stick attacked the dog that had chased him before.

> The big dog chased the boy that had attacked him with the stick before.

> Before, the big boy with the stick chased the dog that had attacked him.

> The boy that had chased the big dog before attacked him with the stick.

> The big dog chased the stick with the boy that had attacked him before.

Anyone at home with an English sentence knows without think-ing that the verb normally comes after the subject and before the object and that modifiers usually go next to the elements they qualify. When words aren't near the words they go with, they go with the words they're near. So if you don't put your sentence components where they belong, you risk confusing your readers or getting laughs you didn't want. Take this sentence, for example:

> Queen Elizabeth read the speech, which was handed to her by the 71-year-old Lord Hailsham, the Lord Chancellor, with the aid of half-moon glasses.

Imaginative readers might picture the lord chancellor handing the queen a furled parchment balanced on a pair of spectacles. The writer should have brought the queen and her glasses together:

> With the aid of half-moon glasses, Queen Elizabeth read the speech handed to her by. . . .

But not all faulty connections yield to simple transpositions. Sometimes you have to reword. Consider this sentence:

> We try to help clients interpret statistics with some sophistication.

Are the clients to interpret rather sophisticated statistics or to interpret statistics in a rather sophisticated way? The article that supplied this example ultimately makes clear that the *with* phrase goes with *interpret*, not *statistics*, but there seems no way to bring verb and phrase closer together. A change to *help clients interpret with some sophistication statistics* would scarcely sound like English, and a change to *help clients with some sophistication interpret statistics* would alter the meaning. In such circumstances you have to open up the sentence and give yourself a little more room to say what you mean:

> We try to help clients develop some sophistication in interpreting statistics.

You can sometimes detect faulty connections in your writing by reading aloud—a practice that can uncover a variety of problems by forcing you to notice individual words that you might skip over in reading silently. But the method is not foolproof, since your familiarity with what you want to say may distort the way you hear your own sentences. You have to train yourself to look at your sentences critically and objectively, and you have to know what to look for. This chapter alerts you to the most common word-order problems and suggests ways of solving them.

PUTTING MODIFIERS IN THEIR PLACES

When an adjective or adverb directly precedes the word it describes, there's no mistaking the connection. Nor is there any problem with a modifying phrase or clause that directly follows the word it describes. But a modifier in an unusual position may fall into the wrong company and form an unsuitable attachment. Though readers can usually figure out what you mean, the momentary misreading can distract them from the substance of what you're saying.

Adjectives

An adjective ordinarily goes before the word it modifies or after a linking verb (e.g., *seem, appear,* or *become*) that ties it to the subject. Occasionally, however, you may like the rhythm or force you get by putting two or more adjectives after the noun they modify, as in *She was an able administrator, strong but tactful.* This sort of variation is fine provided that the adjectives directly follow the appropriate word. In the following sentence, from a pamphlet on money management, the adjectives have gone astray:

> Since dealings with a custodian bank are usually in writing, whether local or out of town, the only difference is a lag of a few days.

It is, of course, the bank that is in or out of town, but the word order suggests that the adjectives modify *writing* (the nearest noun) or, if not, *dealings* (the more prominent of the earlier nouns). To revise, you need only move the words around:

> Since dealings with the custodian bank, whether local or out of town, are usually in writing, the only difference is a lag of a few days.

An adjective modifying the object of a verb expressing opinion (e.g., *consider, think, judge,* or *find*) also comes after the word it qualifies, as in *He found the staff competent* and *I consider her work brilliant.* But if the modifier cannot follow the object directly, the sentence may be hard to read. For example:

> The superintendent of the Ossining Correctional Facility found the community's desire to preserve part of the prison amusing.

Amusing cannot follow *desire,* the word it modifies, because the infinitive phrase claims the same spot; placed after *found,* it would seem to take *desire* as its object (but even a nonverbal adjective—say, *ironic*—would be disruptive in that position). So you would have to restructure the sentence:

> The superintendent of the Ossining Correctional Facility was amused by the community's desire to preserve part of the prison.

Or:

The superintendent . . . found it amusing that the
community wanted to preserve part of the prison.

Sometimes, you may choose to stress an adjective by putting it first in the sentence and setting it off by a comma. *Despondent, the boy left the room* has a force you don't get with *The despondent boy left the room.* An adjective in this position ordinarily modifies the subject of the sentence. Readers will almost always make that connection whether or not you intend it, so be sure to match logic and syntax. Carelessness on this score can produce some bizarre results:

Lightweight and packable, Mom will find this comfortable,
flattering robe indispensable for traveling.

If the adjectives in the example must retain their initial emphatic position, the sentence could read:

Lightweight and packable, this comfortable, flattering robe
will delight Mom and prove indispensable for traveling.

But some might prefer a less frenetic approach:

Mom will find this lightweight, packable robe comfortable,
flattering, and indispensable for traveling.

Occasionally an introductory adjective modifies not the subject of the sentence but the sentence as a whole. In *More important, she finished ahead of schedule,* for example, the meaning is "What is more important is that she finished. . . . " The opening adjective phrase might be considered an aside, tacked onto the sentence rather like an absolute expression (a noun and a modifying participle having no grammatical connection with any other part of the sentence—e.g., *God willing, all things being equal, weather permitting*). You can use a self-contained sentence modifier of this sort if there's no ambiguity, but be careful that it doesn't seem to describe the subject. This sentence, from an article on the exploitation of part-time faculty members, permits misreading:

More subtle but equally important, part-time teachers are
stripped of their professional identities.

To avoid implying that the part-time teachers are more subtle than their full-time colleagues, you could give the adjectives a specific noun to modify:

This practice has another effect, more subtle but equally
important: part-time teachers are. . . .

Perhaps you have been thinking that a sentence modifier like *More important* should be *More importantly.* Many writers do use the adverbial form, and in some apparently analogous sentences an opening adjective would jar. No one would write, for example, *Significant, she finished ahead of schedule* instead of *Significantly, she finished ahead of schedule*. Here, in fact, we seem to be dealing more with idiom than with logic or grammar. Idiom, the normal pattern of the language, sometimes runs counter to both grammar and logic, but it must prevail. A construction that sounds wrong to the educated ear works against you, even though it's arguably correct. Either an adjective or an adverb can modify a sentence as a whole, and if the particular form that comes naturally causes no confusion, let it be—unless you want to consider leaving it out. Writers on style have little to say about this adjective-versus-adverb question, perhaps because there is no hard-and-fast rule, perhaps also because such sentence modifiers are often expendable. If what you write seems important or interesting, you don't have to say that it is. And if it doesn't seem important or interesting, saying that it is won't help. "Being told that something is interesting," William Zinsser says, "[tempts] the reader to find it dull."

Adverbs

Out-of-order adverbs are as common as out-of-order adjectives are rare. A little learning, they say, is a dangerous thing, and a vague malaise about splitting infinitives, the *to* forms of verbs, apparently accounts for a great many oddly placed adverbs. The rule, first of all, only proscribes an adverb after the *to* in a two-word infinitive (*to be, to do, to think*); in a passive or past infinitive—as well as in any other verb phrase that ends with a past participle—the *ed* form of a regular verb, the adverb usually belongs before the participle (*to have sorely needed, to be wholly satisfied, to have been poorly represented; has always wanted, had been justly accused*). And, second, the rule is not sacrosanct. Most accomplished writers respect the integrity of an infinitive—but not at any cost.

The following sentence includes a split infinitive that careful stylists would avoid and another that they would accept, at least if the only alternative were to transpose the adverb:

> To properly assess the situation, you have to carefully weigh planned improvements against anticipated results.

Putting *properly* after *situation* improves the sentence, but if you take *carefully* out of the infinitive, where can you put it? It modifies *weigh*. Placed after the infinitive, it would seem to modify *planned*; before the *to*, it would sound unnatural; after *improvements*, it would separate word groups that belong together; and at the end of the sentence, it would be too remote from the verb it modifies. Although a split in-finitive is preferable to artificiality or ambiguity, you can often avoid all three evils by omitting the adverb or rewording the sentence. In the last example you could easily do without *carefully*—weighing one thing against another implies taking care—but if you wanted to keep it, you could substitute *must* for *have to.*

If you place adverbs by ear, you will usually put them where they belong. Anyone who writes *We have developed recently a plan* or *They have completed just a survey* is either unfamiliar with the sound of Eng-lish or mistaken about the propriety of splitting compound verbs. No native speaker says *They planned recently their budget* or *We checked care-fully our records.* In a conventionally ordered sentence, an adverb modifying a one-word verb ordinarily goes between the subject and the verb, not between the verb and the object; but it may sometimes follow the object if it remains near the verb. When there is no object, the adverb may precede or follow the verb, as the desired emphasis dictates. An adverb modifying a verb phrase goes after the first word in the phrase (*was extremely surprised, has often been said, would certainly have asked*) unless, in verb phrases of three or more words, it modifies only the participle (*had been justly accused, would have been officially ruled*). You usually know instinctively when to put the adverb before the participle, and when you can't be sure, the position probably makes no difference. But H. W. Fowler does offer a helpful hint: Ask whether the adverb and participle naturally suggest a corresponding adjective and noun; if they do, keep them together. Applying this test to the preceding examples, you get *just accusation* and *official rule* but can find no adjective and noun equivalents for either *often* and *said* or *certainly* and *asked.*

Although adverbs generally fall into their proper places automati-cally, they sometimes occur in ambiguous circumstances. Since they can grammatically modify not only verbs but verbals, adjectives, ad-verbs, and whole sentences, they have many opportunities to form misalliances. An adverb placed between rivals for its attention makes readers hesitate, and it may genuinely puzzle them if the context fails to elucidate. For example:

> Critics have raised doubts about attempts to interpret
> Kleist's response precisely because his skeptical statements
> obscure his thoughts.

Following an infinitive and preceding an adverbial clause, *precisely* can modify either. Are the attempts to interpret precisely, or are the doubts precisely because? If *precisely* should modify *interpret*, you might consider putting it before or after that word, but it would either split the infinitive or disrupt the sentence flow—awkward solutions best avoided. Reversing the order of the main and subordinate clauses proves more satisfactory. By putting the subordinate clause first, you automatically separate the competing terms that sandwiched *precisely* in the first version:

> Because Kleist's skeptical statements obscure his thoughts, critics have raised doubts about attempts to interpret his response precisely.

This transposition also works if *precisely* modifies the *because* clause:

> It is precisely because Kleist's skeptical statements obscure his thoughts that critics have raised doubts about interpreting his response.

When you have trouble placing an adverb, don't forget the option of omitting it. Writers tend to use more modifiers than they need, and an adverb that's hard to fit in may also be expendable. You could, for example, do without the ambiguous adverb in *The union leaders recommend strongly demanding a new wage policy.* If *strongly* modifies *demanding,* the sentence has no room for it and would profit from its loss. A strong word like *demanding* functions better without an adverbial boost.

Of course, not all problem adverbs are dispensable. Consider this sparse sentence:

> Writing simply is not degrading.

Since this example comes from an article on the virtues of writing simply, readers would doubtless understand that the adverb means "in an uncomplicated manner" and qualifies *writing.* But without a clarifying context, the sentence would be ambiguous: *simply* might mean "really" and modify the predicate. A change to *simply writing* would give *simply* the sense of "merely," and a change to *simple writing* would make the gerund mean "a piece of writing" instead of "the act of writing." Running out of options, you can't simply delete *simply;* it's the point of the sentence. You have to reword:

> It is not degrading to write simply.

When you read your writing, watch for Janus-faced adverbs like those in the following examples. The suggested revisions—by no means the only ones possible—show alternative interpretations:

> Their willingness to work constantly amazed me.

> ■ I constantly marveled at their willingness to work.

> ■ Their willing and constant labor amazed me.

What you do primarily determines what you are.
- What you primarily do determines what you are.
- Your activities primarily determine what you are.

That interest rates had declined somewhat eased my mind.
- The slight decrease in interest rates eased my mind.
- That interest rates had declined made me feel somewhat easier.

You have to revise such sentences to make sure that others will read them as you do. All the corrections involve some rewording, often the substitution of a noun for one of the two verb forms that vie for the adverb's attention in the original version. This technique, in effect, disqualifies one of the candidates, since adverbs cannot modify nouns.

Four adverbs merit individual treatment because their placement entails special considerations: *also, only, not,* and *however.* Although much of the discussion applies as well to analogous words like *too, just,* and *moreover,* these four cause the most trouble.

Also, though nominally an adverb, seems capable of playing other roles. In *Women, and also men, are facing new challenges,* for example, its adverbial function is not immediately clear. George O. Curme calls *also, not,* and *only* "distinguishing adverbs," which "have the peculiarity that . . . they can direct attention not only to the verb and thus to the sentence as a whole, but also to any person or thing that becomes prominent in the situation as a whole." Whatever the grammatical complexities, *also*—meaning "in addition"—can attach itself to a variety of sentence elements, so that you have to place it carefully to avoid false connections. What element is "in addition" in the following sentence?

I also think he is lying about where he was that night.

Do you give the same answer when you read that sentence as the second of a pair?

She doesn't believe the defendant's alibi for the night of the murder. I also think he is lying about where he was that night.

I think he hated her enough to kill her. I also think he is lying about where he was that night.

The defendant lied about his previous marriage. I also think he is lying about where he was that night.

These examples should demonstrate that *also* in the normal adverbial position can sometimes seem to modify one sentence element and sometimes another, the interpretation varying with the context.

Strictly speaking, the *also* belongs before *think* only when the sentence states an additional thought, as in the second example. Substituting *too* for *also* would more clearly convey the sense intended in the first example, and in the last example *also* belongs between *is* and *lying*.

Theoretically at least, the placement of *only* affects the meaning of a sentence, just as the placement of *also* does. But in practice *I only want one, I want one only,* and *I want only one* all have the same meaning, despite differences in rhythm and emphasis. Although you may have learned that *only* should always directly precede the word it modifies, most contemporary writers on style qualify that rule, pointing out that sentences like these sound stilted and unnatural:

> Maybe millions of people go by, but I have eyes for only you.

> And where it will all end only God knows.

In each of the examples you expect to find *only* where the adverb usually goes, before the verb, and the unnatural placement impedes the reading. You cannot mistake the meaning of a sentence like *In a money market account you are only allowed to write three checks a month* or *Your costs may be higher if you only deal with local suppliers,* and *only* would less effectively signal a qualification if it appeared later. So when *only* falls into its idiomatic place without causing ambiguity, let it stand.

But "without causing ambiguity" is an important qualification. You can sometimes muddle a sentence by putting *only* before the verb instead of before the word it modifies. If, for example, you write that *The committee only seemed interested in their proposal,* readers won't necessarily understand "seemed interested only in their proposal." Perhaps the committee was only feigning interest. Again, if you write *We are only ordering metal desks because they are more durable than wooden ones,* readers may think you're ordering only one type of furniture when you mean you're ordering it for only one reason. So take care with your *onlys.* If you've learned that *only* must precede the word it modifies, make sure that your *only* sentences don't sound artificial. If you've only been doing what comes naturally with *only,* watch out for ambiguity.

Like *only,* the adverb *not* does not always belong where it naturally falls. Force of habit often induces writers to put *not* before the verb even when the negative applies to a different sentence element. The problem usually arises in two kinds of sentences. One type follows this pattern:

> All municipal bonds do not have the same rating.

> All forecasters do not agree that the unemployment figures will decline.

> All stories cannot end happily.

Each of these sentences seems to be saying something negative about an entire group when it means to point out a distinction within the group. Precisely worded, the examples would read:

> Not all municipal bonds have the same rating.
>
> Not all forecasters agree that the unemployment figures will decline.
>
> Not all stories can end happily.

Still, Shakespeare could observe, echoing a proverb, that "all that glisters is not gold," and the illogically placed *not* has persisted (*All is not lost*). But the alternative *not all* wording isn't unidiomatic—it doesn't offend the ear—and it has the virtue of sweet reason. In revising, then, watch for sentences in which entire groups are the subjects of negative verbs. If you find any, move the *not* from the predicate to the subject, as in the preceding examples, unless, of course, the negative does apply to the whole group. Even then you may discover that recasting the sentence with a positive verb produces a clear statement. In the following three versions of the same example, the one with the negative predicate seems least satisfactory:

> All my colleagues will not vote in the next election.
>
> All my colleagues will abstain from voting in the next election.
>
> None of my colleagues will vote in the next election.

The second common misplacement of *not*—traceable, like the first, to the compulsion of idiom—occurs in *not–but* sentences: the adverb precedes the verb but applies only to what follows the verb. As originally drafted, the last sentence unintentionally illustrated this error: *. . . when the adverb does not modify the verb but what follows.* Had the slip gone uncorrected, the sentence would have lacked a positive verb to govern the clause after *but.* A simple adjustment usually solves the problem: *when the adverb modifies not the verb but what follows.* Because a *not–but* pattern emphasizes what is, not what isn't, the preceding verb must be positive; the negative belongs to a subordinate part of the sentence. Even conscientious writers sometimes misplace *not* in this type of sentence; the error comes so naturally, in fact, that you should routinely check for it. You can't miss it if you make a practice of reading the verb with the part of the sentence that follows *but.* Try this test, for instance, on *Do not do as I do but as I say,* and you will quickly revise to *Do as I say, not as I do.* If you want to keep the negative verb in this sort of sentence, you have to supply a positive one as well: *Do not do as I do, but do as I say.*

However, the final adverb singled out for special attention, differs in kind from those we have been discussing. As a pure adverb, meaning "to whatever degree," it modifies other modifiers and invariably appears in its proper place (as in *However brave the knight, he will quake before the dragon* or *However valiantly he fights, the beast will prevail*). More often, though, *however* has a connective or transitional function. When it means "but" or "in spite of that," grammarians call it a conjunctive adverb, and in that role it can be hard to place. Because it highlights what precedes, it should follow the element that contrasts with something stated previously, as in these sentences:

> The Class of 1949 gave the most money; the Class of 1955, however, had the largest percentage of contributors.

> Pauline Kael heaped extravagant praise on *Last Tango in Paris*; Vincent Canby, however, was far less enthusiastic.

> We might consider a compromise; we will not, however, accept the proposal as is.

Problems arise when the contrasting element is long and difficult to interrupt. Then *however* may come too late to serve as a signpost:

> The knights who assembled at the Round Table to discuss what measures to take against the dragon could not, however, devise a plan.

Or it may come too early and emphasize the wrong word:

> They, however, expected the fire-breathing monster to destroy the kingdom if they did not continually supply him with maidens.

You may think—and many would agree—that you can avoid such problems by putting *however* first in the sentence. Or did you learn in your school days never to do that? Some teachers used to argue that a conjunctive *however*, since it stresses what precedes, has no business coming first in the sentence. But Theodore Bernstein contends that an initial *however* points to a contrast between the two sentences it separates and that signaling the contrast at the outset has its advantages. "Incidentally," he adds, "if your elementary school teacher told you never to begin a sentence with *however*, forget it."

While the 1982 edition of the *American Heritage Dictionary* reports that an opening *however* "is now generally considered . . . acceptable," it also acknowledges that "some grammarians have ruled to the contrary." Jacques Barzun, for one, recommends keeping set transitional words like *however* to a minimum and making them as unobtrusive as possible by burying them inside sentences. "For my part," he writes, "*however* is a forbidden word, the sign of a weakness in thought. I use it once in a great while, when I cannot get rid of neighboring *but*'s and do not want to add one more."

Though you need not consider *however* a taboo, you should guard against the common tendency to overwork it, particularly as a sentence opener. In revising your work, think twice about every *however* you use. It is in the right place? Would a different word be better? An internal *however* is less ostentatious than an initial one, and an alternative like *but* or *yet* usually provides a smoother transition. Occasionally, however, you may want to begin with *however* to mark an emphatic contrast between ideas, and it's always better to put it first than to force it inside a sentence that has no room for it.

Verbal Phrases

Participles, verb forms ending in *ing* or *ed* (except for the irregular verbs) and functioning as adjectives, have a well-known tendency to escape the bonds of syntax, to detach themselves from the elements they should qualify. In other words, they dangle. The most notorious dangler is the introductory participle that does not describe the subject of a conventional sentence.

Rhetoric handbooks usually have ludicrous examples of this infamous error, such as *Driving along the highway, a deer leaped in front of the car* or *Laughing and singing around the campfire, the weenies roasted and the popcorn crackled.* The mistakes are hard to miss and easy to fix. You either convert the participial phrase to a clause (*As we drove along the highway, a deer leaped in front of the car*) or make the subject of the sentence the word the participle logically modifies (*Laughing and singing around the campfire, the children enjoyed the sounds and smells of roasting weenies and crackling popcorn*).

But unattached opening participles, however simple to detect and avoid, continue to flourish in real life. A cook-ahead cookbook introduces its recipe for *canard à l'orange* with this sentence:

> Roasted to perfection, carved, and reheated in orange sauce,
> you can serve this duck to the boss.

Failing to bring duck and sauce together, the writer ends up with a mutilated cook. Revised, the sentence could read:

> Roasted to perfection, carved, and reheated in orange sauce,
> this duck is elegant enough to serve to the boss.

A college admissions officer, writing to a prospective applicant, provides another example:

> Having thus expressed a direct interest in [our college], we
> have enclosed the materials you requested along with an
> application form.

Clearly the sentence should read:

> Since you have expressed an interest in [our college], we are sending you an application form along with the materials you requested.

And here's an example from a major metropolitan newspaper:

> Based on information supplied by the victim's brother, the police in Nevada are searching for the body in the same area where the suspect is being sought.

The police, whether based in Reno or Las Vegas, cannot be based on information; *based on* does not yet rank among the participles that have turned into prepositions or adverbs and no longer need modify nouns or pronouns. A number of participles have shed their exclusive adjectival status and evolved into prepositions, parts of prepositions, phrases, conjunctions, or adverbial sentence modifiers (e.g., *speaking of*, *provided that*, *granted that*, *regarding*, and *according to*); others may be traveling in that direction but have not yet established themselves beyond question (e.g., *assuming*, *admitting*, and *acknowledging*). If you don't know whether or not a participle has undergone this metamorphosis, play it safe, or check its part-of-speech label in the dictionary. *Based* remains a participle—a dangling participle in the last example. You could revise by substituting a participle to fit the subject:

> Acting on information supplied by the victim's brother, the police. . . .

A dangling participle can occur anywhere in a sentence, not only at the beginning. When it comes at the end, it may have more than one word to modify. It clearly relates to the subject if no intervening word lures it away, as in *Many actors feel nervous when performing in the presence of the president*, but in a sentence like *Many actors feel nervous in the presence of the president when performing*, readers can't be sure who's performing. In looking for unattached participial phrases, don't be thrown off by a subordinating conjunction like *when*, *if*, or *while* that precedes the participle. You can consider a phrase like *when performing* an elliptical clause, a sequence of words in which a subject and verb are "understood" rather than expressed, but the phrase still needs an anchor. It must, in fact, modify the word that should be understood as its subject. If that relation is not clear, you can always convert the phrase to a clause: *when they are performing* or *when he is performing*.

In the next example, from an advisory pamphlet for investors, the problem arises not because the closing participle can modify either of two nouns but because it has nothing to modify:

> Individual issues in the portfolio should be ignored when reviewing performance.

Since *reviewing* cannot sensibly modify either *issues* or *portfolio,* you have to ask who is reviewing and supply an answer. Here are two solutions:

> When reviewing performance, you should ignore individual issues in the portfolio.
>
> You should ignore . . . portfolio when you review performance.

A closing participial phrase usually either limits the meaning of the immediately preceding noun or describes, without limiting, the subject of the sentence. When the participle follows the noun directly, without intervening punctuation, readers generally take it as a defining, or restrictive, modifier of the preceding word. For example:

> The brochure lists the plays scheduled for next season.
> (The participle modifies *plays,* identifying them as the ones scheduled for next season.)

When a closing participle follows a comma, as in the preceding parenthetical sentence, readers ordinarily interpret it as modifying, but not restricting, the subject of the sentence. For example:

> The shipping department mailed the brochures yesterday, working overtime to meet the deadline. (The closing participle modifies the subject, *department,* without limiting or defining it.)

If a closing participle conforms to neither of these patterns, readers may not immediately see what it modifies. Sentences like these are ambiguous:

> We have often seen celebrities waiting in line to buy tickets.
>
> A giant supermarket will open in the new shopping plaza, drawing customers from a fifteen-mile radius.

You can clear up the confusion by converting the closing participial phrase to the appropriate clause (*when we were waiting . . .* , or *which draws customers*).

Here, finally, is a dangler in the middle of the sentence:

> Such celebrities should be studied seriously, based on full information and guided by good judgment, instead of being left to the idolatrous worship of the marketplace.

Presumably the study of the celebrities should be based and guided, but since the sentence includes no noun, such as *study,* for these participles to modify, readers misattach them and stumble over the illogicality of celebrities studied, based, and guided. You might revise this way:

> Such celebrities should not be left to the idolatrous worship of the marketplace but should be given serious study based on full information and guided by good judgment.

While participles are the verbals most often found dangling or forming improper alliances, some gerund and infinitive phrases have similar problems. A gerund, the *ing* verb form used as a noun, obviously cannot be a modifier, dangling or otherwise; in itself, it serves as a subject, object, or complement. But it can be part of a prepositional phrase that needs something to modify. Such a phrase poses no problem if the subject of the clause in which it appears is also the understood "subject" of the gerund (the person or thing performing its action), as in the first of the following examples, or if a possessive noun or pronoun precedes the gerund and indicates a different subject, as in the second example:

> In running a large office, an administrator must be willing to delegate authority.
>
> In her running of the office, I saw little to criticize.

In contrast, the opening phrases in the next pair of sentences attach themselves incorrectly to the subjects of their clauses:

> In running a large office, a willingness to delegate authority is essential.
>
> In running the office, I could find little fault with her.

Two other examples, accompanied by revisions, show that misattached preposition-gerund phrases can occur anywhere in a sentence:

> Our consultants felt that, instead of cutting back production, new markets should be developed.
>
> ■ Our consultants felt that, instead of cutting back production, we should develop new markets.
>
> Customers have been lost by taking them for granted.
>
> ■ We have lost customers by taking them for granted.
>
> ■ Customers have been lost by our taking them for granted.

A modifying infinitive—one in which the *to* has the sense of "in order to"—may also make the wrong connection if its understood subject is not the same as the subject of the clause in which it appears. A few illustrations should be enough to clarify the problem, since it is the same one that occurs with preposition-gerund phrases. In each of the following examples the infinitive has nothing to modify, and the revision suggests a solution:

> To succeed in this business, opportunities must be sought out and promptly acted on.
>
> ■ To succeed in this business, one must seek out opportunities and act on them promptly.

Hard work is not enough to succeed in this business.

■ Hard work is not enough to ensure success in this business.

The trainees were praised to help build their confidence.

■ We praised the trainees to help build their confidence.

Infinitives and gerunds that are themselves subjects, objects, or complements obviously need not have understood subjects that match the subjects of their clauses. Berkeley's "To be is to be perceived" is flawless, at least in its grammar, and so are *Swimming is fun* and *I enjoy dancing.* Nor does the rule hold for adjectival infinitives or preposition-gerund phrases that directly follow the words they modify. There's nothing wrong, for example, with *The doctor gave a lecture on keeping fit and suggested ways to stop smoking.*

Fortunately, verbals are easier to use correctly than to discuss. Most of them cause no trouble and require no attention, and once you recognize the sort that can go astray, spotting errors becomes almost instinctive. Just make sure that the verbal phrases you use as modifiers, not as nouns, have appropriate words to modify. In reading critically, illogicalities will become obvious and can be readily corrected by applying standard remedies. But if you didn't notice the errors in the last sentence, you still need practice.

Appositive and Contrasting Phrases

An appositive phrase restates, and thus clarifies or defines, the term next to it. Both elements denote the same person or thing. In *General Motors, the giant of the automotive industry, recently recorded impressive profits,* the appositive *giant* phrase identifies *General Motors.* By definition, an appositive adjoins the noun or pronoun it applies to, but sometimes other words intervene, breaking the connection. While such slips rarely confuse, the imprecision makes a poor impression. Often the writer begins a sentence with the appositive, using it as a catchy opener, but fails to make the synonymous term the subject:

One of the most rewarding and trouble-free house plants, I
feel that hoya belongs in every indoor garden.

If the writer could have parted with the humble *I feel that,* all would have been well. Although such phrases are common, you rarely need them to distinguish opinion from fact. But if you insist on *I feel* in such a sentence, either move it out of the way or eliminate the appositive construction:

One of the most rewarding and trouble-free house plants,
hoya, I feel, belongs in every indoor garden.

Or:

> I feel that hoya belongs in every indoor garden, for it is one
> of the most rewarding and trouble-free house plants.

The following sentence illustrates an even more common error in
the use of appositives:

> A resident of Middletown since boyhood, Trent's interest in
> antiquities dates back to his senior year in high school.

In the earlier example the appositive and its principal are not adjacent. Here, strictly speaking, the appositive has no principal. Terms in
apposition should be grammatically equivalent, and no element in the
sentence equates with *resident. Interest,* the noun nearest the appositive, clearly doesn't qualify. We know, of course, that *Trent* and *resident* denote the same person, but the sentence provides *Trent's,* not
Trent. Since a possessive modifies a noun, thus acting as an adjective,
it cannot also function as a noun and anchor an appositive or adjective phrase. Failure to recognize this rule of grammar accounts for
many opening danglers, not only dangling appositives but dangling
verbal phrases as well (*Listening to the melancholy music, my eyes filled with
tears; To be eligible for the race, your application must be filed by 15 July*).
Recast logically, the sentence about Trent might read:

> A resident of Middletown since boyhood, Trent became
> interested in antiquities during his senior year in high
> school.

Some appositive constructions leave readers in doubt about
which terms go together. Be sure that no word intervening between a
noun and its appositive invites a mismatch. For example:

> The association endorses the candidacy of the first man to
> challenge the unfair policies of the incumbent—a civic
> leader well known to all of us, John Milner.

Reversing the order of principal and appositive would prevent the
faulty pairing of *incumbent* and *leader:*

> . . . candidacy of John Milner, a civic leader well known to
> all of us and the first man to challenge the unfair policies of
> the incumbent.

A contrasting phrase, like an appositive one, should follow the
word it applies to. Some grammarians, in fact, call such a phrase a
negative appositive. In the following sentence the antithetical element
is in the wrong place:

> Although government has usurped some parental
> responsibilities, at heart it is still parents who are obligated
> to care for children, not someone else.

Because the *not someone else* is not where it belongs, after *parents*, the sentence seems to say that parents must care for their children and not for someone else. Perhaps the writer settled for this imprecise word order because the plural *are* seemed awkward in the sequence *it is still parents, not someone else, who are obligated.* But you shouldn't have to avoid one problem by introducing another. Instead of allowing the contrasting phrase to make an improper connection, the writer could have recast it as a plural:

> . . . at heart it is still parents, not state agencies, who are
> obligated to care for children.

Prepositional Phrases

Prepositional phrases—units consisting of words like *at, by, in,* and *with* and their objects—will probably figure in most of the faulty sequences you discover in your writing. Since they can modify nouns, pronouns, verbs, adverbs, and adjectives, they usually latch onto whatever precedes, and they lend themselves readily to different interpretations. So keep a sharp eye out for problems.

The blunders that get into print are sometimes so blatant that it is difficult to understand how they escaped notice. For example, a brochure from a Nova Scotia resort, attempting to lure vacationing anglers, offers *sea trout in tidal rivers without need of guides or boats.* But your own lapses may be more subtle and harder to detect, since you read over your sentences with the inflection and emphasis that bring out the meaning you intend. You may have to put yourself in someone else's place before you can recognize the alternative ways of combining elements.

With phrases are among the most troublesome, because *with* can either have one of several specific meanings (e.g., "accompanied by," "by means of," or "having") or serve as a vague connective, a means of tacking on supplementary information that has no precise relation to the other sentence elements. (The *with* entry in *Webster's Third New International Dictionary* takes up more than a column of fine print.) How do you interpret *with* in this sentence?

> The radio's precision controls let you zero in on weak
> signals with a minimum of background noise.

The *with* phrase seems to go with *signals,* but presumably the writer is not defining weak signals as those with the least background noise. If the *with* modifies the verb *zero,* it's hard to know what the preposition means: *zero in on signals with a minimum of background noise* doesn't fit the pattern of "beat an empty barrel with the handle of a broom" or "endure hardship with patience and fortitude." The sentence needs more precision control to help readers zero in on the message:

> The radio's precision controls zero in on weak signals and minimize background noise.

The next example gives some baffling investment advice:

> Owning stocks in a period of declining prices carries the risk of losing large amounts of money with the reward of losing little or no money.

Perhaps the *with* phrase modifies *risk*—"carries the risk that has the reward"—but readers do not readily make that connection when *amounts* and *money* are closer at hand. Changing *with* to *and* and adding *potential* before *reward* would improve the sentence; you can, in fact, correct most *with* problems by substituting connectives less open to misinterpretation—if not *and*, then something more specific, such as *because of* or *when*.

Like *with*, *for* has a variety of definitions and adapts easily to the nearest convenient word. Make sure that the word at hand is appropriate. In the following examples, one from a news story and the other from a letter of application, the *for* phrases make the wrong connections and, as the revisions show, putting them right involves rewording or rearranging:

> The Reagans attended the Joffrey Ballet Saturday to see their son dance professionally for the first time.

> ■ Attending the Joffrey Ballet Saturday, the Reagans had their first opportunity to see their son dance professionally.

> I recently prepared a report on the psychic rewards of working for the personnel department.

> ■ I recently prepared a report for the personnel department on the psychic rewards of working.

By is another commonly misrelated preposition that attaches itself readily to different types of words. You may have to edit out a *by* phrase if you can't put it immediately after the word it modifies. For example:

> The law was formulated in 1662 on the basis of Boyle's measurements by his disciple, Richard Townley.

> ■ Using Boyle's measurements, his disciple, Richard Townley, formulated the law in 1662.

> The Romantic fascination with history led to the replacement of the quest for a universal grammar by a modern historical philology.

■ Reflecting the Romantic fascination with history, modern historical philology replaced the quest for a universal grammar.

As the revisions show, you can sometimes eliminate a placement problem by omitting needless words. In other circumstances the best solution may be to break the sentence in two. For example:

An Amtrak employee who worked the midnight shift in the railroad's nearly deserted electrical substation near Pennsylvania Station was found shot dead early yesterday by a fellow worker.

■ An Amtrak employee . . . near Pennsylvania Station was shot dead last night. A fellow worker found the body early this morning.

Although the preceding examples all involve prepositional phrases that follow the wrong elements, phrases that begin sentences can also cause trouble. Always ask what an initial phrase modifies. If the answer is a noun or a pronoun, the phrase functions as an adjective, and in a conventional sentence the word it modifies must be the subject. The rule here is the same as the one governing introductory participles. In the following quotation the error seems obvious:

Miss Fallaci says that the dream of her life has always been to write novels. At the age of 16, her uncle, who was a journalist, advised her, "First you have to live, then you will write."

The second sentence in the example should, of course, have begun *When she was 16.* Although the reader quickly figures out that the uncle was not the adolescent, the incongruity causes a moment's pause, and the reader who hesitates may be lost to the author. "The man snoozing in his chair with an unfinished magazine on his lap is a man who was being given too much unnecessary trouble by the writer," says William Zinsser, who claims that the average reader has an attention span of about twenty seconds.

Watch especially for dangling opening phrases introduced by *as, like, unlike,* and other prepositions that should compare, contrast, or group their objects with analogous elements. When such words are not in a position to relate corresponding terms, they produce illogical statements. For example:

As a key person in your organization, we are taking the liberty of sending you a press release describing our program for the coming year.

When *as* means "in the capacity of," its object should be a word synonymous with the word the phrase modifies. Here *As a key person* is too far from the *you* it belongs with, but changing the opening phrase is easier than making *you* the subject of the sentence:

> Since you are a key person in your organization, we
> are. . . .
>
> Or:
>
> Recognizing that you are a key person in your organization,
> we are taking. . . .

Here's another example:

> As associate editor, my responsibilities included correcting
> manuscripts and proofs and laying out pages.

As an applicant for an editorial position, the writer would have fared better had he written:

> As associate editor, I was responsible. . . .

In the next example the opening *unlike* phrase lacks an anchor:

> Unlike most industrial companies, all of a bank's assets and
> liabilities other than premises and equipment, trading
> account securities, and other real estate are monetary in
> nature.

Since it is the bank, not its assets, that differs from industrial companies, the sentence should have read:

> Unlike most industrial companies, a bank holds only
> monetary assets and liabilities, except for its equipment and
> premises, its other real estate, and its trading account
> securities.

The last two examples again illustrate the common error of attaching adjective or appositive phrases to possessive forms. Since the possessives themselves are adjectives, you cannot grammatically use adjectives to modify them.

When a prepositional phrase in the *like–unlike* category follows a negative verb, always check to see that the sentence says what it means. Logic may dictate rewording. For example:

> Men have not traditionally depended on others for their
> support, like women.

Although the wording may suggest that both men and women were traditionally self-supporting, the writer doubtless meant:

> Unlike women, men have not traditionally depended on
> others for their support.

Here's one more example:

> Utility shares are not popular with investors in today's
> market, like low-growth stocks in past periods of recovery.

Can you tell whether low-growth stocks were or were not popular in past periods of recovery? The ambiguity disappears when you place the phrase before the negative statement:

> Like low-growth stocks in past periods of recovery, utility
> shares are not popular with investors in today's market.

In addition to *as*, *like*, and *unlike*, the prepositions *in addition to*, *except*, *including*, *excluding*, *among*, and *as well as*, among others that usually introduce adjective phrases, should link their objects to comparable terms. In the following sentence the *among* phrase does not make the proper attachment:

> I enclose my résumé, which among other qualifications
> details my professional training and editorial experience.

To group *qualifications* with the compatible words *training* and *experience*, you could move the phrase to the other side of *details*:

> . . . which details, among other qualifications, my
> professional training and editorial experience.

Or, to avoid the break between verb and object, you could opt for a simpler version:

> . . . which details my professional training, editorial
> experience, and other qualifications.

Having got that far, you might decide to enclose *a detailed résumé* and do without the *which* clause. Prospective employers, after all, know what sort of information a résumé includes.

Another job seeker provided this example:

> As editorial coordinator, I edited all feature articles and
> wrote substantial portions of the news, in addition to the
> other responsibilities listed in my résumé.

The applicant's other responsibilities were not in addition to substantial portions of the news. In fact, no word in the sentence parallels *responsibilities*. *In addition to* needs a verbal object, a gerund, that can coordinate with the verbs *edited* and *wrote*:

> As editorial coordinator, I edited all feature articles and
> wrote substantial portions of the news, in addition to
> carrying out the other responsibilites listed in my résumé.

The next example comes from what must have been a hastily written news bulletin:

> The suspects are being questioned by the police, except the one that was killed.

The exception, of course, is the dead suspect, whom the police are not questioning, not a dead policeman, who is asking no questions. The *except* is in the wrong place, but it doesn't deserve any place at all. Readers know that dead men tell no tales.

The final example for this section comes from an insurance company's letter to stockholders:

> Guardian Life is forming a reinsurance company jointly with the Martin Group Limited, to which we will both contribute capital, along with several domestic and foreign insurance companies.

Here the *along with* phrase seems to modify *capital* instead of *we*. But since the phrase would be disruptive after *we*, you would do better to reword than to rearrange:

> Guardian Life and the Martin Group Limited are jointly forming a reinsurance company, to which we will both contribute capital, as will several domestic and foreign insurance companies.

Clauses

The last example, as you may have noticed, features a misplaced relative, or adjective, clause as well as a misplaced phrase. The original word order suggests that Guardian Life will contribute capital not to the reinsurance company but to the Martin Group Limited. Although a relative clause (most commonly introduced by *who, which,* or *that*) ideally belongs right after the word it modifies, sometimes another element claims the same place, forcing the clause into an ambiguous position. If you read, for example, *The treatise includes an extensive list of virtuous women that Chaucer puts to good use in the Franklin's Tale*, do you immediately know whether Chaucer is using the women or the list? And when you read *Vandalism at Mays Field causes the custodian to spend a lot of time cleaning up junk that might be better used for other things*, do you think about recycled trash?

Given nothing else to go on, readers associate a relative clause with the word that immediately precedes. But often a writer can direct otherwise. In the following version of the Chaucer sentence, for example, the relative clause obviously modifies *list* even though it directly follows *women*:

> In the Franklin's Tale Chaucer makes good use of the
> extensive list of virtuous women that appears in the treatise.

Here the singular verb *appears* identifies *list*, not *women*, as the antecedent of *that*. The trick is to make the relative pronoun the subject of its clause, so that the number of the verb will establish the proper connection. This approach won't work if the ambiguity involves two singular nouns or two plural ones, but you can sometimes avoid that situation. If you write *The qualities in her poems that have received the most critical attention . . .* , the plural verb *have* is no help, but if you substitute *poetry* for *poems*, the syntax becomes clear. Keep in mind, too, that a relative clause will attach itself to a noun preceded by *the* before it will to a noun without the definite article. *The game of cards that I remember best* suggests a memorable game, not memorable cards, but *the game with the cards that I remember best* might refer to a special playing deck or to a fabulous poker hand. Thus, when there's any question about what a relative clause modifies, you can sometimes revise so that only the appropriate word requires the definite article.

When neither of these devices can straighten out the ambiguity that arises when a prepositional phrase separates a noun from its modifying clause, you can usually get rid of the phrase or transpose it. Here are some problem sentences and suggested revisions:

> The issues in labor disputes that are hardest to resolve
> concern job security.

> ▨ In labor disputes the issues that are hardest to resolve
> concern job security.

> The son of the company's founder, who was a compulsive
> gambler, ran the business for only a short time before he
> sold it.

> ▨ A compulsive gambler, the son of the company's founder
> ran the business. . . .

> A key point in the studies that many have overlooked is the
> effect of turnover on efficiency.

> ▨ A key point in the studies, one that many have overlooked,
> is the effect. . . .

Adverbial clauses cause fewer placement problems than adjective clauses do. They generally fit comfortably first or last in the clauses that incorporate them. Since readers know instinctively that a clause introduced by a word like *if, although, because,* or *after* belongs to the predicate, they make the proper connection even if verb and modifier are not adjacent. In the preceding sentence, for example, the two adverbial clauses cannot be misread. Like other adverbial elements, however, an adverbial clause can make the wrong connection if a tempting part of speech comes between it and the word it should modify, as in these examples:

> They told us they would consider our offer when we met them in New York.

> The principal reprimanded the students for screaming after the performance was over.

> The directors were concerned about the reduction in staff that would be necessary before they introduced the new system.

> They went on working after the conference broke up because they had to meet their deadline.

In each of the examples, an adverbial clause that should modify the verb in the main clause seems instead to modify an element nearer by. The solution is to put the disputed clause first in the sentence, at a safe remove from any competition for its attention. In the last example you could begin with either the *after* or the *because* clause.

The adverbial clauses we have been considering form improper attachments to subordinate verbs. Sometimes, though, the problem occurs in reverse: an adverbial modifier intended for the subordinate verb appears instead to modify the main one. For example:

> When this plan was proposed twenty years ago, the editorial claims that hardly anyone greeted it with enthusiasm.

The opening clause looks as if it belongs with *claims*, but it should go with *greeted*. It identifies the time of the unenthusiastic response, not the time of reporting that response. Watch for this common error in your own writing. The pattern is always the same, and the remedy is simple: either put the adverbial clause after *that* or, if you prefer to leave it where it is, add a comma after the main verb and drop the *that*. The second alternative—*When . . . ago, the editorial claims, hardly anyone greeted*—demotes *the editorial claims* from a main clause to a parenthetical interruption within the main clause, which is now *hardly anyone greeted. . . .* The pair of commas enable readers to bridge the gap between the sentence elements to the left and right. Here's one more example to reinforce the point:

> When stock prices are high, the broker observes that hemlines also rise.

The sentence is illogical in more ways than one, but we need consider only the syntax. The bull market should go with short skirts, not with the broker's observation:

> The broker observes that when stock prices go up, hemlines also rise.

Or:

When stock prices go up, the broker observes, hemlines also rise.

Here and throughout, the suggested remedies represent only some of the possibilities. You can usually clarify word-order ambiguities in several ways, and you can always adopt an entirely different approach to a problem sentence. The next section deals with the process of revision in somewhat more detail, showing how you might arrive at particular solutions.

Jockeying for Position

Word-order problems usually arise because two or more modifiers—say, a participial phrase and a relative clause—belong in the same spot. If the word, phrase, or clause that loses its place falls into the wrong company, rewording can be tricky. This section dissects several illustrative sentences and discusses the steps and options that would be involved in revision.

The first example, taken from a publisher's press release, contains only a minor error, but trying to correct it can be instructive:

> The company announced that it has formed a new editorial press in the Metropolitan Detroit Area called International Book Publishers.

Probably no one would fault you for letting that sentence go as it is. The out-of-place *called* phrase isn't much of an obstacle since it obviously modifies *press*. It can't go where it belongs, right after *press*, because the *in* phrase occupying that position has nowhere else to go. If the prepositional phrase were placed before, after, or within the verb phrase it modifies, *has formed*, it would disrupt the sentence flow. Still, the structure is faulty, and if the words were different, it might be confusing (. . . *formed a new editorial press specializing in European authors called International Book Publishers*). You can improve the sentence by reversing the order of the modifiers and adding a pair of commas to keep the *in* phrase from being misread with *called*:

> The company announced that it has formed a new editorial press, called International Book Publishers, in the Metropolitan Detroit Area.

By setting off the participial phrase as parenthetical, the commas enable readers to make the proper connection. In general, though, you shouldn't try to doctor an ailing sentence with punctuation if you can find a better remedy. Besides, the revision has the disadvantage of de-emphasizing what the announcement should publicize—the firm's name. A little more tinkering produces other possibilities:

> The company announced the formation of International Book Publishers, a new editorial press in the Metropolitan Detroit Area.

> International Book Publishers, the company's newly formed editorial press in the Metropolitan Detroit Area, will. . . .

> The company announced that it has formed a new editorial press—International Book Publishers. Located in the Metropolitan Detroit Area, the press will. . . .

Each of these revisions corrects the word-order problem, but one or another would probably seem best in context.

A suburban newspaper editor wrote this caption for the front-page photograph of a town meeting:

> Part of the standing-room-only crowd at Round Hill School that came to an informational meeting last Monday evening on a proposed residential development near the center of Blooming Grove.

The *that* clause should follow *crowd*, but the *at* phrase rightfully claims the same place. Even though the *the* before *crowd* helps attract the clause to the right noun, the gap between them is somewhat awkward. If you put the phrase after *meeting*, you widen the already awkward separation between *meeting* and *on*. In revising, you might begin by deciding that two word sequences are essential: *at* must stay with *crowd*, and *on* has to follow *meeting*. Starting from these fixed points, you could ultimately arrive at this revision:

> Part of the standing-room-only crowd at Round Hill School last Monday evening for an informational meeting on the proposed residential development near the center of Blooming Grove.

A reporter for a neighborhood Manhattan weekly had a similar problem with prepositional phrases:

> After years of often acrimonious debate, the general public got its first opportunity to inspect and question plans for the Convention Center to be built on the site of the 30th Street rail yards during a public hearing sponsored by Community Board 4 last Tuesday. But the general public didn't show, despite the presence of a high-powered panel of experts present to answer their questions.

The opening prepositional phrase, which modifies *got*, occupies the most appropriate place for a long adverbial modifier, relegating the *during* phrase, which also modifies *got*, to a position where it looks as if it modifies *built*. Here again the writing is more awkward than confusing—readers certainly wouldn't think that the center would be built during a hearing—but such sloppiness debases the reporter's by-line. Other lapses betray carelessness—the general *public* at the *public* hearing, the *presence* of the panel *present*, and the *public* considered singular in the first sentence (*its opportunity*) and plural in the next (*their questions*). These sentences might provide a good exercise for journalism students trying to master the *who-what-where-when-why* lead. Here's one possibility:

> At a hearing sponsored by Community Board 4 last
> Tuesday, the public got its first opportunity, after years of
> often acrimonious debate, to inspect and question. . . .

Although the opening might be duller in this version the *after* clause causes less trouble within the sentence than the *during* (now *at*) phrase did, and the new order has the additional advantage of juxtaposing the related elements *first opportunity* and *after*. The surrounding commas mark the *after* phrase as parenthetical and help readers make the proper connection between *opportunity* and the infinitives it governs. Still, the word order is less than ideal, and you might try a different approach:

> Last Tuesday Community Board 4 assembled a high-
> powered panel of experts to answer the public's questions
> about the Convention Center to be built on the site of the
> 30th Street rail yards—but the public didn't show, even
> though the hearing gave them their first opportunity to
> inspect and challenge a plan that for years has been the
> subject of often acrimonious debate.

The final example in this section comes from an account of a murder trial:

> Under cross-examination, both witnesses basically
> substantiated the defendant's alibi that he was helping his
> mother and her family move the day of the killings to
> Ringwood, N.J., from their Sloatsburg home.

Although readers know better than to believe the sentence, it does say that the accused helped move the day of the killings to another town from their home. Slipshod writing that's easily corrected brands the writer as lazy or incompetent. Here you might begin revising by adding a preposition to clarify the role that *the day* plays in the sentence. Then, recognizing that *on the day of the killings* intervenes between sentence elements that belong together, you could put the disruptive phrases after *that* to get them out of the way. Finally, you might reverse the order of the last two prepositional phrases and make them more compatible with each other (one naturally moves from here to there, not to there from here, and one more logically moves from one town to another than from a home to a town):

> Under cross-examination both witnesses substantiated the defendant's alibi that on the day of the killings he was helping his mother and her family move from Sloatsburg, N.Y., to Ringwood, N.J.

CLARIFYING THE STRUCTURE

Any discussion of faulty word order naturally concentrates on modifiers, since these are the components most commonly misplaced. While the main sentence elements—the subjects, verbs, and objects—pose fewer problems of this sort, writers sometimes arrange them in ways that obscure the syntax. Even if readers can't tell a predicate from a preposition, they instinctively look for the basic components that shape a sentence. They can't make their way through it unless they can see its framework. A subject may have so many qualifications that readers forget what it is before they find out what it does. If the description builds up in front of a subject, they can get lost on the way to the main clause. The word order may suggest that an element plays a different role from the one intended, or a verb and an object may be so far apart that the connection between them dissolves. This section discusses the obstacles that keep readers from recognizing how the structural parts of a sentence fit together.

Subject–Verb Connections

A sentence in which the subject consists of a noun modified by a long string of phrases and clauses preceding the verb that says what the subject does may be hard to read. The last sentence is a case in point. When complicated modifiers separate subject and verb, readers may have trouble connecting the two, as in this sentence:

> People for whom the nuclei of atoms are as real as the bacon and eggs they have for breakfast are exceedingly rare.

You can usually eliminate an overlong subject easily enough, though the method will vary with the particular sentence. Here you might simply invert the sentence:

> Rare indeed are people for whom the nuclei of atoms are. . . .

Or you could shorten the subject:

> People for whom the nuclei of atoms are as real as their
> breakfast bacon and eggs are exceedingly rare.

Or you could restructure the sentence, either by eliminating the original predicate or by converting the original subject to a clause and choosing a different subject:

> Very few people find the nuclei of atoms as. . . .
>
> Or:
>
> Though some may consider the nuclei of atoms as real as
> their breakfast bacon and eggs, such people are exceedingly
> rare.

The last approach often provides the fastest way out of the difficulty. Here's what it would do for the deliberately wordy sentence that opens this paragraph:

> If a long string of modifiers separates a subject from its
> verb, the sentence may be hard to read.

While you should avoid amassing words between subject and verb, you should also avoid long-winded modifiers before the subject, lest you sidetrack your readers before they find out what you're talking about. Here's an example:

> Still persisting almost twenty years after the assassination,
> with its truth or falsehood probably never to be convincingly
> proved despite the negative conclusions of repeated
> investigations, the rumor of a conspiracy to kill President
> Kennedy has fueled yet another work of fiction.

When you find yourself spinning out such an opening, start again. If you can't move some of the preliminary comments into the predicate, you'll probably have to break the bulging sentence in two:

> Despite the negative conclusions of repeated investigations,
> the rumor of a conspiracy to kill President Kennedy persists,
> probably never to be convincingly proved or disproved.
> Now, more than twenty years after the assassination, it has
> fueled yet another work of fiction.

Not all problems in establishing the proper link between subject and verb occur in long sentences, as the next example shows. It illustrates the common fault of placing a verb where it can attract the wrong subject:

> Our representatives know that we oppose the pending
> legislation and do not expect it to pass.

Is it our *representatives* or *we* who do not expect? The context might make the answer clear; the sentence itself does not. To clarify, you either have to give each verb a subject of its own or eliminate one of the verbs. The revision, of course, would depend on the meaning intended. Here are two possibilities:

> Since our representatives know that we oppose the pending legislation, we do not expect it to pass.

> In view of our opposition to the pending legislation, our representatives do not expect it to pass.

The next example, sad to say, comes from an early draft of this chapter:

> A lazy writer will let the misplacement stand and argue that no one can misunderstand the meaning.

The sentence means, of course, that the writer will *let* and *argue,* but *stand* and *argue* seem to go together. The revision replaced *let stand* with *keep* (. . . *will keep the misplacement and argue* . . .), but adding *will* before *argue* would also have worked, since putting the verbs in parallel form would mark them as a pair.

Words play different roles in different sentences, and their placement in any context determines the way readers understand them. An *ing* verb form, for instance, can be a noun or an adjective, and often only its relative position in a sentence reveals its function. In the last example confusion arises because *stand,* the infinitive form without the *to,* looks like the present tense, and the context permits either interpretation. (Idiom calls for dropping the *to* before an infinitive that follows *let*; *let it stand* is equivalent to *allow it to stand.*) Other ambiguities stem from the duplicity of the *ed* verb form, which can be either the past tense or the past participle. For example:

> I realized why they had failed and regretted taking part in the program.

The word order suggests a link between *failed* and *regretted,* though the writer meant *and* to connect *realized* and *regretted.* Either of these revisions would give the intended meaning:

> I realized they had failed, and I regretted taking part in the program.

> Realizing why they had failed, I regretted taking part in the program.

Whenever you write a sentence in which a third verb follows a main verb and a subordinate verb and looks as if it could pair with either, read it with the subject of each clause and you'll see the potential misinterpretation. Here's one more example from an early draft of this chapter:

> Most adjectives modify the nouns they precede or follow
> linking verbs.

Did you link *precede* and *follow* and then falter when you got to *linking verbs*? Adding an *either* before *modify* to balance the *or* before *follow* would couple those two verbs and make misreading less likely. But since *precede* and *follow* form a natural pair, it would also help to reverse the order of *modify* and *precede*:

> Most adjectives either precede the nouns they modify or
> follow linking verbs.

If you always pay attention to what the connectives *and* and *or* seem to join, you should be able to detect and disentangle mismatched pairs. This simple check can save you from many awkward sentences.

Ambiguous Words

Look-alike verb forms are not the only sentence elements subject to mistaken identity. Words that can serve as different parts of speech take on the roles the context assigns, but sometimes the context leaves the matter in doubt. For example:

> Careful preliminary work should result in the investor's
> speaking to no more than a half dozen money managers,
> with two or three more likely.

On first reading, the sentence may seem to contradict itself. If there will be no more than six managers, how can two or three more seem likely? The question arises only for those of us who take *more* in a sense different from the writer's. We read it with *two or three*, interpreting it as a pronoun meaning "additional money managers," but the writer apparently intended *more likely* as a comparative adjective form. Replacing the *with* phrase with *and probably only two or three* makes the meaning unmistakable.

Unfortunately, specific examples of ambiguous word usage have little general application. The ways to go wrong are infinite. But if you try to look at your work from a reader's point of view, you may find sentences that are open to misinterpretation. One problem involves the possibility of confusing nouns and verbs, since many words can be either. Consider, for example, these phrases (or sentences?): *the frantic dance to the point of collapse, the British camp across the river, the triumphant shout "Eureka!"* Although such word sequences are not ambiguous once the context enables you to classify the disputed word correctly, they may be stumbling blocks, and you can speed readers along by revising. For example:

> She has examined all the records and reports that the witnesses have provided contradictory accounts.

■ She has examined all the records and finds that. . . .

> The writer condemns heavily modified subjects and objects that they muddy the sentence structure.

■ The writer condemns heavily modified subjects and argues that. . . .

> The article cites the escalating prices and charges that the services are demanding undue profits.

■ Citing the escalating prices, the article charges that. . . .

If in each of these sentences you first read the second verb as a noun, then you must also have misread the *that* clause as a modifier. This ambiguity reflects a fairly common problem. When a *that* clause directly follows a noun, make sure that readers can immediately tell whether it functions as a noun or as an adjective. The noun function is clear-cut in *We tell callers that they can expect overnight delivery,* but in *We told the messenger service that we always used to schedule daily four o'clock pickups,* readers can take the *that* clause as the object of *told* or as the modifier of *service.* (Was the usual messenger service told to schedule four o'clock pickups, or was the service told what we always used to do?) In revising, you would have to get rid of the confusing *used to schedule* sequence: *We told our regular messenger service to schedule . . .* or *We told the messenger service that daily four o'clock pickups had always been scheduled.*

You can often omit *that* before a noun clause (*No wonder you're pleased, I thought they would agree*), but you sometimes need it to keep the subject of the clause from looking like the object of the introductory verb. In each of the following sentences the missing *that* permits an initial false connection, requiring readers to pause and make an adjustment:

> I believe the economic forecast was self-fulfilling.

> They reported the warehouse explosion wiped out their inventory.

> I understand the upsurge in the market reflects an anticipated decline in interest rates.

The insistence on *that* in such sentences may strike you as overfussy, but if you imagine a line break after the subject of each noun clause, you may change your mind.

Placement of Objects

When a hiatus occurs between verb and object or between preposition and object, the connection may not be clear, and often the two kinds of difficulties occur together. Some verbs need prepositions to relate them to the objects they act on—you approve *of* something, talk *about* something, and look *for* something—whereas others, of course, take direct objects and need no intervening prepositions—you like something, discuss something, seek something. Problems may arise if verbs seem to share an object that belongs to only one of them (*We should meet and discuss our common enemy*), if verbs require different prepositions to relate them to the same object (*They never participate in or, with few exceptions, contribute to such charitable endeavors*), or if the direct object of one verb is also the object of a preposition that follows the other (*We do not have to explain and certainly we need not apologize for our refusal*). Ideally, when two verbs govern the same object, neither should need a preposition or both should need the same preposition.

A headmaster's letter announcing noontime parent-teacher conferences illustrates the risk involved in giving a direct object to only the second of a pair of verbs:

> A buffet will be served in the cafeteria during the visiting
> hours, so that parents can eat as well as meet their children's
> teachers.

Here *teachers* looks like the direct object of two verbs, permitting a ludicrous misreading. One solution is to give the first verb an object of its own:

> . . . so that parents can eat lunch as well as meet their
> children's teachers.

In the next example the relation of verb to object gets lost in the distance between them:

> Please read and let me have your department's views on the
> attached marketing proposal.

It's hard to connect *read* and *proposal*, especially when the intervening *department's views* looks as if it goes with both *read* and *let me have*. Adding a pair of commas, one after *read* and the other after *on*, would clarify the structure, but the awkward break between verb and object would remain. You can usually correct this sort of problem by placing the object after the first verb and using the appropriate pronoun in the prepositional phrase that follows the second:

> Please read the attached marketing proposal and let me have
> your department's views.

Here, however, you could simply omit *read* and begin *Please send me,* since presumably no one comments on a written proposal without reading it first. When a sentence needs revision, tightening is often the best approach.

In the following sentence, different prepositions share the same object:

> He always conferred with, or asked the approval of, his
> colleagues.

The sentence is clear but bumpy. To smooth it out, bring *with* and its object together:

> He always conferred with his colleagues or asked their
> approval.

In the next example the first verb lacks the preposition necessary to connect it to the object:

> For many years employees not only complied but did not
> question the office dress code.

You would have to add the missing *with* after *complied* and then bring preposition and object together:

> For many years employees not only complied with the office
> dress code but did not question it.

Here, though, you might prefer to substitute a verb that, like *question,* needs no preposition to connect it to an object:

> . . . employees neither violated nor questioned the office
> dress code.

Although Jacques Barzun objects to examples like the last, which involve a break between preposition and object, he sees nothing wrong with pairing verbs in which only the second requires a preposition before the object. He allows sentences like *Expect and prepare for setbacks* because the preposition and object are adjacent. But sometimes such constructions tempt readers to associate the preposition with both verbs. Here's the specific sentence that Barzun cites as acceptable:

> His experience makes him the best person to tackle and
> succeed in this difficult task.

Readers may not only attach the *in* phrase to *tackle* but also momentarily mistake *him* for the best person to tackle. Here the standard solution—*the best person to tackle this difficult task and to succeed*—won't work; *the best person to succeed* doesn't make much sense. You could open up the sentence:

> His experience makes him the person best qualified to tackle
> this difficult task and the most likely to succeed.

Or you could tighten it:

> His experience makes him the person most likely to tackle
> this difficult task successfully.

While you should generally try to keep prepositions and objects together, short gaps are easy to bridge and readers take them in stride. You needn't change *plays on and off Broadway* to *plays on Broadway and off it* or replace *looked up and down the street* with *looked up the street and down it*. If doing what you think is correct results in a sentence that sounds awkward or artificial, do something else. Anything that sounds odd is likely to make readers falter, and your aim is to keep them moving right along. In some contexts idiom condones a preposition at the end of a clause and the object at the beginning. No one still recommends, for example, *You get that for which you pay* and *About which rules are you talking?*

As a reader, you've undoubtedly run into sentences that stop you cold because they don't make sense. Though the ideas may be simple enough, the presentation is so poor that you have to read the words again and again before you can begin to get their drift. You're obviously not going to devote this sort of frowning concentration to a sentence unless you're intensely interested in it—unless you're reading, say, a letter from your lover or instructions for assembling a bicycle. As a writer, you can't expect readers to grope for the meaning you intended to convey.

While faulty word order can make a sentence well-nigh impenetrable, it usually doesn't. Readers are not hopelessly literal-minded or insensitive to logic, and they can generally recognize your intention even though you haven't expressed it precisely. Still, faulty connections damage your prose. They are stumbling blocks, distractions that dissipate whatever spell you're trying to weave. Efficient writing makes effortless reading. It never calls attention to itself.

Ill-matched Partners

3 Many familiar lines of prose and poetry owe their place in Bartlett's to their balanced cadences. "Marriage has many pains," says Samuel Johnson, "but celibacy has no pleasures." "The Puritan hated bear-baiting," Macauley explains, "not because it gave pain to the bear, but because it gave pleasure to the spectators." Deprived of their parallel structure, some famous quotations lose their punch:

> I come for the purpose of burying Caesar, not to praise him.
>
> Was this the face that launched a thousand ships and was responsible for the burning of Ilium's topless towers?
>
> . . . brought forth on this continent a new nation that had its conception in liberty and was dedicated to the proposition that all men are created equal.
>
> Many are called, but God doesn't choose more than a few.
>
> . . . that all men . . . have certain unalienable rights: to life, liberty, and to pursue happiness.

The originals mangled here echo insistently enough to demonstrate their superiority. And though you need not strive for the perfect symmetry of, say, the Sermon on the Mount (a style best reserved for special occasions), parallel constructions have an important role in all writing. Appropriately matched components can make the difference between a sentence that runs smoothly and one that jerks along in fits and starts.

Most sentences meet the test of parallel structure when the elements presented in series or pairs belong to the same grammatical category, that is, when all are adjectives, nouns, active verbs, infinitives, phrases, or clauses. Just as you can't add apples and oranges, at least not without reducing them to pieces of fruit, you can't yoke disparate parts of speech or different types of constructions and expect them to function together efficiently. To write *He is determined, a fighter, and has a quick mind* or *We need employees with specific skills and who can work as a team* is like harnessing a horse, a goat, and a camel to a troika or designing a chair with a rocker on one side and a pair of legs on the other.

To some extent parallel constructions are idiomatic. Children chant, or used to, *Doctor, lawyer, merchant, chief*; romantic heroes are *tall, dark, and handsome*; Pal Joey's ladylove is *bewitched, bothered, and bewildered*; Caesar said, *I came, I saw, I conquered*; and Lincoln spoke of a government *of the people, by the people, and for the people*. More often than not, parallel structure comes naturally to us. We might describe the typical Swede as fair, blond, and blue-eyed or as having fair skin, blond hair, and blue eyes; we would be unlikely to say that the stereotype is fair, a blond, and has blue eyes. Such imbalances make us uneasy. You don't have to know the rules of rhetoric to sense that something is wrong with *We are told to live our own lives and that we should not interfere with how others behave*, but an experienced editor would immediately recognize that the infinitive phrase and the *that* clause make a lopsided pair. To right the balance, you could substitute *not to interfere* for *that we should not interfere*, and perhaps someone arrived at that point before coming up with the inspired *to live and let live*. For while we're naturally attracted to parallel pairs and series, they don't always come readily to mind. As Wilson Follett observes, felicitous writing "seems inevitable, but if we could contemplate the doing of it from a little in advance of the fact, we should see nothing marked out as foreordained, but rather a labyrinth of ways to go wrong."

UNBALANCED PAIRS AND SERIES

You can detect most errors in parallel structure by routinely checking the words or word groups you join by *and* and *or* and making sure that they match. In other words, the elements linked as compound subjects, objects, verbs, and modifiers should have the same grammatical form. When they don't, you can either bring them into line or change the structure to eliminate the need for parallelism.

Since faults in parallel structure are easy to spot, their abundance in print is somewhat surprising. But deadlines often leave little time for polishing, and revisions can be tricky. When you find an imbalance, first try to put the coordinate items in the same form, converting an adjective and a noun, say, to two adjectives or two nouns. Sometimes, though, the right terms prove elusive, and forcing two elements into the same structure may make the sentence wordy or stilted. The serial items are not parallel in *The new clerk is intelligent, conscientious, and wants to change the system,* but . . . *is intelligent, conscientious, and desirous of changing the system* isn't much of an improvement. While the form of the series is flawless, the artificial wording calls attention to itself.

Serial or paired items that are hard to balance may not belong together; they may resist alignment because they are not logically similar. The solution then is to uncouple the combination, to subordinate one component to the others instead of making them all coordinate: *The new clerk, who is intelligent and conscientious, wants to change the system.*

The following examples represent some of the most common types of mismatches, and the alternatives suggest possible revisions:

> The proposed transmission line is ugly, unsafe, and an environmental danger.
>
> ■ . . . ugly, unsafe, and hazardous to the environment.
>
> The process is slow, prone to politics, and robs all concerned of direct responsibility.
>
> ■ . . . slow and prone to politics, robbing all concerned of direct responsibility.
>
> The applicants were all college graduates, of similar socioeconomic background, and interested in business careers.
>
> ■ . . . all college-educated, similar in socioeconomic background, and interested in business careers.
>
> Your cover letter should include information about your present employment and why you want to change jobs.
>
> ■ . . . should include information about your present employment and explain why you want to change jobs.
>
> The problem is on the minds of millions of Americans, young and old and in all parts of the country, not only in Louisiana.
>
> ■ . . . on the minds of millions of young and old Americans in all parts of the country, not only in Louisiana.

The mismatched pairs and series in the above examples involve such combinations as adjective and noun, adjective and verb, noun and prepositional phrase, and noun and clause. Some imbalances are less pronounced than these and are not even universally regarded as flaws. Still, they leave room for improvement. If, for instance, you've coordinated an active verb with a passive or linking one, consider substituting two active verbs or recasting the sentence to avoid the ill-matched compound. For example:

> Farm failures contributed to the 1917 revolution and were one of the reasons for Khrushchev's ouster in 1964.

> ▓ Farm failures contributed to the 1917 revolution and to Khrushchev's ouster in 1964.

> He has worked for the bank for many years, is knowledgeable about nearly all areas of banking, and will be an excellent addition to top management.

> ▓ Employed by the bank for many years and knowledgeable about nearly all areas of banking, he will be an excellent addition to top management.

> She ranks as the country's top railroad analyst and is often consulted by financial writers and stockbrokers.

> ▓ As the country's top railroad analyst, she is often consulted by financial writers and stockbrokers.

Combinations of nouns and gerunds can also be jarring, though less so than those involving different parts of speech. Since a gerund is the *ing* verb form used as a noun, it might seem a fit associate for a purebred noun, but when its verbal side is insistent, the two don't work well together. Apparently, however, not all experts would agree. One author, in analyzing various sorts of writing errors, makes no apology for this sentence:

> When people have to write from a point of view not their own, they . . . betray this by hedging, blustering, an uneasy choice of words, and syntactical looseness.

In this context the gerunds suggest people doing something—hedging and blustering—and this active element is absent from the noun phrases in the series. But the items do not go gently into parallel structure:

> . . . by hedging, blustering, misusing words, and lapsing into syntactical looseness.

> Or:

> . . . by an uneasy choice of words, syntactical looseness, and a tendency to hedge and bluster.

The difficulty in making the terms grammatically compatible suggests that they are not logically equivalent, and you might decide to restructure the sentence. Here's one possibility:

> When people write from a point of view not their own, they
> hedge and bluster, betraying uneasiness in their choice of
> words and their loose syntax.

In the next example one conventional noun intrudes in a series of gerunds:

> The technical reforms needed to protect Social Security
> include curtailing preferential federal pensions, bringing
> federal employees into the system, raising the retirement age
> to sixty-eight, modification of the indexing policy, and
> increasing military careers to thirty-three years.

It's hard to understand how anyone could use *modification of* instead of *modifying* in that sentence. Similarly mystifying is the choice of *the construction of* over *constructing* in this one:

> The plan entailed razing the entire business district—
> thirty-four buildings dating from the nineteenth century—
> and the construction of a modern shopping plaza.

In some series, however, gerunds and conventional nouns mingle without friction, either because the grouping is loose enough not to require precise parallelism or because the verbal qualities of the gerunds do not surface. Whatever the explanation, you can usually tell instinctively whether or not a gerund is out of place in a group of straight nouns. In the earlier examples the change in form brings you up short, but in the following series you hardly notice it:

> Among the many aspects of credit examined are credit
> scoring, debt burden, the cash analysis system used by
> banks, the difference between charge and credit cards, debt
> servicing, credit ratings for women, denial of credit profiles,
> and the personal judgment factor.

An accomplished writer may occasionally use an unbalanced pair or series for a specific reason—perhaps to imitate a style of speech or to achieve a comic effect. Few would quarrel with Lorenz Hart's "I'm wild again, beguiled again, a simpering, whimpering child again" or with the riddle that asks "What's big and red and eats rocks?" (Answer: "A big red rock eater.") But if you set aside the rules of parallelism, know what you're doing and why. Unintentional violations reflect laziness or ignorance.

PARALLELISM AND CORRELATIVE CONJUNCTIONS

Whatever leeway you allow yourself in balancing coordinate elements in general, you should enforce a rigid parallelism on those connected by the so-called correlative conjunctions—principally, *either . . . or, neither . . . nor, both . . . and,* and *not only* (or an equivalent like *not just, not simply,* or *not merely*) *. . . but also* (or *but* if what follows seems to intensify rather than to supplement). These double connectives emphasize the correspondence between the word groups they introduce, and it offends logic not to make the companion pieces grammatically equivalent. The first one makes readers anticipate a mate, and it's unsettling for those expecting a second shoe to drop to hear instead the thud of a chair or the shattering of a teacup.

When you're roughing out a first draft, the conjunctions may not fall where they belong (*I not only sent a copy to my supervisor but also to the head of the division*), but be sure to put them right when you revise (*I sent a copy not only to my supervisor but also to the head of the division*). A good editor never reads over correlative conjunctions without checking what they introduce and correcting any inequities. A sentence like the next one should never have got past the newspaper's copy desk:

> The officers were not only well respected professionally but
> they also often went hunting and fishing with their
> colleagues on the state police and local sheriff's department.

The following revision at least meets the technical requirements of parallel structure:

> Not only were the officers well respected professionally but
> they had often gone hunting and fishing with their
> colleagues on the state police force and in the local sheriff's
> department.

This alternative corrects not only the improper placement of the correlative conjunctions but also the imbalance between *state police* and *local sheriff's department*; in the original the two law-enforcement agencies were linked as compound objects of *on,* but *on the . . . department* is unidiomatic. The solution to the *not only–but also* problem is less satisfactory, since *were respected professionally* and *had gone fishing* make an odd couple. Though each correlative now introduces a coordinate clause, the ideas are not in balance. You can get better results by changing the word order and finding a more compatible verb to pair with *respected*:

> The officers' colleagues on the state police force and in the
> local sheriff's department not only respected the men
> professionally but regarded them as friends, having often
> gone hunting and fishing with them.

Devising an acceptable version of the last example took considerable effort, and perhaps the news item came in too late to rewrite. But many mistakes in the use of correlatives are easily fixed. Sometimes you need only transpose one of the conjunctions or add an article or a preposition. The elements after correlative conjunctions should correspond exactly; if, for example, the first conjunction precedes a preposition that governs both elements, you should either repeat the preposition after the second conjunction or move the preposition ahead of the first conjunction. Here are some typical errors and corrections:

> From the beginning this faction has been critical both of the motivation and the tactics of the new government.

> ■ . . . has been critical of both the motivation and the tactics. . . .

> The end can neither be known nor imagined.

> ■ . . . can be neither known nor imagined.

> He began to stay late at the office, either because the work was piling up or to impress his staff.

> ■ . . . either to clear away the work that was piling up or to impress his staff.

> ■ . . . either because his work was piling up or because he hoped to impress his staff.

> These virtues are not only the heart of liberal learning but they also perform a critical social function: they constitute the glue that holds the community together.

> ■ These virtues not only constitute the heart of liberal learning but also perform a critical social function: they serve as the glue. . . .

> ■ These virtues are not only the heart of liberal learning but also the glue that holds the community together. (Is there any need to point out that holding the community together is a critical social function?)

> The company not only dominated the town's business but also the way the residents lived and thought.

> ■ The company dominated not only the town's business but also the way. . . .

> In pointing out the dangers of nicotine, the surgeon general is not only referring to smoking cigarettes but also chewing tobacco.

> ■ . . . surgeon general is referring not only to smoking cigarettes but also to chewing tobacco.

In highlighting the matching parts of a sentence and thus showing which elements go together, correlative conjunctions sometimes provide a useful means of avoiding ambiguity. In the last example, for instance, the misplacement of *not only* is especially awkward because it mismatches *referring* and *chewing*, suggesting that the surgeon gen-

eral was chomping on a wad of tobacco when he made his announcement. But since the correlatives—especially *not only . . . but also* and
both . . . and—are emphatic devices, don't squander them on compound elements that don't need them. Using correlative conjunctions
where a simple *and* would do is like driving in a thumbtack with a
sledgehammer. For example:

> I have the figures for both the first quarter and the second.

> I read not only your report but also the list of
> recommendations you attached.

Although the correlative conjunctions must precede parallel parts
of the sentence, the terms that make up these pairs do not invariably
function together. Each can operate alone. In particular, you can use
not only without necessarily going on to *but also* or *but. Not only* always
promises more to come, but the rules of rhetoric allow alternative
ways of keeping that promise:

> It is not only our country that faces this problem, most
> Western nations have high unemployment rates.

> Not only our country but also most other Western nations
> have high unemployment rates.

The comma after *problem* in the first of these examples shows that the
sentence is not yet complete. *Not only* signals something to follow.
This construction is one of the few that permit the junction of independent clauses without a stronger mark of punctuation or a coordinating conjunction.

PARALLELISM AND CLARITY

As the preceding sections emphasize, the proper management of parallel structure has a great deal to do with a pleasing writing style, and
you should mix and match your sentence components as attentively
as the well-dressed coordinate their outfits. The difference between a
carefully assembled sentence and one just thrown together is the difference between a Neiman-Marcus mannequin and a cornfield scare-
crow.

But the value of parallel structure goes beyond aesthetics. While
the eighteenth-century essayists used perfectly balanced clauses primarily for rhetorical effect, the matching of parts within clauses often
serves a more practical purpose. It points up the structure of the
sentence, showing readers what goes with what and keeping them on

the right track. Without this sort of coordination a sentence may be not only awkward but open to misinterpretation. For example:

> Emphasis is placed on explaining the company's controls and how effective those controls can be.

What two elements does the *and* connect here? Neither of the possibilities on its left, the gerund *explaining* and the noun *controls,* matches the *how* clause on the right, so that readers can't be sure which elements function together. They can guess, of course, but any structure that requires guesswork also requires revision. If *controls* is the first element in the pair, you can improve the sentence by converting the *how* clause to a modifier-noun combination:

> Emphasis is placed on explaining the company's controls and their effectiveness.

But since *controls* and *their effectiveness* do not seem distinct topics, a more condensed revision might be more precise:

> Emphasis is placed on explaining the effectiveness of the company's controls.

If the gerund and the clause are the compound elements, you can convert the clause to a verbal phrase:

> Emphasis is placed on explaining the company's controls and on demonstrating their effectiveness.

Let's look at another example:

> The article on American agriculture explains the interacting forces of technology, government policies, fluctuating demand, international politics, inflation and recession, surpluses and subsidies, land values, the real cost of borrowed capital, and how fallow fields can earn more than fertile ones.

You might think at first that the final *and* introduces the last item of the long series and that the clause should be made compatible with the other items in the series—converted, say, to *the potential of fallow fields to earn more than fertile ones.* But if you pay attention to the meaning, you can see that the original *how* clause does not belong in the list of interacting forces. Rather, it parallels *forces,* functioning as a second object of *explains.* The revision could read:

> . . . explains how various forces interact to affect farming— technology, government policies . . . borrowed capital—and how fallow fields can earn more than fertile ones.

In many contexts you have to repeat a subordinating conjunction, a preposition, an article, or an auxiliary verb before each element in a pair or series to reinforce the parallelism and prevent misalliances. For example:

> Limit the candidates to those managers who can provide independently measured results or firms that can provide good recent references.

Here readers might initially see _results_ and _firms_ as joint objects of _can provide_. Though they would quickly reject this pairing in favor of _managers_ and _firms_, a _to_ before _firms_ would have prevented the flicker of hesitation.

You usually don't have to repeat an article before each noun in a pair or series (_a pair or a series_, for example, might be called pedantic, schoolmarmish, or overrefined—the adjective depending on which usage critic you consult). Strict grammarians recommend using an indefinite article before each coordinate term when one word requires _a_ and the other _an_, but this rule can also go by the board in informal contexts (_Eat an apple, peach, or pear every day; He wasn't wearing a hat or overcoat_). When articles do need repeating, we generally include them automatically. If you attend a meeting with two business acquaintances, for example, you might say you went _with a broker and a banker_. _A broker and banker_ would imply a single companion who wears two hats. When you use correlative conjunctions, an article must appear with the second element if it does with the first. Though you may say _Get me a hammer and nail_, you would have to say _I don't have either a hammer or a nail_ or _I have neither hammer nor nail_. Occasionally you need articles before both nouns in a pair to prevent the second one from being misread as a verb. Another _a_ would be helpful, for example, in _Whenever I attend a seminar or lecture on the new technology I become depressed_.

Duplicate whatever words help to establish the relation between compound elements. You needn't repeat articles and prepositions that don't contribute to clarity, but you shouldn't omit those that provide guidance. Without pointers to the contrary, readers assume that an _and_ or _or_ connects the word group on its left to the corresponding one on its right. A second _about_ would serve no purpose, for example, in _I talked about my predecessor and his influence on our policy_, where _and_ obviously links the two objects of the preposition. The sentence permits no other interpretation. But in _I talked about my predecessor's influence on our policy and the steps I plan to take_, you need another _about_ after _and_ to keep readers from seeing _policy_ and _steps_ as joint objects of _on_. Since _and_ does not connect the terms adjacent to it, you have to take precautions against misreading.

Be sure to treat all items in a series consistently. Don't repeat a preposition or a conjunction with only some of them. The function word should either serve the entire series or reappear in each item. Faulty sentences of this sort are common:

> There is a feeling that the government is lagging, that
> business is looking ahead with enlightened self-interest, and
> labor is busy trying to sandbag against today's problems.

The illogical omission of *that* before the last serial item jars readers, whether or not they recognize what's wrong, and it might lead some to interpret the final clause as the second part of a compound sentence, balancing *There is a feeling*, rather than as the third in a series of subordinate clauses.

Since putting paired and serial elements in the same form helps identify them as compounds, using parallel structure for components that do not function together can be misleading. In one fairly common type of flawed sentence, readers have to choose a coordinate pair from a matched threesome in which two grammatically compatible elements precede *and* or *or* and one follows. Sometimes the conjunction follows both a verb in the main clause and a verb in a subordinate clause and precedes a verb that looks as if it could pair with either. The question is whether the third goes with the first or with the second. Chapter 2, on word order, includes a few examples of this problem. Here are two more:

> The program became a successful model from which other
> programs developed and pioneered a variety of major
> innovations in management education.

> We take pride in the work we do and appreciate your
> comments and suggestions on ways to serve you better.

In sentences like these, usually the simplest solution, though not necessarily the best, is to add a comma before the conjunction and a subject before the following verb (adding only a comma would separate the two verbs that belong together as well as the two that do not): *. . . work we do, and we appreciate. . . .* Sometimes, though, you can produce a better sentence by editing out the odd verb:

> The program became a successful model for other programs
> and pioneered a variety of major innovations in
> management education.

> We take pride in our work and appreciate your
> suggestions. . . .

If you can't easily eliminate the problem verb, you can take a different approach. Consider this sentence:

> We discovered that our competitors had increased their
> market share and decided to introduce an improved product.

Here *decided* can pair with either *discovered* or *increased*—that is, its subject may be *we* or *competitors*. Assuming that the subject is *we*, you can clarify the sentence by repeating the pronoun before the second verb:

> We discovered that our competitors had increased their
> market share, and we decided. . . .

Or you can eliminate the ambiguity about what *and* joins by eliminating *and*—in other words, by subordinating one of the verbs:

> When we discovered that our competitors had increased
> their market share, we decided to. . . .

Of course, if the *decided* of the original version parallels *increased*, not *discovered*, you could make the connection clear by adding *had* before *decided*:

> We discovered that our competitors had increased their
> market share and had decided to introduce an improved
> product.

The problem of misleading parallel structure is not restricted to verbs. The next sentence allows some confusion about which nouns function together:

> The development of new electronics industries and the
> country's changing demographics will cushion the
> unemployment problem.

Some readers may see *industries* and *demographics* as objects of *of* before they recognize *development* and *demographics* as subjects of *will cushion*. Among the various ways of avoiding this possibility, certainly the easiest would be to reverse the order of the compound elements:

> The country's changing demographics and the development
> of new electronics industries will cushion. . . .

Since no confusion arises when *and* links the terms adjacent to it, the transposition solves the problem. Whenever you have paired nouns like those in the preceding example, try to put the odd noun last. That is, make the noun followed by the prepositional phrase the second of the pair. Another possibility, as always, is to change the coordinate structure to a subordinate one:

> Along with the country's changing demographics, the
> development of new electronics industries will. . . .

Or you could shift to a passive construction, if you could justify it, and put the parallel elements in matching *by* phrases:

> The unemployment problem will be cushioned by the development of new electronics industries and by the country's changing demographics.

This approach wouldn't work, of course, if there were another *by* phrase to obscure the structure:

> The unemployment problem will be cushioned by the new industries created by the electronics revolution and by the country's changing demographics.

In pairing phrases or clauses, as in pairing verbs or nouns, watch out for three of a kind. For example:

> We understand that you plan to discontinue the incentive program that you adopted last fall and that the union has protested.

Is the third *that* clause the second one that modifies *program* or the second direct object of *understand*? Admittedly, you could avoid confusion by introducing the adjective clause, or clauses, with *which* instead of *that*, but not if you follow the advice of the usage critics who would restrict *which* to nonrestrictive clauses. You might better clarify by eliminating the odd *that* and leaving only the parallel pair. These two revisions correspond to the two possible meanings:

> As we understand it, you plan to discontinue the incentive program that you adopted last year and that the union has protested.

> We understand that the union has protested your plan to discontinue the incentive program that you adopted last year.

The next sentence has a confusing number of *of* phrases:

> In the absence of any evidence of coercion of clients or of opposition to the proposal, I see no reason why we should not go ahead.

Are both evidence and opposition absent, or are both coercion and opposition unproved? If you start with *Since there is*, you can pin down the meaning by using *either . . . or* or *neither . . . nor* to mark the elements intended as coordinates:

> Since there is no evidence either of coercion of clients or of opposition to the proposal, I see. . . .

> Since there is neither opposition to the proposal nor evidence that clients were coerced, I see. . . .

Correlative conjunctions almost always provide a way of identifying parallel pairs where there is any ambiguity. Although you shouldn't resort to this emphatic device frivolously, it can be useful if you find that you haven't clearly established what elements an *and* or *or* connects. Here's one more example, this one involving a trio of infinitives:

> The dean said that she hoped to persuade the board to
> authorize the new curriculum and to increase the faculty in
> several disciplines.

Either the dean hoped to persuade and increase, or she hoped that the board would authorize and increase. Adding *both* after *hoped* or after *board* would eliminate the doubt.

In the preceding examples, where coordinate elements have the same form as some other element nearby, the parallel structure can mislead readers about what goes with what. Less commonly, parallel structure can mislead, not because it creates ambiguity about the matching parts but because it suggests a correspondence between elements that are too disparate to be associated. When Lewis Carroll groups cabbages and kings or Alexander Pope writes of husbands and lap dogs breathing their last, the effect is intentionally comic. Don't impose parallel structure on incongruities unless you're aiming at humor, because the result is likely to be ludicrous:

> The police found no alcohol in his bloodstream but a loaded
> gun in his car.

> Nylon tricot sleepwear will make her glamorous and still
> practical for traveling or lounging.

The proper management of parallel structure involves guiding readers smoothly through sentences by signaling the elements that work in pairs and series. There are, as Follett says, "a labyrinth of ways to go wrong." The following examples, both from printed sources, illustrate some of the ways not covered in the preceding discussion of specific flaws. Above all, these sentences show that putting parallel ideas in parallel form is essentially a matter of thinking straight, of recognizing how the various sentence components fit together. Elements that have the same relation to another element should have a family resemblance, and those that do not function together should not look as if they do.

Our first example contains two types of faulty parallelism—one relatively subtle, the other blatant:

> Downsizing encompasses smaller cars, houses, and families,
> as well as conservation efforts; all of this affects iron and
> steel production, and rubber, lumber, glass, copper, and
> other basics.

The less obvious flaw lies in the first clause, where the serial items and the *as well as* phrase don't mesh. *Cars* and *houses* match well enough, but certainly *families* are not in the same category. The *as well as* phrase compounds the problem by bringing *conservation efforts* into the picture. When you stop to consider the logic of this grouping, you quickly realize that smaller cars and conservation efforts are not parallel notions. If nothing else, one is concrete, the other abstract. The writer has not thought through what the sentence should say, and judging from the quotation alone, you might have a hard time guessing. Here I happen to have inside information, so that I know what the author had in mind:

> Downsizing encompasses smaller cars and houses, which in turn reflect conservation efforts and the trend toward smaller families. . . .

The last part of the sentence is also inexact: *production* does not belong in the same series with a list of basic materials. The second clause should read:

> . . . all this affects the production of iron, steel, rubber, lumber, glass, copper, and other basic materials.

The final example in this section reflects the same sort of poor quality control that has cost American manufacturers business:

> The Japanese machine cost $60,000 less than the American model, was judged to be more flexible and have better controls, greater accuracy—and could be delivered faster.

You might begin attacking this sentence by making the verbs parallel. You can't convert the two passive verbs to active ones and still have a compound predicate, since they would require different subjects, but you could make the first verb passive to match the others. You might then put the cumbersome second serial element at the end, where it causes less trouble:

> The Japanese machine was priced $60,000 below the American model, could be delivered faster, and was judged to be more flexible and accurate and to have better controls.

Looking at this version, you might consider the parallel structure forced and try a different approach. What about that unwieldy ending? If *better controls* means only "controls permitting greater flexibility and accuracy," you could simplify:

> Not only was the Japanese machine judged more flexible and accurate than the American model, but it was priced $60,000 lower and could be delivered faster.

But if *better controls* is not implicit in this version, what precisely does the phrase mean? A more specific statement might also be more graceful:

> . . . judged easier to operate and more flexible. . . .

OTHER INCOMPATIBLES

In addition to checking pairs and series for parallel structure, pay attention to the elements you compare and contrast. These too should be parallel in form, though disparate wording is probably the most innocuous of the ways that comparisons can go wrong. There's nothing seriously amiss with this sentence:

> In the early stages of market declines, the risk of making less money is more palatable than the risk of substantial losses.

Nevertheless, wouldn't anyone with half an ear compare *the risk of substantial losses* with *the risk of reduced returns* rather than with *the risk of making less money?* More often, a faulty comparison involves elements compatible in form but incompatible in substance. Both may be nouns, for example, but nouns denoting entirely different sorts of things. Not all the precepts of grammar seem logical, but the rule that you can only compare like things is patently sensible. Though no one would say that *five is better than blue* or that *eating is better than Sunday*, comparisons just as witless often find their way into print, not because the authors are simple-minded but because they don't write what they mean. For instance:

> The newspaper has been around since 1870, but its editorial style is as aggressive as a publication started yesterday.

Clearly the author means to say that the style of the paper is as aggressive as that of a newspaper started yesterday, but the stated comparison is between a style and a publication. It doesn't mislead us, because we know better than to believe what it says, but the wording is sloppy. We all make slips in talking, and if anyone calls us on them, we're likely to say, "Oh, you know what I mean." But in writing, where presumably we have a chance to look over what we've set down, there's less excuse for imprecision.

The last example illustrates a common sort of inexact comparison, and you can usually correct it simply by adding *that of* or *those of* to provide a fitting balance for the left-hand side of the comparison. Here are two more examples, with the corrections in brackets:

> Salary levels for bank portfolio managers are at least a third less than [those for] investment managers in brokerage houses.
>
> The cost of renovating the offices was estimated to be considerably below [that of] leasing new space.

It's even simpler to straighten out faulty comparisons in this form:

> New York's taxes are higher than most other states.

Here *taxes* is compared with *states*, but you need only add an apostrophe after *states* to make the statement logical, since *taxes* would be implicit after the possessive. Of course, you use *that of* or a possessive form, not both. The *that of* is redundant in this example:

> Butte's downfall may be similar to that of Detroit's.

In this sort of sentence the apostrophe works better than a *that of* construction. A demonstrative that refers to a noun preceded by an adjective seems to stand for the combination—here for *Butte's downfall*, not just *downfall*. Similarly, the sentence *Sales taxes are worse than those imposed by the IRS* is inexact, because *those* points to *sales taxes*, not just *taxes*.

A comparison is open to misinterpretation if it fails to indicate whether the word that follows *than* or *as* contrasts with the subject or the object of the preceding clause. You can usually clarify the meaning by adding a verb, or a subject and verb, to the second part of the comparison. For example:

> Japanese workers fear automation less than their American counterparts [do].
>
> The mayor considers the vigilantes more threatening than [she does] the criminals.

Sometimes you only need a preposition to show how the right-hand element fits into the sentence. This one-word addition provides an elliptical clause, enabling readers to understand an implicit subject and verb. For example:

> The book deals more with the wonders of high technology than [with] the implications for labor.
>
> Our earnings last year were slightly higher than [in] 1979.
>
> We imported more oil from Saudi Arabia than [from] Mexico.

While imprecisely stated comparisons are usually more slovenly than confusing, some are genuinely unclear. Left uncorrected, the last example, for instance, could mean either that Saudi Arabia supplied more oil than Mexico did or that we imported more oil than Mexico did. Similarly, the earlier comparison involving vigilantes and criminals could mean either that the mayor finds the vigilantes more threatening than she does criminals or that she finds them more threatening than criminals do. This sort of ambiguity, though easily clarified, is a common fault, so watch for it in your own writing. You should, in fact, look critically at all your comparisons to make sure that they make sense.

If a comparison is too muddled to salvage by inserting a word or two, you may have to scrap it and start over. Certainly that's what the author of this sentence should have done:

> The tract influenced Mill, and he claimed to have reached a
> state of mind differing less from that of the sect than existed
> previously.

Elliptical constructions work when readers automatically infer the missing words from those already stated. But in this example what words are they to understand between *than* and *existed*? What existed previously? The only possibility the sentence provides is *a state of mind*, but repeating that phrase doesn't solve the problem:

> . . . he claimed to have reached a state of mind differing less
> from that of the sect than the state of mind that existed
> previously.

Readers need to add something more on their own to keep *state of mind* from seeming parallel to *that of the sect* instead of to the earlier *state of mind*:

> . . . he claimed to have reached a state of mind differing less
> from that of the sect than his previous state of mind had
> differed from the sect's.

Obviously, readers aren't going to work that hard to do what the author should have done for them. Besides, though the reconstructed sentence verges on clarity, it's stunningly awkward.

Most writers are capable of drafting such poor sentences, but they should also be capable of recognizing and rectifying their errors when they revise. Before you can recast a badly tangled comparison, you have to figure out exactly what terms you intend to contrast. It takes time and concentration to rework the example we have been discussing:

> The tract influenced Mill, and he claimed that his state of
> mind now differed less from the sect's than it had before.

Of course, as the author, you might decide to jettison *state of mind* as more trouble than it's worth:

> . . . he claimed that he now differed less from the sect than he had before.

Let's look at one more example:

> The report on credit explains why lending institutions may regard ownership of an old car more favorably than a new one.

The sentence illogically compares *ownership* and *new one*, but you can't correct it by simply adding *that of* after *than*. That remedy only serves when the *of* phrase shows possession, and you have a different situation here. Although you can say *the hood of the car* or *the car's hood*, you can't say *the ownership of a car* or *a car's ownership*; ownership does not belong to a car.

When you start working on the sentence, you might decide to restate the comparison so that it involves the two terms that naturally contrast with each other, *an old car* and *a new one*. Using some form of the verb *own* instead of the unwieldy noun *ownership* would give you more flexibility in rewording. The revision would have to fit the context, of course, but here are two possibilities:

> The report explains why owning an old car rather than a new one may be in your favor when you apply for credit.

> The report explains why lending institutions may consider you a better credit risk if you own an old car than if you own a new one.

Just as the elements you compare should be in the same category, so should any elements that you group together. Not all related items are linked by coordinating conjunctions. Phrases introduced by words like *along with, together with, similar to, like,* and *unlike* should have objects of the same sort as the words the phrases modify. Chapter 2 discusses the importance of placing such phrases so that they seem to modify the appropriate words. It is even more important to include the appropriate words. In the following sentence, for example, the *among* phrase has no anchor, no word grammatically compatible with its object:

> Federal reserve banks distribute currency, transfer funds, and pay government bills, among other responsibilities.

You can correctly say that *distributing currency* is among the banks' responsibilities but not that *distribute currency* is among their responsibilities. Here are a few more sentences, along with revisions, to illustrate the problem:

> Unlike taking care of other pets, fish are hardly any trouble.

■ Fish, unlike other pets, are hardly any trouble to care for.

> Along with his other faults, he never met deadlines, so we had to discharge him.

■ His failure to meet deadlines, along with his other faults, forced us to discharge him.

> When we go out to lunch, she always plays the fool, like asking for chopsticks in an Italian restaurant.

■ When we go out to lunch, she always does something silly, like asking for chopsticks in an Italian restaurant.

It is possible, at least theoretically, to overindulge in parallelism. An addiction to elaborately balanced clauses could result in an artificial, mannered style. But few writers today sin in that direction. You are not likely to go wrong if you concentrate on putting comparable sentence components in parallel form. Although accomplished writers can sometimes justify setting the rules aside, guard against careless violations by routinely checking for them:

1. Look at the items you present in series to see that they match in grammatical form, that you haven't intermingled nouns with verbs or adjectives, infinitives with gerunds, or phrases with clauses. Make sure, too, that you have been consistent about repeating initial prepositions, conjunctions, possessive pronouns, or articles; you usually have to include such words with all serial items or with only the first. If you can't put all the items in the same form, consider recasting the sentence to eliminate the series; the grouping may be illogical.

2. Notice the elements connected by *and* and *or* and make sure that they are grammatically equivalent. Then ask yourself whether readers will immediately recognize what terms the conjunctions link. If the sentence components that look like a pair are not the ones you intend, revise to preclude misreading. Pay particular attention to the words that follow correlative conjunctions and make sure that they match exactly. If you cannot put coordinate elements in the same form without sounding unnatural, consider uncoupling them; they may be incompatible.

3. Finally, look closely at the elements you compare, especially those that follow *as* or *than*, to see that they are logically and grammatically similar, that you are comparing like with like. Also make sure to group like with like; check prepositional phrases that begin with words like *along with, together with,* and *among* to see that their objects belong in the same category as the words the phrases modify.

If you review your writing in these ways, you should detect any errors in parallel structure you've let slip by. Checking for mismatches becomes automatic after a while, and eliminating them will go a long way toward improving both the fluency and the clarity of your writing.

Mismanaged Numbers and References

4 Those scornful of prescriptive grammar have attacked many of its precepts, but they have generally not challenged the rules that require the agreement of subjects and verbs in person and number and the agreement of pronouns and antecedents in number, person, and gender. Though some language scholars do argue strongly for replacing *his or her* with an inconsistent *their* in a sentence like *Everyone is taking his or her seat,* they usually do not practice what they preach, nor do they recommend the consistent but unidiomatic *Everyone are taking their seats.*

SUBJECT–VERB DISAGREEMENT

Most of us make most of our subjects and verbs agree most of the time, and we do so without thought or effort. Usually, in fact, it's hard to do otherwise. Apart from the verb *to be,* English verbs do not differ in form for any subject except a third person singular—*he, she, it,* or whatever one of these pronouns can stand for. The variation occurs in the simple present tense (*he works;* but *I, you, we,* or *they work*) and in any other tense or mood formed with an auxiliary verb that changes in the third person singular, from *are* to *is, were* to *was, have* to *has,* or *do* to *does* (*it is working, she was working, he has worked, it does work*). The distinctive form always ends in *s.* In standard verbs the *s* or *es* attaches itself to the root form (*walks, thinks, passes*); in the irregular auxiliary verbs *be* and *have* it does not (*is, was, has*).

The last paragraph may seem a little complicated if you're not comfortable with the grammatical terms, but it merely describes the changes that you automatically make to bring subjects and verbs into line. Errors in agreement, a singular subject matched to a plural verb or vice versa, do not reflect faulty arithmetic or an inadequate grasp of verb forms. If you make a mistake, you have either misidentified the number of the subject or, more likely, lost sight of what words go together.

Thus, to avoid errors in subject-verb agreement, you have to know how to pick out the subject for every verb you use and how to tell whether that subject is singular or plural. Few sentences will give you trouble on this score. It is only certain types of construction that may tempt you to go wrong. Once you know the danger spots and master a few analytical techniques, you can easily detect and eliminate any faults.

Compound Subjects

Usually a subject consisting of two or more words joined by *and* requires a plural verb: *My pad is on the desk* but *My pad and pencil are on the desk.* Compound subjects rarely pose problems in conventional sentences, but when writers invert the normal order, putting the verb before the subject, they sometimes fail to prepare for a double subject. In the following examples the correct verb form appears in brackets:

> Enclosed is [are] my application and a check for the fee.
>
> Also on my list of all-time great comedies is [are] *A Night at the Opera* and *Tight Little Island.*
>
> More rewarding than the salary is [are] the public exposure the job offers and the opportunity to influence developments in your field.

You usually have to plan ahead for compound subjects in asking questions, too, since the verb usually precedes the subject in an interrogative sentence. Here are a few examples:

> How important to your operation is [are] your West Coast office and your Washington bureau?
>
> Has [Have] the domestic unrest and the international opposition begun to affect government policy?
>
> Does [Do] an orange and a grapefruit have the same number of calories?

Train yourself to check for subject-verb agreement whenever you use an inverted sentence order. If you mentally put the subject before the verb, any mistake should become apparent. Pay particular attention to inverted clauses that begin with *there* and a singular verb form, and make sure that the subject that follows doesn't need a plural verb. These examples show how easy it is to go wrong:

> There is [are] a police officer at the front door and two reporters at the back.
>
> In those days there was [were] only optimism and the prospect of continued expansion.
>
> There seems [seem] to be at least one factual error and several false assumptions in this report.

If the plural verbs sound wrong in these sentences, you can doubtless sympathize with writers who would choose ungrammatical singulars. In informal writing and especially in conversation, where there's no time to plan, the singular verb in such constructions is at least excusable. Theodore Bernstein points out, moreover, that some writers favor a singular verb when a singular noun is the first of the linked subjects that follow. Edwin Newman, the popular word watcher, would seem to be one of them, judging from a letter he wrote to the *New York Times*:

> According to a Washington dispatch in your edition of June 30, "There were shrimp, smoked salmon, roast beef . . ." at Secretary of State Haig's party.
>   I take it that the reporter was answering an editor's question: "What were there to eat?"

Perhaps Newman means to suggest that the *shrimp* series is a singular concept—the food served—and thus should not have a plural verb; in any event he does imply that the plural verb is stilted and unnatural. But Bernstein finds a plural verb "unexceptionable" in such constructions and says that "the singular verb might put [you] in the position of having to defend [yourself]." Fortunately, if grammar requires a form that sounds awkward to you, you can always rewrite to avoid the issue. You could, for instance, convert the last three examples to *There are two reporters at the back door and a police officer at the front; In those days, with the prospect of continued expansion, there was only optimism;* and *This report seems to contain several false assumptions and.* . . .

Occasionally a subject made up of two words connected by *and* designates not separate entities but the same person, thing, or concept; thus it properly takes a singular verb. Examples include frozen phrases like *sum and substance, part and parcel,* and *the long and the short of it.* The singular is also correct in a sentence like *A friend and colleague of mine is in charge of the arrangements,* in which *friend* and *colleague* denote the same person. If both a friend and a colleague were in charge, the article would appear before the second noun as well as the first, and the verb would be plural. But the omission of the second article in such sentences does not necessarily mean that the subject is singular. In each of the following examples, the subject arguably consists of two words designating one idea:

> One crucially important linkage and desperately needed collegial contact is between community college teachers and the university faculty.

> The trial and conviction of Alger Hiss is becoming as much a cause célèbre as the Sacco and Vanzetti case.

Examples like these are hard to find. Only occasionally does *and* join words to form a single concept. When *and* is part of your subject and you have used a singular verb form, make sure that you can justify your choice. Ideas may be closely associated and yet distinct. Any doubt on this issue should incline you toward a plural verb. If you set readers wondering about your grammar, you've distracted them from what you're saying. The singular verbs in the following sentences are at best questionable, whereas the plurals, shown in brackets, would not have given anyone pause:

> His education and background gives [give] him an important advantage in dealing with academics.

> George Eliot understood how much resentment and suppressed rage there was [were] in women.

> My own experience and that of my colleagues argues [argue] that. . . .

> Your concern and tangible aid is [are] very much appreciated.

Some writers whose logic is better than their grammar consider a subject plural when it consists of a singular noun followed by a phrase beginning with a preposition like *together with, along with, in addition to,* or *as well as.* If you write *My father, as well as my mother, prefers tea to coffee,* you are, of course, talking about two persons, but you don't have a grammatical plural. A preposition cannot substitute for the conjunction *and,* which alone can link words to form a compound subject, and the object of a preposition cannot be the subject of a verb. A coordinating conjunction like *and* joins sentence elements of equal grammatical weight; a preposition shows the subordinate relation its object bears to some other sentence element.

Though in each of the following examples the writer made the mistake of using a plural verb, the commas show that the singular

subject is what the sentence is essentially about and that the prepositional phrase provides only supplementary information:

> The strength of the dollar abroad, along with the rising costs
> of domestic resorts, have [has] made European travel
> attractive to American vacationers.

> The senator, together with several advisers, are [is]
> preparing a bill that would restrict a utility company's right
> of eminent domain.

> Calling for a rent strike, Richards said that the inadequate
> heat, in addition to the landlord's failure to make needed
> repairs and to maintain the halls, have [has] made the
> building almost uninhabitable.

Subjects Subverted by Other Words

Sentences like *Life is just a bowl of cherries, You are my sunshine,* and *Old
King Cole was a merry old soul* conform to the equation $x = y$ and, of
course, can reverse to $y = x$: *and a merry old soul was he.* The subject is
always on the left of the linking verb, and the complement, the word
that equates with the subject, is always on the right. Whether x or y is
the subject depends on which precedes the verb. Word order indicates the subject, and the subject determines the number of the verb.
But when subject and complement differ in number, writers sometimes get confused, as in these sentences:

> My chief concern in opposing tuition tax credits are [is] the
> metropolitan public schools.

> The first item on the agenda are [is] the recommendations
> on cost-cutting measures.

In each of these examples, the verb agrees with the complement
rather than with the subject. Admittedly, the complement exerts a
strong pull on the verb, especially when the subject is at a remove,
and the sentences may seem awkward when you substitute the correct verb forms. Here again, your best bet may be discreet evasion (*In
opposing tax credits, I am chiefly concerned with . . . ; First on the agenda are
the recommendations . . .*).

Just as a complement can distract a writer from the subject, so too
can a modifier that separates subject from verb. The problem generally arises when a plural noun, usually the object of a preposition,
intervenes between a singular subject and its verb. For example:

> Support from a few foundations and federal agencies for
> curriculum reform and collaborative research have [has]
> added significant resources to English and other disciplines.

> Naturally the council suggests that greater attention to public activities—those that capitalize on demographics—are [is] necessary.
>
> One of the most dangerous macho games involve [involves] two cars accelerating toward a head-on collision, the "chicken" being the first to swerve out of the way.

Errors like these occur because writers lose track of what they're talking about. If you routinely trace verbs back to their subjects, you won't have this problem. It's especially easy to overlook a singular subject like *one, anyone, everyone, each, either,* or *neither* when, as in the last example, it precedes an *of* phrase with a plural object. Writers frequently fall into the trap of discarding the individual in favor of the group. Here are a few more examples of this common mistake:

> Neither of the athletes are [is] at fault.
>
> Each of the colleges and universities take [takes] a different approach.
>
> Not one of the witnesses have [has] mentioned seeing a blonde woman talking to the child just before the accident.

Whether a relative pronoun—usually *who, which,* or *that*—is singular or plural depends on the number of the word it stands for, and that word is always the noun or pronoun the relative clause modifies. When a relative pronoun is the subject of its clause, the verb should agree with the pronoun's antecedent. You would naturally write *the child who is* and *the children who are;* but when the relative pronoun does not immediately follow its antecedent, the correct choice may require conscious effort.

Many writers who invariably keep *one* in sight as the subject of a sentence, resisting the lure of intervening plurals, have become so obsessed with *one* that they want to make it the subject of every verb in its vicinity. Consider this sentence:

> One of the areas that has suffered most from the economic cutbacks is education.

Here the writer uses a singular verb not only in the main clause, where it is appropriate, but also in the relative clause, where it is incorrect. The subject of the subordinate verb is *that,* not *one,* and the antecedent of *that* is *areas.* The relative clause limits *areas* to those that have suffered. *Education* is not the one area that has suffered but one of those that have suffered.

This error must be one of those that occur most frequently in the work of accomplished writers. Although strongly condemned in most usage guides, it crops up everywhere—in a column by an eminent drama critic, an article by a well-known book reviewer, an essay by a respected scholar. Permissive critics take the popularity of this construction in learned circles as a sign that usage is changing on this point, and they are probably right. But logic remains on the side of the conservatives, and violations are not yet above reproach. Here are a few more examples:

> He is one of those actors who has [have] a brilliantly secure technique and who never gets [get] anything but rave reviews.
>
> Eva Perón was one of those figures who seems [seem] to exist outside history.
>
> Marijuana may be one of many environmental agents that adversely affects [affect] genetic development in subtle ways.

And here's an author who not only makes *one* the subject of the wrong verb but fails to make it the subject of the right one:

> One of the things that was [were] missed when my presentation was taped were [was] some acknowledgments.

While the one-of-those-who construction is probably the most likely to trick writers into mistaking the number of a relative pronoun, it is not the only offender. When a relative clause does not directly follow the word it describes, writers sometimes let intervening words determine the number of the pronoun. For example:

> The museum has postponed the exhibition of Picasso's late paintings that were [was] scheduled for the fall.
>
> It is the number of runs batted in, not the number of hits, that decide [decides] the ball game.

In each of these examples the verb in the dependent clause should be singular because its subject, *that,* stands for the singular noun that precedes the prepositional phrase, not for the plural object of the preposition.

What, All, and *None* as Subjects

Contrary to what many writers seem to believe, the pronouns *what, all,* and *none* are not invariably singular or plural. Their number depends on their context, but unlike the relative pronouns, they do not derive their meaning from their antecedents.

The pronoun *what* that concerns us here is not the one that asks a question but the one that means "that which" or "those which," or "the thing that" or "the things that," and serves as the subject of a clause. While you should construe *what* as singular if you have nothing else to go on, don't hesitate to make it plural if you'd replace it with a plural. In sentences like *What seem to be diamonds are only rhine-stones* and *The collection includes what are generally considered these writers' best works, what* clearly means "the things that." But beware of letting a plural complement seduce you into using a plural verb when *what* sensibly means "that which," as in *What the school needs is more paying students* and *What concerns me most is the increasing numbers of unemployed.*

Writers commonly betray their uneasiness about *what* by trying to make it mean both "that which" and "those which" at the same time, giving it a singular verb in its own clause and a plural verb in the main clause. For example:

> What is now being challenged are the principles of humility
> and self-sacrifice associated with Christianity.
>
> What is missing here are the boldness and originality that
> characterized his work in the past.

Watch out for such double-dealing *whats* in your own writing and revise as necessary. You have to make up your mind whether the force of *what* is singular or plural and correct the verb that's out of line. In the above examples the singular sense should prevail. In the next two the writers should probably have chosen the plural:

> What is [are] even more striking than these recurring figures
> are the ships and trains that lurk on the fringes of de
> Chirico's paintings.
>
> What appears [appear] to be humility and an unwillingness
> to assume the throne are really affectations designed to
> ensure his ascension.

In the next sentence you could perhaps justify either a singular or a plural *what*:

> What makes a good secretary are not only topnotch skills
> but such qualities as efficiency, conscientiousness, and
> affability.

What you cannot justify is both the singular verb and the plural one. If the sentence seems awkward or unidiomatic when you bring the two into line, revise: *A good secretary must have not only topnotch skills but such qualities as. . . .* Remember that you never have to choose between clumsiness and faulty grammar. In some problem sentences—for example, the one about de Chirico—you can simply omit the *what*: *Even more striking than these recurring figures are the ships and trains. . . .* Or you can rearrange a sentence so that *what* governs only one verb. The sentence about Christian principles, for example, might read *The Christian principles of humility and self-sacrifice are what is now being challenged.*

If you don't stop to think about the pronoun *all,* you're probably more likely to consider it plural than singular. And when it means the

total number in a group, it is unquestionably plural. You would not
be tempted to use a singular verb in a sentence like *All have sinned* or
The ship has gone down, and all are lost. But in a different context you
could correctly write *all is lost,* since the sense is clearly singular when
all means "everything" or "the only thing." Whenever you use *all* as
a subject, take a moment to ask yourself what it means, and make
sure that your verb is compatible with your answer. The lyricist got
the grammar right in "All I want for Christmas is my two front teeth,"
but the writers of the next two sentences let the plural complements
distract them:

> All that matters now are your continued loyalty and
> support.
> All that is missing are the copies of the original invoices.

The easiest way to correct each of these sentences is to reverse the
word order:

> Your continued loyalty and support are all that matters now.
> The copies of the original invoices are all that is missing.

The pronoun *none,* of course, derives from *no one*; and many English teachers, especially in the past, have insisted that it can have no
other meaning, classing it with such invariably singular indefinite
pronouns as *everything, nobody, anyone,* and *each.* Most contemporary
grammarians, however, contend not only that *none* can be plural,
meaning "not any ones," but that the sense is more commonly plural
than singular. Even in a sentence in which *none* is clearly singular,
such as *None of my work has paid off* or *None of this advice seems valid,* the
meaning is not "no one" but "not any" or "no part of."

When *none* precedes a prepositional phrase with a singular object,
you needn't worry about your verb choice; the singular is both inevitable and correct. In many other contexts *none* can as easily mean "not
a single one" as "not any ones," and you can make it singular or
plural as you see fit. Not even traditionalists like Fowler and Follett
would call you wrong for writing either *None of us are going to the
meeting* or *None of us is going to the meeting.* Bernstein says, though, that
you're usually better off with the plural unless you emphatically
mean "not a single one," and in that case, he adds, maybe that's what
you should say. Compare, for example, *I consulted five doctors, but none
was able to help me* with the stronger *I consulted five doctors, but not a single
one was able to help me.*

The only writers who are likely to get into trouble with *none* are
those who believe that the pronoun must be singular and who thus
trap themselves into absurdities of this sort:

> None of the houses on that side of the street looks alike.
>
> Obviously, none of the parallel roads meets.
>
> None of the parts fits together.

A singular *none* makes no sense in such sentences, and you can use the plural with nearly everyone's blessing. But if you remain unconvinced, out of loyalty to your English teacher or to the etymological sense of *none*, avoid using it when logic calls for a plural. Instead of writing *None of the parts fits together,* you could say *No two parts fit together.*

Other Tricky Subjects

Are words like *government, group, chorus, orchestra, team, pair, majority, variety,* and *number* singular or plural? They can, of course, be either: if the collective noun denotes a unit, make it singular; if it refers to the individuals the group comprises, make it plural. In reading over what you have written, pay attention to collectives as subjects and see whether you've given them appropriate verbs. Just use common sense. If you say *A number of critics disagree,* you mean "Several disagree," and you obviously want the plural. In *The number of highway accidents rises every year, number* denotes a singular statistic, not the individual collisions. Bernstein offers the helpful hint that *a number* properly takes a plural verb whereas *the number* properly takes a singular one.

In general, while you can correctly treat a collective noun as singular or plural, one or the other interpretation will usually seem better in a particular context. You will probably choose the appropriate verb if you recognize that the choice is yours. Writers who decide on an unsuitable singular usually do so because they think that nouns singular in form must take singular verbs or that the plural "sounds funny." Americans, unlike the British, are not comfortable with combinations like *the government are prepared* or *the committee are meeting.* This reluctance to regard collective nouns as plural accounts for illogical sentences like these:

> The department comes from a variety of backgrounds.
>
> The board of trustees differs from one another on the best way to solve the problem.

The department as a unit does not come from different backgrounds, and the board of trustees as a single entity cannot disagree. Of course, making subjects and verbs agree is a two-way street. If you don't like the way a plural verb sounds with a collective noun but the plural interpretation makes more sense, you can find a plural subject that permits a more idiomatic sentence. In the preceding examples, for instance, you could substitute *department members* and *the trustees.*

Although a collective noun can be singular or plural, it cannot be both at once, as the subjects try to be in these sentences:

> At the end of the ceremony the class jumps up and throws their hats into the air.
>
> When E.T. "dies," the audience reaches for their handkerchiefs.
>
> The couple is spending their honeymoon in Florida.

While the plural pronoun *their* in each of these examples shows that the writer considers the subject plural, the singular verb suggests the opposite. Such mistakes are common, either because writers fail to recognize collective nouns as permissible plurals or because they do not see the connection between the pronoun and the verb. Once you are alert to this sort of error, you can easily avoid it. You should routinely check personal pronouns to make sure that they have clear antecedents, and when you trace a plural pronoun to a subject, make sure that the subject has a plural verb.

If you use a collective noun repeatedly in a passage, keep it consistently singular or plural. Even though it is logical to construe *staff* as plural in *The staff expect annual salary increases* and as singular in *The staff has one view, the management another,* the shifting from singular to plural may be distracting if the sentences occur close together. Decide whether the collective noun is dominantly singular or plural and reword sentences that require the exceptional interpretation. If you have used *staff* primarily in a singular sense, you might substitute *employees* where you need the plural.

Just as collective nouns that look singular can be plural, some words that look plural can be singular—notably, words ending in *ics,* such as *politics, economics, ethics, tactics,* and *acoustics.* These words are plural when they denote activities (*Gymnastics take up much of the morning*) or characteristics (*The acoustics of the new theater are excellent*) but singular when they mean a science or an art or a field of study (*Ethics interests students more than metaphysics does* or *Mathematics is the study of numbers*).

The distinction, though, is not always obvious. Depending on what you mean, you can correctly write either *Athletics fascinates me* or *Athletics fascinate me.* When a subject ends in *ics,* choose the verb form that shows the sense you intend. If you're not sure, the context may help you make up your mind, and sometimes the dictionary entry will provide guidance. Often the number of the predicate noun makes one or the other choice seem more logical (*The most popular athletics are swimming and tennis* or *Politics is a field for the power hungry*); the verb still depends on the subject, but when the subject can be either singular or plural, the predicate noun can influence the interpretation. It is not, however, a sure-fire indicator. Consider *Gymnastics are a way of shaping up* and *The ambassador's ethics are what is at issue here, not his diplomatic ability.* A *the* or a possessive before the questionable term provides another clue, suggesting a plural. If searching your soul and analyzing the context still leave you in doubt about the number of an *ics* word, make it singular.

A few other singular nouns ending in *s* include *congeries*, derived from the Latin, and *bathos* and *pathos*, derived from the Greek. The literary or scholarly writers likely to use these words are unlikely to mistake them for plurals. But a similar singular, *kudos* (meaning "acclaim"), has strayed into general use, where it commonly appears with a plural verb. All the usage guides would call *kudos is in order* correct, but whether *deserves a kudo* and *kudos are in order* are incorrect depends on which dictionary you read. While the *American Heritage Dictionary* recognizes only the singular *kudos*, *Webster's Ninth* lists in addition the singular *kudo*, with the plural *kudos*, as an acceptable back-formation from the singular *kudos*.

Some writers are also confused about the numerical status of nouns that name singular objects consisting of a pair of connected parts. Words like *scissors, pincers, tongs, pliers, tweezers, pantyhose, trousers*, and *pants* are plural; the things they represent, Curme says, "are never simple in their make-up, so that the plural idea is uppermost in our minds." But the dictionaries acknowledge that all or most of such terms for tools, but not for garments, are singular or plural in construction. A plural verb is always appropriate, but if you want to use the singular, make sure that your dictionary gives you this option. Since dictionaries sometimes disagree on points of usage, consult one authority consistently.

Foreign plurals thriving in English are another problem. Among the forms most often misconstrued as singular are *criteria, curricula, media, phenomena*, and *strata*. All these should govern plural verbs; the corresponding singulars are *criterion, curriculum, medium, phenomenon*, and *stratum*. In contrast, some originally foreign plurals have become accepted as English singulars—for example, *agenda* (the original singular, *agendum*, has been lost) and *insignia*, now regarded as either singular or plural (the singular *insigne* barely survives). While *data* and *trivia*, the plurals of *datum* and *trivium*, are going the same route, traditional critics still object to construing these words as singular; *data are* and *trivia are* remain safe choices. In general use, some foreign plurals have given way to English forms—*focuses* is preferred to *foci, indexes* to *indices, appendixes* to *appendices*—but *alumni* and *loci*, for example, show no sign of losing out to *alumnuses* and *locuses*. The explanations advanced for the varying fates of such words do not provide a practical test for determining whether a foreign plural retains its form and number. When in doubt, check the dictionary.

Still another type of troublesome subject is a quantity or an amount stated in plural form but construed as singular when taken as a unit. Sums of money, for example, are often singular, as in _Eighty-five thousand is only an asking price, Twenty dollars buys considerably less than it did ten years ago,_ and _Is sixty thousand an adequate advertising budget?_ Similarly, a period of time expressed in plural form often requires a singular verb, as in _Two weeks is the usual time allowed for a vacation_ and _Six months in jail is too lenient a sentence for that offense._ But the plural seems more natural in _Our two weeks on the island were sheer heaven,_ where the connotation is fourteen days counted one by one. Often either a singular or a plural interpretation is defensible. When a subject of this sort gives you pause, you're probably safe with one or the other, but once you've made your choice, stick with it. You have to be more decisive than this writer was:

> The first few weeks on the expedition have not dampened
> my enthusiasm but, I am beginning to suspect, has
> disappointed my colleagues.

Alternative Subjects

Because compound subjects—subjects consisting of nouns or noun equivalents joined by _and_—require plural verbs, some writers make the mistake of also giving plural verbs to subjects joined by _or_. For example:

> We verge in somewhat different ways on as dark an age as
> Santayana or Yeats—name your own dark prophet—have
> foretold.

Obviously the sentence means "as Santayana has foretold or as Yeats has foretold"—that is, as either one or the other has foretold, not as both have foretold. While a dog _and_ a cat _make_ good pets, a dog _or_ a cat _makes_ a good pet, and neither a dog _nor_ a cat _is_ desirable if there are allergies in the family, because either a dog _or_ a cat _is_ likely to set off sneezes. Of course, if _or_ or _nor_ joins plural words, the verb is plural: either _cats or dogs inspire_ affection.

Once you realize that subjects linked by _or_ or _nor_ independently govern the verbs they share, you should have no trouble, provided that both subjects have the same number. But when one of the alternative subjects is singular and the other plural, what do you do about the verb? While some rhetoric handbooks say that in this situation the verb should agree with the nearer subject—_Neither my parents nor my_ *brother is here,* but *Neither my brother nor my parents are here*—Follett and Barzun condemn this practice, and Bernstein and Fowler find it the least desirable way out of an awkward situation. As Follett says, "the construction that drives a plural and a singular in one harness always poses a choice of evils." This problem, the pundits agree, calls for discretion rather than valor, evasion rather than confrontation. Sometimes you can replace the questionable verb with an equivalent that has the same form whether the subject is singular or plural. To avoid having to choose between *has* and *have* in *Either the parents or the child has to make some adjustment,* you could write *Either the parents or the child must make some adjustment.* Another device, though somewhat more ostentatious, is to provide each subject with its own verb: *My brother is not here, and neither are my parents.*

What is true of subjects linked by *either . . . or* and *neither . . . nor* seems to apply as well to those connected by *not only . . . but also,* even though the last pair do not present alternatives. *Not only . . . but also* appears more like *both . . . and* than like *either . . . or,* but there is a nuance of difference: when *both* and *and* precede subjects of the same verb, the verb serves the two subjects together; when the correlatives are *not only* and *but also,* the verb goes with each subject in turn, as in an *either-or* construction. Whatever the explanation, *not only . . . but also* cannot introduce a compound subject in the same way that *both . . . and* does. The plural verb is jarring in *Not only the students but also the teacher are at fault,* though *Both the students and teacher are* is idiomatic. Logic and grammar sometimes appear at odds, and bringing them together may require ingenious rationalization. For this reason, perhaps, not many handbooks of English discuss *not only–but also* subjects. Among those that do, the usual advice is to make the verb agree with the nearer subject, but that reasoning seems no more valid for *not only . . . but also* than it does for *either . . . or.* Here again, evasion seems the best tactic. Substitute *both . . . and* if that suits your purpose, or use the verb with only the first subject: *Not only are the students at fault but also the teacher.* Or settle for a simple compound: *The students and the teacher are both at fault.*

PRONOUN-ANTECEDENT DISAGREEMENT

With a few exceptions, notably the indefinite pronouns (such as *one, some,* and *any*) and the impersonal *it* of *It's raining,* pronouns stand for nouns or for indefinite or relative pronouns. The words they replace are called their antecedents or principals. One of the most logical rules of grammar requires that a pronoun match its antecedent in person, gender, and number.

Shifts in Person

Making pronouns and antecedents agree in person usually comes naturally, but accidents do happen. As you know, the first person is *I* or *we*; the second person is *you*, singular or plural; and the third person is *he, she, it, they,* or any of the words that these pronouns can refer to. Here are a few examples of unwarranted shifts, along with suggested revisions:

> If a person wants to succeed in corporate life, you have to know the rules of the game. (Change to *A person who wants to succeed in corporate life has to know . . . ,* or change *a person wants* to *you want,* or begin the sentence with *To succeed.*)
>
> I play the part of a poor young woman who has to depend on the bounty of my stingy old uncle. (Change *my* to *her.* The antecedent of the possessive pronoun is *who,* not *I*; and *who*—since its antecedent is *woman*—is the third person singular, as the verb *has* shows.)
>
> As Americans who have seen the erosion of our standard of living, we know that the government's policies are not working. (Change *our* to *their*; the antecedent is *who,* which has the number and person of its antecedent—*Americans.* But you might better write, *As Americans whose standard of living has eroded, we. . . .*)
>
> When one tires of visiting museums and cathedrals, you can renew your strength in one of London's lovely parks, sitting by a lake and watching the English at play. (Change *one tires* to *you tire,* or change *you can* to *one can* and *your* to *one's.*)

In the last example you might think that *he can* and *his* would be preferable to the *one* forms, which sound stilted to American ears and seem especially objectionable when accompanied by *one* in other senses. But in strict usage—quite apart from the question of sexist language, discussed below—*one's* and *oneself* must be used with the indefinite *one,* as opposed to a *one* that is limited in some way (*one of my friends* or *the one who lives in London*) or to a *one* that serves as a substitute for *I,* a usage more common in England than in the United States (*My American cousins keep saying, "Fly over and see us"*—as if one were a swallow or something). If you use *one's* and *oneself* to refer to the indefinite *one,* you avoid the ambiguity that might result with *his* and *himself.* Here's Fowler on the subject: "The difference between *One hates his enemies* and *One hates one's enemies* is at once apparent if to each is added a natural continuation: *One hates his enemies and another forgives them; One hates one's enemies and loves one's friends.* The first *one* is numeral, the second impersonal, and to make *his* and *one's* exchange places, or to write either in both places, would be plain folly."

The impersonal *one* construction, however, can lead to the awkwardness of repeated *ones*. If it does, avoid it. You can substitute *you* if it suits the tone of your writing and you use it consistently, but the second person is informal and not always appropriate. *We* denoting you and your readers, or all Americans, or the whole human race is also a possibility in some contexts, provided again that you keep its antecedent constant and don't let *we* sometimes mean one group and sometimes another. Or you could use a plural noun that names the group the *one* belongs to; for instance, you could make the last example read:

> When sightseers have exhausted themselves visiting museums and cathedrals, they can regain their strength in one of London's lovely parks, sitting by a lake and watching the English at play.

Gender Problems

If you have been thinking that many avoid the excessive-*one* problem by substituting *a person* or *a man*, you are right. A writer who chooses to use *one* presumably wants the third person singular, not the first person plural, the second person, or the third person plural, so that the obvious way to revise the last example might seem to be this:

> When a person has exhausted himself visiting museums and cathedrals, he can regain his strength. . . .

The contemporary objection to this solution is, of course, that the masculine pronoun refers to a person who may be a woman. Although pronouns should agree with their antecedents in gender as well as in number, this requirement did not trouble most writers until the women's movement alerted them to the issue of sexist language. In our patrilineal society *he* has long served to denote someone of unspecified sex, and grammar books in the past, perhaps because they were invariably written by men, invariably recommended *he* over *he or she* in such contexts. Several current guides, in fact, continue to endorse the traditional usage, eloquently defending the integrity of the language against the inroads of reformers who would sacrifice graceful prose to social or political ends. Roy H. Copperud, for one, finds the use of *he or she* "not only clumsy but unnecessary. It is a well-established convention that in such instances the masculine form (*he*) is taken as applying to both sexes." And Ebbitt and Ebbitt, after presenting the argument against sexist language, explain that they use *he* "to refer to *student* and *writer* not because of bias or obtuseness but in the interest of economy and style."

Among the opponents of that expedient, Watkins and Dillingham argue that "there are as many 'she's' as 'he's' in the world, and one pronoun should not be selected to represent both." Still, no one advocates the awkward repetition of *he–or–she* combinations. Bemoaning the lack of a third-person singular pronoun to designate a person of either sex, some critics have proposed adding a new pronoun to the language to meet the need. Others have recommended using *he/she, s/he,* or an ungrammatical *they.* At this point, however, none of these suggestions seems to have any chance of winning general approval.

Although finding acceptable alternatives presents a challenge, fewer and fewer writers seem comfortable with the so-called generic *he* or, for that matter, with *man* to denote a human being or the species and with compounds of *man,* such as *policeman* and *mailman,* that have unexceptionable genderless equivalents (*police officer, letter carrier*). It is hard not to see the validity of the objections to practices that relegate women always to "the other," to the second sex, and foster a sense of inferiority. Studies have shown that readers associate *he* primarily with a male person and that they envision a man when they read about "the doctor and his patients," "the lawyer and his clients," and "the artist and his work." A woman does not automatically identify with *he*; she may feel left out when she reads that *Anyone can achieve whatever he wants to.*

If you care about good prose and also about social justice, what are you to do? You will, of course, have to decide for yourself; but if you use *he, he or she,* or *they* to refer to a singular antecedent of unspecified sex, you're going to irritate a good many readers. It would at least seem advisable to avoid controversy whenever you can do so without compromising what you want to say. While some writers— women among them—still accept *he* for any person, they explain in a note that their *he* means "he or she"; but the need for such an explanation undercuts the argument that the generic *he* has wide recognition and acceptance. The first person plural, the second person, or the third person plural often provides a way of avoiding the issue. Sometimes the best evasive tactic, though one not always available, is to eliminate the personal pronoun. Thus, *Relations between a teacher and his student, a social worker and his client, and a pastor and his parishioner have some traits in common* would become *between teacher and student, social worker and client, and pastor and parishioner.* . . . The following examples illustrate some controversial uses of the masculine pronoun and suggest revisions that should be acceptable on both stylistic and ideological grounds:

> When a man fears that his words are being taken down,
> that his associations and movements are under scrutiny, that
> neighbors and associates may be babbling about him to the
> police, he does not speak or act with the freedom and

candor that Americans are accustomed to regard as a
birthright.

■ When citizens fear that their words are being taken down,
that their associations and movements are under scrutiny,
that neighbors and associates may be babbling about them
to the police, they do not. . . . (In some contexts you might
prefer recasting the passage with *we* or *you*.)

Students who have not yet wrestled with the great questions
that have immemorially engaged humane and civilized
men . . . can be invited to collaborate with us in posing the
questions of most immediate concern to them. In so doing,
the student may more readily perceive that the unexamined
life is not worth living and that Aeschylus, Shakespeare, or
Yeats can assist him in his efforts at self-discovery.

■ Students who have not yet wrestled with the great questions
that have immemorially engaged humane and civilized
thinkers . . . can be invited to collaborate with us in posing
the questions of most immediate concern to them. In so
doing, they may more readily perceive that the unexamined
life is not worth living and that Aeschylus, Shakespeare, or
Yeats can assist them in their efforts at self-discovery. (The
first sentence does not have a gender-agreement problem—
the revision differs from the original only in replacing *men*
with *thinkers*—but it shows that the writer found a plural
subject acceptable and that the switch to the troublesome
singular in the second sentence was as gratuitous as it was
mistaken.)

A teacher may be ever so sincere in his belief in
communism, but can he at the same time be a sincere
seeker after truth?

■ Can a teacher who is a sincere believer in communism be at
the same time a sincere seeker after truth?

Any employer wishes to have a considerable amount of
freedom in the selection of his subordinates who require
special trust. Even after a man has been hired, his employer
wants the power to dismiss him if found unworthy of
confidence.

■ Any employer wants considerable freedom in selecting
subordinates who require special trust and in dismissing
those found unworthy of confidence.

While many writers apparently want to avoid the charge of sexist
language, their consciousness seems to be at half-mast. They carefully sidestep some controversial masculine pronouns, even at the
cost of good grammar, but fail to notice other lapses. For example:

> If a driver buckles his seat belt, the person beside him will
> buckle theirs.

Even though the *theirs* probably reflects an effort to avoid an ambiguous *his*, not a generic one, it tacitly recognizes that the passenger may be either a man or a woman. But the writer keeps a man in the driver's seat.

Shifts in Number

Until the generic *he* came under attack, handbooks of grammar had little to say about pronoun-antecedent agreement in gender. The primary concern was agreement in number, especially the misuse of *they, their,* and *them* to refer to a singular noun or to a singular pronoun like *everyone, each, anybody, nobody.* The women's movement may be contributing to this error, since many who would write *Everybody believes that he has the right to decide for himself* will use *they* and *themselves* in that construction sooner than go to *he or she* and *himself or herself.* Even well-intentioned nonsexist writers have trouble staying with the *he–or–she* format, as this example shows:

> After a series of portfolio disasters, the astute business
> person realizes that he or she is speculating with a
> significant portion of their net worth.

In colloquial use the third person plural commonly refers to a singular antecedent of undetermined sex, and some contemporary writers on style urge general acceptance of this practice. In *The Handbook of Nonsexist Writing* Casey Miller and Kate Swift point out that at one time *you* was only a plural pronoun but that it eventually became the singular as well "in the days before prescriptive grammarians were around to inhibit that kind of change. English needs a comparable third-person singular pronoun, and for many *they* meets the need." Certainly there's plenty of historical precedent for this use. The *Oxford English Dictionary* says that *they* was "[o]ften used in reference to a singular noun made universal by *every, any, no,* etc., or applicable to one of either sex." Among the writers quoted in evidence are Fielding, the Earl of Chesterfield, and Ruskin.

While the argument for *they* in singular constructions is not without merit, those who favor this usage have not yet prevailed, and if you adopt it, expect to have your grammar challenged. Miller and Swift persuasively insist that *he* cannot mean either a man or a woman because *he* cannot shed its male connotation. Now that the eighteenth-century grammarians have imposed their logic on the language, can *they* shed its plural connotation and mean "he or she"?

Will we learn to say *they is*? Or will *they*, though construed as singular, retain the plural verb form?

Others try to bring *everybody* and *their* into line by a somewhat similar route. They contend that since *everybody* is plural in meaning, *everybody should take their seats* makes perfect sense. But though words like *anybody, everybody,* and *each* often mean essentially what *all* does, they remain syntactically singular. No one advocates, for example, *Everyone are at their wits' end.* Bernstein says that "the writer of craftsmanship and taste will reject the grammatical inconsistency of the combination of a singular noun and a plural pronoun" and will change one or the other. Usually a shift to a bona fide plural provides the most graceful way out of the dilemma. Here are a few examples:

> The classic parka was designed for the rugged wear a backpacker expects from their gear and clothing.
>
> ■ . . . for the rugged wear that backpackers expect. . . .
>
> The coach responds to this human frailty by asserting the hierarchical right to monitor each player closely, forcing them to stick to their job.
>
> ■ . . . to monitor the players . . . their jobs.
>
> Or, if the coach is in charge of a single-sex team:
>
> ■ . . . to monitor the players closely, forcing each to stick to her [or his] job.
>
> When the professor asked who had read the assignment, everyone raised their hands.
>
> ■ . . . assignment, all the students raised their hands.
>
> ■ . . . assignment, everyone's hand shot up.

A similar error in agreement occurs when a plural pronoun stands for a collective noun that governs a singular verb. Obviously a collective noun cannot be simultaneously singular and plural. Train yourself always to check the verbs and pronouns you use with collective nouns to make sure that you have been consistent. If you find a disagreement, decide whether the singular or plural seems more appropriate and revise accordingly. For example:

> In addition, PROTECT plans to serve as a watchdog over CPOC. They [It] will mount a large-scale advertising, fund-raising, and membership campaign throughout Orange County.
>
> The firm compensates their [its] managers in an unusual manner.
>
> The spectral cast of adventurers gathered in the opening scene does [do] not feel that their destinies have been completed.

OTHER DISAGREEMENT PROBLEMS

Some writers have trouble keeping to the plural point of view they begin with. They start off talking about a group as a whole and then shift their attention to an individual within the group. As Follett says, "The axiom that if one person has one head, heart, or torso two persons have two seems to be a stumbling block to a good many writers." For example:

> Humanists forever keep one foot in art and one in behavior.

Clearly humanists as a group have more than two feet among them; the sensible change here is to *The humanist forever keeps.* . . . This sort of lapse from logic comes easily. The author of a popular newspaper column on language supplied the next example, in which several thinkers share a forehead:

> This is the line being peddled behind the furrowed brow of
> the most earnest and nonpartisan politicians.

Of course, changing *brow* to *brows* won't help if you're troubled by the notion of peddling a line behind a brow, but that's not the issue here. In the following sentence the unwarranted shift from singular to plural requires a little more effort to correct:

> These chefs would even slice up their grandmother and
> season her with parsley just so they could put on the menu
> "Assiette de grand-mère."

Presumably the chefs did not have the same lineage, but converting to *grandmothers* would create another problem—a sentence in which the third-person plural pronoun sometimes has one antecedent and sometimes another. If all the chefs in question are men, the sentence could read:

> Such a chef would even slice up his grandmother. . . .

If you don't mind either *his* or *his or her* for a person of unknown sex, you could shift to the singular even if the group included women. But if *chefs* must remain plural, you would have to use *grandmothers* and find some way to avoid making it the antecedent of a pronoun:

> The chefs would even slice up their grandmothers and
> sprinkle on some parsley for the chance to put "Assiette de
> grand-mère" on the menu.

The following examples of faulty noun agreements, with the corrections shown in brackets, are more typical:

> Lawyers are told that if they do not become a partner [become partners] by age forty they never will.
>
> Colleges that have [A college that has] an attractive campus near a major city naturally have [has] an advantage that less well situated schools do not.

Of course, some combinations of plural subjects and singular objects make perfect sense. If two persons share an apartment, you can say *They keep their apartment neat.* An abstract quality characteristic of several persons is properly singular, as in *They all showed courage* or *They were all driven by ambition.* Figurative words also remain singular: *We earn our bread and butter in nine-to-five jobs.*

Occasionally you may have trouble deciding whether or not a noun should remain singular when a related noun is plural, but you can usually rely on either logic or your ear for idiom to guide you. If you question such a usage, try out the plural; if it sounds unnatural, reject it. You wouldn't change *heart* to *hearts* in a sentence like *They took heart from the situation* or *eye* to *eyes* in *A small painting near the doorway caught our eye.* But guard against making two or more share something concrete that they don't have in common. Statements like *We all got our driver's license at the age of seventeen* and *All in favor raise their right hand* are careless and illogical.

Managing most numbers, in fact, is primarily a matter of care and common sense. You can't have the joint venture of one person. A group regarded as a unit can't fight with one another. The authors of the following sentences simply weren't thinking:

> The project is the result of the combined efforts of each participant [all participants] working toward a common goal.
>
> The discontinuity [discontinuities] of language present in the Chinese examples and in Trakl's poetry has [have] different origins.

Some errors in noun agreement occur because writers fail to note the connective between two numerical adjectives modifying the same noun. You should say *between the fourteenth and fifteenth centuries* but *from the fourteenth to the fifteenth century.* Similarly, you should say *the fourteenth and fifteenth centuries* but *the fourteenth or fifteenth century.* In other contexts, too, writers forget that their choice of *or* instead of *and* affects the number of a related noun. For example:

> The only medicines [medicine] to cure wild inflation are [is] the snake oil of wage-price controls or the castor oil of periodic hard times.
>
> In Shakespeare's principal tragedies—*Hamlet, Macbeth, Othello,* or [and] *King Lear*—the hero fits [heroes fit] the classic pattern.

Still another common problem arises when the same noun must serve two constructions, one requiring a singular form and the other a plural, as in *one of the best, if not the best, deals I ever made.* In the example, *deals* goes with *one of the best,* but *if not the best* needs a *deal* it doesn't get. You could, of course, write *the best deal, or at least one of the best deals, I ever made,* but you can avoid the repetition by writing *one of the best deals, if not the best, I ever made.* In Fowler's words, "the place from which the understood word [here *deal*] is omitted is after, not before, the word from which it is to be supplied [here *deals*]; for from a word that has already been expressed the taking of the other number is not forbidden." In other words, make sure that the completed phrase precedes the elliptical one.

Contemporary writers on style do not comment on phrases like *one or two things,* which are probably well on their way to acceptance, but in formal contexts Fowler's principle should apply here as well. In this example *things* agrees with *two* but not with *one;* precise usage would require *a thing or two.* Similarly, *Let me make one or two more points* would become *Let me make another point or two.*

One other type of faulty agreement involves the demonstrative adjectives: *this, that, these,* and *those.* As you know, most adjectives in English remain the same whether they modify singular or plural nouns; the demonstratives are the exception. *This* and *that* should precede singular nouns, *these* and *those* plural ones. Most grammarians regard constructions like *these kind of plays* and *those type of windows* as violations of this rule; the plural object of the *of* phrase tricks writers into using the plural demonstrative, but the word modified is not the plural noun but the singular *kind* or *type.* (Curme disagrees, arguing that *kind of* and *type of* are adjectives in such contexts, but the weight of opinion is against him.) The preferred choices are *this kind of play* and *that type of window* or *these kinds of plays* and *those types of windows.* Routinely check such constructions; if you find disagreement, change the demonstrative to fit the noun or the noun to fit the demonstrative. Or you can make the plural object of the prepositional phrase change places with the noun the phrase modifies. Thus, instead of *these kinds of plays,* you could write *plays of this kind;* instead of *those types of windows,* you could write *windows of that type.*

Whether the object of the preposition in such constructions should be plural or singular is another matter. Use the singular when you're talking about a classification—*these kinds of farce, these types of behavior*—and the plural when you mean the individuals within the class—*these kinds of stories, these types of events.* Often you can justify either number; you're within your rights to regard the object of the preposition as the class or as the individuals within it: *these types of activity* or *these types of activities.* Just make sure that the demonstrative adjective before the singular *sort* or *kind* or *type* is *this* or *that*, not *these* or *those*.

FAULTY REFERENCES

Most pronouns, the indefinite ones excepted, derive their meaning from their antecedents. Unless you make clear exactly what a pronoun stands for, your readers will have to pause to guess. Even if they rapidly figure out your intention, their momentary doubt is an obstacle to efficient communication.

Reference-of-pronoun errors are easy to spot if you're willing to look for them. Just trace every pronoun back to the word it replaces and make sure that the antecedent is an appropriate part of speech appropriately placed and uniquely qualified to do the job. In the throes of composition, few authors bother to use pronouns precisely, but a conscientious writer eventually makes the necessary repairs. When you're generally satisfied with your final draft, read through it again checking only pronouns. You'll almost certainly find some that need clarifying.

Missing Antecedents

Writers frequently use a pronoun—especially *this, which,* or *it*—to refer loosely to an idea or to something implicit but not stated in what precedes. Vague at best, such a pronoun is at worst misleading; lacking a clear-cut antecedent, it may associate itself with the wrong word. Let's look at some examples, the first from a true-crime best seller:

> I had come to his office as a . . . sympathizer and if, as the
> trial progressed, questions arose in my mind, this wasn't out
> of personal hostility to either him or his client, as he
> apparently took it to be.

What wasn't out of hostility? The *this* has no word to stand for, and the subsequent *it* that goes back to *this* compounds the difficulty. Because the reference is imprecise, readers may initially take *it* to mean *hostility,* discarding this possibility only when they realize that it makes no sense. Readers would not stumble if the writer had corrected the sentence to read:

> . . . questions arose in my mind, they did not stem from
> personal hostility to either him or his client, as he
> apparently thought they did.

The vague *this* is among the most common of pronoun faults. The next two examples come from a newspaper's editorial pages:

> The investors claimed a further deduction because the property was sold at a paper loss. The Justice Department can argue that this is illegal, but. . . .

The *this* has several preceding nouns well situated to serve as its antecedent, but it actually refers to claiming a deduction, an idea that does not appear in the sentence in a form that can anchor the pronoun. To correct this sort of error, you need only convert the demonstrative pronoun to a demonstrative adjective—that is, give *this* a noun to modify:

> The Justice Department can argue that this practice is illegal, but. . . .

Here's another example, with the correction shown in brackets:

> The School Board is expected to decide at its next meeting whether to have elementary pupils attend schools 40 minutes less every day. This [ruling] would leave the children with the state minimum of five hours of daily instruction.

The vague *which* crops up at least as often as the vague *this*. For example:

> The plans proposed for Indian Point have the look of an Achilles' heel, which is why critics are focusing on them.

The sentence structure makes *heel* look like the antecedent of *which* (cf. *Achilles' heel, which was his vulnerable point,* where *heel* is the antecedent), but presumably the critics are focusing on the plans not because of a heel but because of the plans' vulnerability. To state the idea precisely, you could edit out the *which* clause:

> Critics are focusing on the plans for Indian Point because these proposals have the look of an Achilles' heel.

You can't say "because they have the look . . . ," since the *they* might then seem to refer to *critics.* If you wanted to forgo the causal idea for the sake of conciseness, you could write:

> Critics are focusing on the plans for Indian Point, which have the look of an Achilles' heel.

Here's another example:

> On days when everything seems to go well, which hardly ever happens, you can sometimes forget the odds against success.

What hardly ever happens is that everything goes well, but that idea is not expressed in a form that *which* can replace. You could write:

> On days when everything seems to go well—which hardly ever occur—you. . . .

In the revision *which* refers clearly, logically, and grammatically to *days*. But rewording to eliminate the relative clause produces a smoother sentence:

> On those rare days when everything goes well, you can. . . .

In the following sentence, too, you should probably excise the problem *which*:

> Some instructors choose not to participate in this activity, which may be a telling fact in itself.

You might choose one of these remedies:

> Some instructors choose not to participate in this activity, and their refusal may be a telling fact in itself.

> That some instructors choose not to participate in this activity may be a telling fact in itself.

Occasionally *which* or *this* can refer clearly to the whole preceding clause, not to a specific word, and most guides accept this usage (*They hired us immediately, which makes me think that we are underpricing our services*). But these pronouns are so frequently abused that you are better off sinning on the side of caution.

A third pronoun that tempts writers to looseness is *it*. But not every *it* needs a preceding reference word. In idiomatic phrases like *It's raining* and *It's cold out*, the impersonal *it* requires no antecedent. Also, in statements like *It is true that money can't buy happiness* and *It is important to work hard*, the subject *it* stands for the noun clause or infinitive phrase that follows the verb and explains what *it* means. The *it* you have to worry about is the one that, like *which* and *this*, refers to some notion embedded in what precedes but not in a form that can serve as an antecedent. For example:

> The principal claimed that he had not heard about any muggings of younger children by high school students but that he would investigate it.

The *it* has no legitimate antecedent in the sentence. The writer should have either replaced the pronoun with a noun—say, *the matter* or *the complaint*—or dropped the unanchored *it* and ended the sentence with *investigate*. Here's another example:

> The doctors wanted to operate at once, but the boy's mother would not allow it.

It stands for an unexpressed "the operation" or "them to operate." Even though the infinitive *to operate* functions as a noun in the sentence, it's not the antecedent of *it*; you could not replace *it* with *to operate* and have the sentence make sense. But you could write:

> The doctors urged an immediate operation, but the boy's mother would not allow it.

Or you could keep the original but substitute *them to* or *consent* for *it*:

> The doctors wanted to operate at once, but the boy's mother would not consent.

In the next sentence the easiest solution is to replace the vague *it* with a noun:

> Fewer chips are passing across the gaming tables these days, and Las Vegas is feeling it [the loss].

An *it* that begins a clause and refers to what you have just said always deserves scrutiny. Does the *it* have a clear antecedent in what precedes, or does it simply refer to what you have been saying in general? Consider this example:

> When my grandmother was ten, she wheedled a quarter from her father so she could see the circus that had come to town and then, while standing in line to pay admission, gave the money to a stranger who offered to buy the ticket for her; she never saw him again—or the circus—and it made her distrustful of everyone for the rest of her life.

Presumably the *it* stands for the incident just related, not for a single word, but it's inadequate for the job and perhaps even misleading, since it may seem at first to refer to *circus*. The writer should have substituted a summarizing noun for *it*—*this experience*, perhaps.

Although *this, which,* and *it* are probably the pronouns that most often lack clear-cut antecedents, they are by no means the only ones. A vague *that*, for instance, is fairly common. Here's one example, along with a suggested revision:

> She refuses to perform in any state that has not ratified the ERA, and that means a Chicago concert is out.
>
> ■ Since she refuses . . . , a Chicago concert is out.

The next sentence not only fails to give *those* an appropriate antecedent but suggests an inappropriate one:

> Sales are way off, and even those still making money are cutting production.

Here the solution is to replace the demonstrative pronoun with a noun—say, *companies*. In the next example *they* lacks an explicit antecedent:

> The little town of Florida, New York, is the onion capital of the United States, and they are [its produce is] shipped all over the country.

That sentence requires readers to manufacture an antecedent (the plural *onions*) from an adjective (the *onion* in *onion capital*). The next example makes the same unreasonable demand:

> At the end of the term, the instructor invites student comment on the course, and they often make constructive suggestions.

The sentence includes no plural noun that *they* can replace, and if readers weren't paying attention to probable meaning, they would find it easier to convert the singular *instructor* to *instructors* than to make a plural noun from the adjective *student*. To solve the problem, you could simply change *invites student comment* to *invites students to comment*.

Theoretically, since the possessive forms of nouns function as adjectives, they too are unsuitable antecedents for pronouns—except, of course, for pronouns that are also in the possessive case. By strict standards the following sentence is incorrect:

> The president's outrage when he heard about the incident led him to demand the secretary's resignation.

With *president's* technically an adjective, the *he* and *him* have no noun to stand for. To correct the sentence, you would have to get *president's* out of the possessive case:

> The incident so outraged the president that he demanded the secretary's resignation.

Not many writers are careful about honoring the possessive's adjectival function, and infractions rarely threaten clarity or call attention to themselves. Still, if you respect grammatical precision, you may want to observe the rule.

Obscure Antecedents

When you check your pronouns, first make sure that those requiring antecedents have explicit ones. Then notice where you have put the antecedents; generally, of course, they should antecede the pronouns. One exception already noted is the deferred "antecedent" that follows an anticipatory *it* construction. But even in other contexts a briefly postponed principal may sometimes be less of a problem than the wording adopted to avoid it. For example, *In his time Joe Louis was a great source of pride to his people* seems easier to read than *Joe Louis, in his time, was a great source of pride to his people.* But keep the pronoun close to the word it stands for. Readers have to wait too long to find out what this sentence is talking about: *A legend in his own time and a great source of pride to the black people during the years when the white-dominated sports world offered little else, Joe Louis. . . .*

Even pronouns preceded by appropriate antecedents may give readers trouble. An antecedent may be too far back to serve as an easy reference. For example:

> When the judge reported the jury's request for clarification of the incident, the defense attorneys began to have second thoughts about the stress they had placed on it, especially when they heard his instructions.

The *his* can refer only to *judge,* but did you hesitate a moment before you made the connection? The distance between antecedent and pronoun is too great for comfort. The *it* may also have made you falter. The intended antecedent, *incident,* lacking a dominant position in the sentence, fails to assert itself. A pronoun refers more easily to the subject or object of a preceding verb than to the object of a preposition or to a word buried in a parenthetical phrase. The difficulty is compounded if some other noun of the appropriate number and gender is in a better position to attract the pronoun. For example:

> The current problem is coded into the computer, and it then shows what the cause is.

Obviously *it* has to mean the computer, but you can see that *problem,* the subject of the preceding verb, strongly attracts the pronoun, even though the real antecedent, the object of a preposition, is closer. To clarify, you could convert the second coordinate clause to a relative clause modifying *computer:*

> . . . computer, which then identifies the cause.

In each of the following examples the revised version is easier to read because it takes the antecedent out of the background and gives it prominence as the subject of the sentence:

> When she moved to the small apartment over the Landons' garage, she had the peace and quiet she needed for her work, and its simple furnishings pleased her.
>
> ■ The small apartment she now rented over the Landons' garage gave her the peace and quiet she needed for her work, and its simple furnishings pleased her.

If after four years in college you still cannot earn enough money to support yourself, you may think that they were a waste of time.

■ Four years in college may seem a waste of time if they don't enable you to earn enough money to support yourself.

This view is endorsed in an editorial in the November issue, and it makes a strong case.

■ An editorial endorsing this view appears in the November issue, and it makes a strong case.

Ambiguous Pronouns

A pronoun can have a specific and compatible antecedent in a dominant position not too far back and still fail to make itself clear. Readers cannot immediately recognize what a pronoun stands for if two or more preceding words qualify syntactically for the role of antecedent. In *Mary says that Ellen always gives her children too many presents,* whose children is Ellen spoiling? A pronoun with two possible antecedents can be so confusing that readers cannot tell what the writer has in mind. More often, though, such a pronoun is only technically ambiguous, since the context reveals what the writer intends. Still, the questionable syntax distracts readers. They may initially misinterpret the pronoun and then have to backtrack when logic shows that the pronoun cannot mean what the wording suggests. Sometimes the misinterpretation is ludicrous, as in Lady Diana's comment to reporters about her $55,000 engagement ring: "I can't get used to wearing it yet. The other day I even scratched my nose with it, because it's so big." The nervous princess-to-be apparently heard the ambiguity herself, for she quickly added, ". . . the ring, I mean."

Although sometimes, like Lady Di, you can detect a faulty reference by saying your words aloud, a more reliable technique is to trace every pronoun back to its antecedent and make sure that no confusion is possible. As we have seen, a noun in a dominant position preceding the pronoun is in a stronger position to serve as the antecedent than, say, a noun in a prepositional phrase or in a parenthetical element. It is also true that a pronoun tends to identify itself with the nearest preceding noun. Ambiguous pronouns are usually pulled in two directions—toward a nearby noun in a comparatively weak position or a more distant noun in a stronger position or toward two nouns in equally strong positions. Unfortunately, no set way of positioning antecedent and pronoun will ensure clarity in such contexts. The many variables make any general rule impractical.

Worrying about unclear pronouns in the early stages of writing can only impede your progress. But be sure to check for ambiguities when you review your final draft. I've never read a manuscript that is free of these errors, and they abound in print. When you find a pronoun whose identity is questionable, you usually have to substitute a noun or reconstruct the sentence. Here are a few examples, the first one from a newspaper's theater page:

> I wonder how the show will go over in Washington now
> that it has turned conservative.

Here the *it* could refer either to the nearer noun, *Washington,* or to the one in the strong position, *show.* The sentence, written shortly after President Reagan took office, does mean that the capital turned conservative, but another interpretation is possible: the show could have been revised to meet the prevailing taste. In fact, the story later quotes the producer's suggestions for interpreting the scenario as Republican. Still, the context does ultimately make the *it–Washington* connection, and you could clarify the sentence most easily by changing *it* to *the government.*

The next example also comes from a newspaper article:

> "Tell Them" was written, incidentally, by the songwriter
> Paul Dresser, the brother of the novelist Theodore Dreiser,
> whose "My Gal Sal" will be sung at stops along East 20th
> Street.

Readers probably realize that the songwriter, not the novelist, wrote "My Gal Sal," but they need to infer this connection. A relative pronoun ordinarily refers to the immediately preceding noun—here, *Dreiser*—and the failure of *whose* to do what's expected is a stumbling block. You could revise this way:

> Incidentally, both "Tell Them" and "My Gal Sal," the song
> that will be sung at stops along East 20th Street, were
> written by Paul Dresser, the brother of the novelist
> Theodore Dreiser.

In the last example the ambiguity might give readers a moment's pause; in the next one it stops them cold:

> Many people fear that a boa constrictor will choke a person
> for no reason at all. They don't realize that the snake will
> only attack another animal when it is feeding.

Since either *snake* or *animal* could qualify as the antecedent of *it,* those not up on their herpetology may well wonder whether the boa attacks to protect its own food or to steal another's. Eliminating the direct object of *attack* would also eliminate the ambiguity:

> . . . that the snake will only attack when it is feeding.

But in the unlikely event that a snake will only attack a feeding animal, you could write:

> . . . that the snake will only attack an animal that is feeding.

Here's one more example in which the identity of the pronoun is anyone's guess:

> The bachelor policeman became Mr. Smith's legal guardian,
> and the young man, who recently turned eighteen, moved in
> with Officer Jones, who lives with his mother.

The news story does eventually straighten out the ambiguity, but the writer could have avoided the problem by rearranging the sentence so that the masculine pronoun can refer to only one preceding noun:

> Officer Jones, a bachelor policeman who lives with his
> mother, became Mr. Smith's legal guardian, and the young
> man, who recently turned eighteen, moved in with him.

You can also create ambiguity by repeating a pronoun in a sentence and giving it first one meaning and then another. Once readers know what a pronoun refers to, they tend to understand successive uses in the same way, and a shift in midstream can leave them floundering. Although you can sometimes swap horses so clearly and unobtrusively that no one notices, such a feat is an exception. Fowler's succinct rule is "One pronoun, one job," and violating it is risky. Here's an example:

> Getting European Jews to Palestine during World War II
> involved first getting them to the Mediterranean, past
> German army guards and their many European
> sympathizers.

The *them* refers clearly to *Jews,* and readers expect the possessive form of the pronoun to have the same antecedent. But why would it be difficult to get Jewish refugees past their sympathizers? To avoid this confusion you would have to eliminate one of the pronouns, perhaps by writing:

> . . . past German army guards and the many Nazi
> sympathizers in Europe.

The error is more serious in this example:

> Miss Brown said that until her arrest for the holdup of an
> armored truck she did not know about her roommate's
> hidden past.

Can you tell who was arrested? Part of the problem is that the first *her* refers to an "antecedent" that does not antecede the pronoun. Sentences that concern two men or two women often pose reference-of-pronoun problems, and usually, as here, the best solution is to replace the ambiguous pronoun with a noun, even at the cost of repetition, a lesser evil. Since the news story that includes this sentence does identify Miss Brown's roommate by name, you could reword this way:

> Miss Brown said that she did not know about her
> roommate's hidden past until Miss Black's arrest for the
> holdup. . . .

The next sentence involves a somewhat more complicated shift-in-antecedent problem:

> The teacher's job is to work with students as they struggle
> to form their ideas, capture them in writing, shape them
> through rewriting, and finally succeed in conveying them to
> others and, equally important, to themselves.

The *they, their,* and *themselves* refer to *students,* the *them* to *ideas.* You might consider shifting to *the student,* but using the singular would create gender problems. The revision here does not come easy, and since the ambiguity is more theoretical than real, expedience might lead you to connive at the violation. But if there's a will—not to mention world enough and time—you could devise a way:

> The teacher's job is to work with students as they struggle
> to form and express their ideas—ideas that they must
> capture in writing, shape through rewriting, and finally
> convey to others and, equally important, to themselves.

The ambiguity in the final example is self-evident:

> If the heat in your building goes off, get an extension cord,
> plug it into your electric blanket, and wrap it around you.

To revise, you have to edit out one of the *its.* You could substitute *blanket* for the last one or you could write:

> If the heat in your building goes off, wrap yourself in an
> electric blanket plugged into an extension cord.

Getting your pronouns right should be less difficult than this discussion may suggest. Despite the many ways to go wrong, only a few pronouns are likely to pose problems. You can usually check a sentence for pronoun faults as quickly as you can read it. Correcting the errors you find can take a little longer, but if you value clear and unobtrusive prose, the time will be well spent.

Problems with Punctuation

The main reason for punctuating a sentence is to clarify its structure and prevent misreading. Building sentences correctly, phrasing and placing the parts to show their relations to one another, reduces the need for punctuation and avoids most problems. "The workmanlike sentence," Follett says, "almost punctuates itself." When you have trouble getting the commas right, chances are you're trying to patch up a poorly structured sentence. Instead of using punctuation marks as Band-Aids, you'd do better to perform some basic surgery.

Punctuation can not only guide readers through a sentence but contribute substance as well. Just as the same words can have different senses depending on their arrangement, the same words in the same order can convey different information depending on how you punctuate them. If you write *I recognized the young man who was wearing a red carnation*, the *who* clause tells readers which young man you mean. By inserting a comma after *man*, you indicate that there was only one young man you could mean, that no other was present. You show, in other words, that the phrase *young man* is enough, in context, to identify the person you're referring to, that the information about his boutonniere is merely incidental, not defining.

Contemporary writing lacks many of the commas that weigh down eighteenth- and nineteenth-century prose, since the tendency over the years has been toward an increasingly "open" punctuation style. "Apply punctuation sparingly, like salt," current advisers say, or "When in doubt, leave it out." But as recently as the fifties some teachers were still telling students to insert punctuation wherever pauses would occur in speaking and to use commas, semicolons, co-lons, and periods to signify successively longer stops: "Count one for a comma, two for a semicolon. . . ." While rhetorical punctuation—punctuation to show how words should be read aloud—has its place even today, it is confined to contexts in which structure neither re-quires nor proscribes punctuation. In these places you may punctuate to mark a pause, to add emphasis, to indicate how you want your words read. Though you don't need punctuation in *Smith stared blankly for a moment and then abruptly turned and ran,* you could add a comma or a dash after *moment* to stress the sharp change in Smith's behavior, or you could highlight *abruptly* by enclosing it in commas. But such punctuation is basically decoration. It does not affect the clarity of what you have to say. Far more important is the punctuation that points up the sentence structure, that keeps some words apart and groups others together, enabling readers to move effortlessly through a sentence. It is that punctuation which chiefly concerns us here. This chapter does not pretend to cover all marks of punctuation, or even all uses of those it includes. Concentrating on common faults that can obscure or distort meaning, it disregards conventions that are not crucial to clear communication, as well as those that educated writers almost never violate, such as ending statements with periods and enclosing direct quotations in quotation marks.

Some writers profess to have no idea where to put commas, and they willingly relinquish the responsibility to copy editors. Others clearly have the wrong idea and insert commas that impede rather than facilitate reading. This cavalier attitude is surprising in serious writers, since imprecise punctuation can be as damaging as poor wording to what they have to say. The rules of punctuation, more-over, are fairly simple, and every handbook of composition includes them. The difficulty, perhaps, is that these rules are invariably ex-pressed in the language of grammar. There is no other efficient way of presenting them. Writers who have never learned the fundamen-tals of sentence structure cannot check the logic of their punctuation. If you cannot tell an independent clause from an adverbial phrase, you should bone up on syntax before going on with this chapter (see appendix A).

COMMAS—GOOD, BAD, AND INDIFFERENT

Commas are both the most common marks of punctuation and the most troublesome. Yet you need them in only four basic circum-stances, apart from dates, addresses, and other special forms. Else-where they are incorrect or at best optional.

Helpful Commas

Before Conjunctions Joining Independent Clauses

A comma almost always belongs before a coordinating conjunction—*and, but, for, nor, or, yet,* or *so*—that links the two parts of a compound sentence. The punctuation prevents the conjunction from seeming to connect smaller sentence elements. For example:

> In the forties girls studied home nursing, and boys took shop. (The comma prevents *boys* from looking like the second object of the girls' study.)

> We must stop wasting our resources, or our children will face dire need. (The comma prevents *children* from looking like the second object of *wasting.*)

> He never worked, for his father had left him a fortune. (The comma prevents the misreading of *for his father* as a prepositional phrase.)

> I have now seen all Shakespeare's major plays performed, but *Hamlet* remains for me the most gripping. (The comma prevents the misreading of *but* as a preposition.)

This comma rule has two notable exceptions: (1) a semicolon should generally replace the comma when the conjunction joins heavily punctuated clauses; (2) the conjunction needs no preceding punctuation if the clauses are short and closely related, provided that a comma is not necessary to prevent misreading.

Between Adjacent Parallel Items

In a series of coordinate words, phrases, or clauses in which a conjunction precedes only the final item, a comma should follow every item except the last. For example:

> On the New York Stock Exchange yesterday the industrials were up 9.5, the transports were down 4.35, and the utilities were unchanged.

> The agency lists openings in publishing, broadcasting, advertising, and public relations.

Most magazines and newspapers, in keeping with the trend toward minimal punctuation, do not use a comma before the final item in a series, but many writers on style and usage consider that comma essential. Follett points out the fallacy in regarding it as superfluous: a conjunction, which connects, cannot do the job of a comma, which separates. Without the comma the final item may seem to be a compound. In the last example, for instance, dropping the second comma might turn *advertising and public relations* into a single field. Routinely omitting the comma before the conjunction also makes it possible for readers to mistake certain word combinations for series:

> The mailing went out to educators, teachers and administrators.
>
> In this study of power plants, coal-fired systems and nuclear facilities compare unfavorably with hydroelectric operations.

Neither of these sentences includes a series. The first involves two nouns in apposition to another; the second, a compound subject following an introductory prepositional phrase. If the serial comma were obligatory, such sequences could not be misconstrued.

Commas should also separate consecutive coordinate adjectives modifying the same noun, but not all adjectives that precede a noun are in this category. In the phrase *an intelligent, conscientious worker* the adjectives are parallel, but in *the average city dweller* they are not. In the first phrase, the coequal adjectives both qualify the noun; in the second, the first adjective modifies the unit made up of the second adjective and the noun. Since *average* describes *city dweller*, a comma between *average* and *city* would be inappropriate. Similarly, commas would be wrong in *the old oaken bucket, my sweet little alice-blue gown,* and *his shiny brown leather shoes.* Adjectives denoting color, age, size, or material are rarely coordinate with other adjectives. Coordinate adjectives sound idiomatic if you reverse their order or read *and* between them. You can change *the delicate, subtle flavor* to *the subtle, delicate flavor* or to *the subtle and delicate flavor,* but both *his leather brown shiny shoes* and *his shiny and brown and leather shoes* sound peculiar.

Some writers add a comma after the last of a series of coordinate adjectives, but the final comma in *an engrossing, readable, and informative, book* is as wrong as the comma in *an informative, book.* The error, if not merely careless, may reflect some confusion about the rule for setting off an adjective phrase that contrasts with another adjective modifying the same word (*steady, but hardly rapid, progress*). While such a phrase needs enclosing commas, a series of simple coordinate adjectives needs only intervening commas. When parenthetical elements are not involved, a comma should not separate a modifier from the word it modifies.

Around Parenthetical Elements

In this chapter the term *parenthetical element* refers to any word, phrase, or clause that should be set off from the rest of the sentence by enclosing commas—or, if there's a sharper break in the continuity, by dashes or parentheses. When such an element begins or ends a sentence, the single comma that follows or precedes is one of an implicit pair.

A pair of commas mark the words they set off as outside the mainstream of the sentence—as either nonessential to the basic meaning or disruptive of the flow. The enclosing commas help readers bridge the gap between the structurally related parts that come before and after. Perhaps the most common and serious of punctuation mistakes is the use of only one comma in a context that calls for a pair. Half a loaf here is worse than none: the single comma separates words that belong together, thus inviting misreading, whereas a pair would highlight the structure by setting off the extraneous or intrusive. The error appears in this sentence:

> The current five-year expansion program, culminating in
> approximately 100 building materials supermarts by the end
> of fiscal 1980 is continuing on schedule.

The expendable *culminating* phrase separates subject (*program*) from verb (*is continuing*), and the single comma simply reinforces the separation. But a pair of commas—the second after *1980*—would effectively bring the two together by setting off the intervening words. Here's another example:

> The expertise afforded by the exceptionally well qualified
> staff, along with the dedicated leadership promises a
> continuation of the division's highly successful record.

A second comma, after *leadership*, would help readers connect subject (*expertise*) and verb (*promises*), but no commas at all would be better than only one. Readers would then take the *along* phrase as crucial to the sentence. Dedicated leaders and an expert staff might well be equally important to continued success, and perhaps the writer wanted that interpretation and inserted the comma only to keep *leadership* from seeming parallel to *staff* instead of to *expertise*. The single comma, though, adds more confusion than clarity, and recasting the sentence would have been preferable. If you excise *expertise*—after all, what else would one expect of an exceptionally well qualified staff?— you avoid any question about what goes with what: *The exceptionally well qualified staff and the dedicated leadership promise continued success* or, if the staff seems more important than the leadership, *The exceptionally well qualified staff, along with the dedicated leadership, promises. . . .*

Nonrestrictive Modifiers
The last example, like the opening one about the young man with the carnation, shows that the absence or presence of commas around a phrase or clause can affect not only the sound but the sense of what you want to say. Using no commas makes the modifier essential, using two commas makes it expendable, and using only one can turn

your statement into nonsense. If you write *Executives who never take advice are pigheaded,* you are limiting your criticism to executives who do not take advice. Enclosing the *who* clause in commas would make the sentence mean that all executives are pigheaded, as their failure to take advice bears out. Similarly, the sentence *The spectators horrified by the gory scene left immediately* implies that some spectators stayed behind when the squeamish ones left. If all the spectators walked out, the *horrified* phrase belongs in commas.

While you can punctuate some sentences to mean one thing or another, others offer no choice. Only one meaning is possible and only one punctuation decision is correct. Commas do not belong around a modifier that defines or restricts the meaning of the word it applies to; they would make vital information look dispensable. The punctuation makes no sense in this sentence: *A mother, willing to sacrifice her baby for a good cause, is a rarity.* Treating the *willing* phrase as nondefining leaves the ridiculous statement *A mother is a rarity.*

Appositives and adjective phrases and clauses. The modifiers most likely to raise the restrictive-nonrestrictive question are appositives, participial phrases, and relative clauses (adjective clauses usually introduced by *who, which,* or *that*). An appositive introduced by *for example, that is,* or *namely,* for instance, is invariably nonrestrictive. So too is an appositive that consists of a synonym preceded by *or:*

> The chipmunk, or ground squirrel, hibernates in winter.

The comma is inappropriate, of course, if *or* introduces not another name for the same thing but a different thing (*a dog, or canine, is . . . ,* but *a dog or a cat is . . .*).

Modifiers or appositives that follow proper nouns are almost always nonrestrictive. For example:

> Stonehenge, that mysterious assemblage of giant stones, was the next stop on the tour.

> The Yucatán, which offers beaches as well as ruins, is a popular vacation area.

> Judy Garland, Liza Minnelli's mother, is most famous for her role as Dorothy in *The Wizard of Oz.*

> The Woolworth Tower, located in downtown Manhattan, was once the tallest building in the world.

Proper nouns usually retain their identity however you describe them (unless there is more than one person or thing with the same name and the context permits confusion about which of the two you mean: *The John Smith who lived next door to us is not the same John Smith who married Mary Jones*). The Yucatán remains the Yucatán no matter what you say about it, and Judy Garland is the same celebrity whether she's identified as a child star of the thirties or Vincente Minnelli's first wife or an American singer who wowed them at the Palladium. Still, writers often omit the commas required around phrases or clauses that modify proper nouns, and you should routinely check the punctuation in such contexts. While most modifiers that follow proper nouns are nonrestrictive, some are restrictive, not because they define the noun, but because they limit it to a particular circumstance. In a sentence like *I remember Judy Garland singing "Over the Rainbow"* or *I regretted finding Stonehenge fenced off from the crowd*, the participle provides essential information. Here again, the question that determines the punctuation is, Would deleting the modifier alter the meaning of the sentence? In the last two examples, the answer is clearly yes.

A noun does not have to be proper to have an unalterable identity. In context *John's kitchen table* or *my mother* or *the red house next door* or *our history textbook* would be unlikely to have a modifier that affected its meaning. The following paired examples of nonrestrictive and restrictive modifiers should clarify the difference between them:

        Nonrestrictive: Gray, a popular color this season, is not becoming to me.
           Restrictive: The color gray is not becoming to me.

        Nonrestrictive: My archaeology teacher, who has spent years in Greece, claims that Delphi is the most interesting site.
           Restrictive: An archaeologist who has spent years in Greece claims that Delphi is the most interesting site.

        Nonrestrictive: The detective novel, which almost always requires a puzzling crime and an ingenious solution, poses special problems for the writer.
           Restrictive: A detective novel that features a hard-boiled private eye may not appeal to fans of Jane Marple and Hercule Poirot.

        Nonrestrictive: My younger sister's mother-in-law, sitting on my left, chattered incessantly.
           Restrictive: The woman sitting on my left was my younger sister's mother-in-law.

Adverbial phrases and clauses.   Like adjective modifiers, adverbial phrases and clauses can be classified as restrictive or nonrestrictive, but their punctuation often depends on other considerations. For example, a comma follows any long adverbial element—restrictive or not—that precedes the subject of the sentence. Similarly, commas set off disruptively placed adverbial phrases and clauses even if they convey crucial information. The restrictive-nonrestrictive question arises primarily with adverbial modifiers at the ends of sentences. A comma precedes only a nonrestrictive adverbial phrase or clause in that position. For example:

> Nonrestrictive: I woke up this morning at exactly seven, when my neighbor began playing the trumpet. (Since the exact time of waking is stated, the *when* clause provides only supplementary information.)
>
> Restrictive: I woke up this morning when my neighbor began playing the trumpet. (Here the *when* clauses defines the moment of waking.)

> Nonrestrictive: Please be on time, as you promised.
> Restrictive: Please do as you promised.

> Nonrestrictive: We ran all the way to grandmother's house, over the bridge and through the woods.
> Restrictive: We ran over the bridge and through the woods to grandmother's house.

> Nonrestrictive: Ask me any time, as often as you like.
> Restrictive: Ask me as often as you like.

In the preceding examples the adverbial elements are clearly restrictive or nonrestrictive, but in some sentences they could be either, the interpretation resting on the use or omission of a comma. The sentence *You should water the plants, as Jim suggested* indicates that Jim thought the plants needed water, but without the comma the sentence would imply that he suggested a particular way of watering the plants—say, twice a week from the bottom. The comma has a similar effect in these sentences:

> A talent scout discovered her in 1959 (,) when she was performing in a small club in Chicago. (Without the comma the *when* clause limits the time of the discovery to that period during 1959 when the entertainer was working at the Chicago club; with the comma the clause merely gives supplementary information about the entertainer's place of employment when she was discovered.)

> Our capital investments began to pay off (,) most dramatically after we automated the Hudson plant. (The comma makes the worthwhile return on investment the point of the sentence; omitting the comma shifts the emphasis to a particularly successful investment.)

> I also read the novel (,) because a friend had recommended it. (The comma makes the reason for reading the novel incidental; left unpunctuated, the sentence primarily concerns the reason for reading it.)

When a comma does not separate a positive verb from a clause or phrase introduced by *since, because,* or some similar word, the emphasis is on the explanation the phrase or clause contains. But when the explanation follows a negative verb, the absence of punctuation often leaves the sentence ambiguous. For example:

> We did not lose the contract because of our references from former employers.

Does the sentence mean that our references kept us from losing the contract or that we lost the contract for some reason other than our references? Adding a comma before *because* makes the first meaning clear. Omitting the comma makes the second meaning probable. As Follett analyzes the situation, the comma makes the *because* clause go with the negative verb; without the comma the negative force shifts from the verb to the explanation, so that the "*because* contradicts a false reason why." In other words, a comma belongs before a phrase or clause that gives the reason for a negative statement but not before a phrase or clause that gives an incorrect explanation. Omitting a comma, however, does not ensure the proper reading. You would do better to use a positive verb and put the *not* before the explanation:

> It was not because of our references from former employers that we lost the contract.

A clause introduced by an *as* that means "in the way that" can also be ambiguous after a negative verb:

> Employees are not shirking their responsibilities, as the editorial states.

Is the editorial defending or accusing the employees? Since dropping the comma would slant the sentence toward an accusing editorial, the comma presumably suggests an approving one; but readers shouldn't have to analyze a sentence to follow its drift. *As the editorial states, employees are not shirking their responsibilities* is clear; so is *Employees are not shirking their responsibilities as the editorial states that they are.*

When a clause introduced by *because* or *as* follows a negative statement, make sure that neither the punctuation nor the wording leaves room for ambiguity. Here are some problem sentences and suggestions for clarifying them:

> They did not publicize the impending distributors' strike because they wanted to avoid a run on supplies.

▇ . . . strike, because they. . . .

> Environmentalists are not primarily responsible for the troubles of the nuclear power industry as the article implies.

▇ . . . as the article implies they are.

Women are not silly creatures, as Ibsen's play suggests.

■ As Ibsen's play suggests, women are not silly creatures.

Expletives and Other Deletables

Like nondefining modifiers, various other types of by-the-way sentence elements require enclosing commas. Obviously in this category are exclamations, polite or vulgar; interjections like *well, yes,* and *oh*; and any name you use in directly addressing someone—*darling, stupid, Senator, Pat, Mom,* or whatever. So too, usually, are transitional expressions like *on the other hand* and *to begin with* and interpolated asides like *perhaps, incidentally, I believe,* and *I understand*—though such expressions are more often punctuated because of their position in the sentence than because of their expendability.

Commas should also set off an alternative or contrasting phrase that refines or embellishes another word but does not contribute essential information. For example:

Their performance was hilarious, however serious its intent.

Her family was well off, perhaps even rich by some standards.

He does the job satisfactorily, though certainly not impressively.

A contrasting phrase is essential, though, if it limits the sense of the first adjective:

A poor but happy person is hard to find.

Studies suggest that strict but loving parents are preferable to parents whom children perceive as indulgent but uncaring.

In such sentences adding commas would only destroy the intended meaning.

One other sort of phrase that does require commas is the absolute construction—a noun and a modifying participle that are syntactically independent of the rest of the sentence. Here are a few examples:

We will be there, weather permitting, by six on Saturday.

I prefer a more conservative program, conditions being what they are.

The play having started, the usher refused to seat the latecomers.

Interrupters

A subordinate element, whether restrictive or not, must be set off by commas if it disrupts the sentence flow. The enclosing commas enable readers to link what precedes the interpolation with what follows. One common type of interrupter is the complementary phrase that separates words that function as a unit—adjective and noun, for example, or preposition and object. When two sentence elements conclude with the same word, commas around the second enable readers to carry over the first to the ending both share:

> She was interested in, but also apprehensive about, the new project.
>
> His lackluster, though technically correct, performance inspired only faint praise.
>
> Sightseeing on the Bowery can be a fascinating, yet rather sobering, experience.
>
> They had contempt for, and refused to cooperate with, the other tenants.

But it is often better to reword to avoid such broken links (*They had contempt for the other tenants and refused to work with them*). Other disruptive elements separate subjects from verbs, verbs from objects or complements, or nouns or verbs from modifying clauses. Here are several examples:

> The president himself, since he believed strongly in the project, offered to speak at the meeting.
>
> What I often do, perhaps unconsciously, is to alternate tough assignments with easy ones.
>
> Their deceit should come as no surprise to anyone who has ever doubted, even for a moment, that honesty is the best policy.
>
> We were relieved, therefore, when the bank offered to extend the loan.
>
> You were, if I remember correctly, the last person to agree.
>
> She is an old-fashioned artisan, they explained, who will never use synthetic materials.

Most parenthetical interpolations are out-of-order or nonrestrictive modifiers, or both. But not all words that intervene between related sentence elements are parenthetical. A restrictive adjective modifier between subject and verb does not disrupt the sentence flow, because it is an essential, defining part of the subject (*The wheel that squeaks gets the grease*). A single-word adverb conventionally placed between subject and verb evokes no pause and needs no commas (*I always do my best*). While commas should set off most out-of-order modifiers, punctuation should not separate the main sentence elements—subject, verb, object, or complement—however they are arranged. For example:

> The final arrangements the president makes himself, paying personal attention to every detail. (The order is object, subject, verb.)
>
> Blessed are the meek. (The order is complement, verb, subject.)

But any parenthetical element in a sentence of this sort would, of course, require the usual enclosing commas: _The final arrangements, which are always left to the last minute, the president. . . ._ When you are not sure whether or not a phrase is disruptive, reading the sentence aloud may help. If you naturally pause before and after the questionable element, add the commas. Rhetorical tests can be definitive where the rules for punctuating by structure leave room for doubt.

Introductory Modifiers

You generally need a comma after an adverbial or adjective phrase or clause, restrictive or not, that begins a sentence in which the subject precedes the verb. While such a modifier cannot be considered disruptive, it is out of its normal order, and the position dictates the punctuation, as this series of examples indicates:

> Running toward us, the man was shouting something and waving a newspaper. (A comma usually follows an adjective phrase that precedes the subject of the sentence.)
>
> The man running toward us was shouting something and waving a newspaper. (Commas do not enclose a restrictive participial phrase in its normal position after the word it modifies.)
>
> Running toward us was a man shouting something and waving a newspaper. (A comma does not follow a participial phrase that comes first in an inverted sentence and complements the subject.)

It is usually natural to pause after a modifying phrase or clause that opens a conventional sentence, and a comma helps readers get their bearings, signaling a delayed subject. Unless required for clarity, however, a comma is optional when a short restrictive adverbial phrase or clause begins the sentence. An opening like _At noon_ or _Before you go_ does not delay the subject for long, but adding a comma may serve a rhetorical purpose.

Most writers recognize the need for commas after opening modifiers in sentences like these:

> After a day of unremitting pressure and difficult decisions at the office, who doesn't deserve a martini?
>
> Although I don't mind taking an occasional trip for a change of pace, traveling two weeks out of every four is more than I care to do.

> Playing games on city streets, children endanger not only
> themselves but also passing motorists and pedestrians.

If the same modifiers were in their normal positions, only the nonrestrictive ones would take commas:

> Who doesn't deserve a martini after a day of unremitting
> pressure and difficult decisions at the office? (The *after*
> phrase limits the question to a specific situation.)
>
> Traveling two weeks out of every four is more than I care to
> do, although I don't mind an occasional trip for a change of
> pace. (The subordinate clause, merely an afterthought, does
> not affect the meaning of the sentence.)
>
> Children playing games on city streets endanger not only
> themselves but also passing motorists and pedestrians. (The
> participial phrase defines the subject.)

In Sequences Where Needed to Prevent Misreading

Sometimes you have to insert a comma to keep readers from making a false connection. For example, though a comma is ordinarily optional after a short introductory clause, it becomes essential if the clause ends in a verb form that might make the subject of the sentence look like a direct object, as in these sentences:

> If he enjoys driving, a car would make an ideal graduation
> gift.
>
> Once you know, the answer seems obvious.

Again, since words of the same form joined by a coordinating conjunction appear to be parallel sentence elements, you have to use a comma before the conjunction if they are not. Here are two examples:

> I expected them to be selected, and prepared for this
> eventuality. (Without the comma, readers might link *selected*
> and *prepared* instead of *expected* and *prepared*.)
>
> Melissa was talking about dancing, and demonstrating the
> various steps she had learned. (Without the comma, readers
> might link *dancing* and *demonstrating* instead of *talking* and
> *demonstrating*.)

But introducing an unconventional comma is rarely the most satisfactory way to prevent misreading; the comma may separate words that belong together as well as those that do not. In the last example, for instance, the comma that keeps readers from mistaking *demonstrating* for a gerund also keeps apart the compound participles. If Melissa had been talking about, say, choreography instead of dancing, *demonstrating* and *talking* would emerge as obvious parallels, so that there would be no need for the comma. Before inserting a preventive comma that is objectionable, not simply optional, you should look for a better solution. Consider this example:

> The obsession leads the candidate to solicit and accept
> money from those most able to provide it, and to adjust his
> behavior in office to the need for money.

The comma added to avoid a faulty junction between *to adjust* and *to provide* has the harmful side effect of separating the parallel elements *to solicit* and *to adjust*. Rather than settle on the comma as the lesser of evils, you could get rid of one infinitive:

> The obsession leads the candidate to solicit and accept
> money from those most capable of providing it and to adjust
> his behavior in office to the need for money.

In Special Contexts

Since the specialized functions of the comma have little to do with sentence structure, they are of only peripheral interest here. Nevertheless, it may be helpful to run through the rules for the most common conventions, those you are most likely to use in your own writing.

In dates written in month-day-year order, use commas both before and after the year: *He wrote on November 13, 1972, that. . . .* The first separates consecutive digits, and the second prevents the misgrouping that might result from using only one comma. But omit the commas if you use the day-month-year order or give only the month and year, since there are then no consecutive digits: *He wrote on 13 November 1972 that. . . .*

In addresses incorporated into the text, put commas after the addressee, the street, and the city: *Send applications to L. H. Dreher, 506 High Street, Cranford, NJ 07016.* But do not use commas at the ends of lines when you write an address in block form, as in correspondence.

A comma between consecutive uses of the same word sometimes, though not always, facilitates reading: *He says that what provisions there are, are hardly enough for six weeks, but I doubt that that's true.* Punctuated as shown, the sentence seems clearer than it would without a comma between the *ares* or with one between the *that* and *that's*. But it is often better to reword to avoid such juxtapositions: *He says that the provisions we have are hardly enough for six weeks, but I doubt that he's right.*

Use a comma to indicate an ellipsis (an omission of words that readers "understand" without seeing spelled out) if the structure might otherwise be unclear. In the following example the first two ellipses require commas, and the last one does not: *The first guests to arrive brought champagne; the second, flowers; and the third, dessert; the first had spent a lot of money, the others very little.*

Commas are conventional around a title or an affiliation, abbreviated or not, that follows a name: *George Jones, Jr., and Susan Hart, Esq., joined Thomas Conway, S.J., on the panel.*

A comma should separate the two parts of an idiomatic construction like *the more . . . the merrier* unless they are short and verbless. In the following sentence only the first of the two examples requires a comma: *The fewer members who know about this plan, the better our chances will be; for the wider the publicity the greater the risk.*

A comma separates a direct quotation from the verb of saying that precedes or follows: *She said, "I wouldn't bother to clean up." "I promised I would," I replied.* When two marks of punctuation belong in the same spot—a comma and a question mark, say—use only the stronger one: *"Don't you mind?" she asked.* When a quotation other than actual dialogue serves as the subject or object or complement of some other sort of verb, omit the comma: *"Sorry" doesn't help, but try "I'll make it up to you."* (Incidentally, do not use quotation marks around *yes* and *no* in a sentence like *I said yes* or *The answer was no.*) Use a comma before an unquoted direct question that you incorporate into a sentence: *The question we have to ask is, By what criteria do we determine our priorities?*

Harmful Commas

If you understand where to use commas, you can readily infer where not to use them. A single comma keeps words apart; it is harmful if the words it separates should interact. A pair of commas set off a parenthetical unit; they are harmful if the words they group do not go together or do not qualify as parenthetical. By marking the words they enclose as disruptive, nonessential, or out-of-place, a pair of commas help readers connect the related sentence elements that come before and after; a single comma used where the context requires a pair obscures the structure.

A single comma should not divide subject from verb, verb from object, preposition from object, or attributive adjective from modified noun. Nor should a comma precede a coordinating conjunction joining two parallel subordinate elements—words, phrases, or dependent clauses. Except in special circumstances, only a coordinating conjunction between independent clauses or before the final item in a series takes a preceding comma. Similarly, a comma should not separate correlative pairs—*both . . . and, neither . . . nor, either . . . or,* and *not only . . . but also* (or *but*)—unless the correlatives precede independent clauses.

The *not only–but also* pair often tempts writers to use superfluous punctuation. Many reputable authors would prefer a comma before *but* in a sentence of this sort:

> This comprehensive history not only provides new details about the famous actors of the American stage but also includes accounts of some interesting lesser-known players.

Perhaps because readers usually pause before *but,* the conjunction often attracts a preceding comma, and an older convention required one. Today, however, with rhetorical considerations no longer ascendant and with open punctuation generally preferred, this comma seems needless. Since the *not only–but also* construction is emphatic in itself (you lose considerable force if you substitute *and*), the added emphasis of the comma only paints the lily. Authors, in fact, tend to overuse these correlatives, accentuating elements that don't warrant the extra attention. That *and* can, and often should, replace *not only . . . but also* shows that the construction is a linking one and supports the argument against inserting a comma.

While *not only . . . but also* connects the parallel elements it governs, a *not–but* construction contrasts them. Thus the punctuation rules are different. You can treat the *not* element in a *not–but* pair as parenthetical and enclose it in commas:

> I go to Los Angeles about six times a year, not because I enjoy the city, but because I have business there.

If the negative seems as important as the affirmative, you can omit both commas. Or you can make the entire construction parenthetical and use a comma only before *not,* indicating that your main point is what you do, not why you do it. Using a comma only before *but,* however, would make no sense; the *not* element alone can be parenthetical but not the *but* element alone, as you can see if you try reading the sentence with a pause only before *but.*

The following examples summarize where *not* to put a comma. The commas in these sentences are at best superfluous and at worst misleading:

> Between subject and verb:
>
> Teachers who care more about instructing and inspiring students than about doing original research, receive little recognition in American universities. (When you're tempted to use a comma after a subject, you've probably taken too long to reach the verb. Consider revising: *American universities give little recognition to teachers who care. . . .*)

Between verb and object:

The senator argued during the committee hearings, that the tax cut would not have the desired effect on the economy. (To correct the sentence, you could either delete the comma or add a second one, before *during,* to make the prepositional phrase parenthetical.)

Between the parts of a compound subject:

The owner of the dog that barks all night, and the neighbor who set out the poisoned meat are going to court over the incident.

Between the parts of a compound object:

They have a pedigreed black cat with wonderful green eyes, and a multicolored dog of mixed ancestry. (Although the comma keeps readers from linking *eyes* and *dog,* it remains objectionable because it also separates a pair; you can easily avoid the problem by recasting the sentence: *They have a multicolored mongrel and a pedigreed black cat with wonderful green eyes.*)

Between parallel subordinate elements:

The restaurant is located opposite Central Park, and slightly west of the Plaza.

After the last item in a series (only the final comma in these examples is incorrect):

She gasped, stared, and then broke into a grin, when she saw the otter in the bathtub. (Here the comma separates the verb from a restrictive modifying clause.)

A haggard, bent, trembling, old man held out his hand for money. (Here the final comma separates the three preceding coordinate adjectives from the term they modify—*old man.*)

All these *do nots* apply to single commas separating parts of the sentence that should flow together; a parenthetical interpolation between such elements obviously needs enclosing commas. The final prohibition refers to a pair of commas used incorrectly to set off an essential part of the sentence.

Before and after a restrictive modifier:

Among the Reagan supporters, who read the *Times* account, the consensus was that the newspaper should not have given the story front-page coverage.

Discretionary Commas

While logic or convention mandates some commas and proscribes others, a number of contexts neither require nor preclude commas but accommodate those that function rhetorically. In view of the current preference for light punctuation, you should generally opt to omit optional commas. If you do use them, do so advisedly. Commas call attention to words. They make readers pause and take notice. Unless you want that effect, don't use commas that the sentence structure doesn't require.

Earlier sections of this chapter mention several kinds of constructions that could be correct with or without commas, depending on the sense intended—clauses, for example, that you might or might not construe as defining. But in these circumstances the punctuation is not optional from your point of view, since it either does or does not reflect your meaning. Sometimes, though, your decision will depend less on whether or not you consider an element restrictive than on whether or not you want it to stand out. The comma will affect the tone of the sentence but not the sense. In the contexts illustrated below the commas in parentheses are permissible but not essential.

After a Short Introductory Phrase or Clause
In these examples you would probably omit the comma unless you had some reason to stress the opening modifier:

> By 1952 (,) he was ready to forsake the literary life for a
> steady job.
>
> In the afternoon (,) the committee reconvened.
>
> When she called (,) she sounded optimistic.

The fate of the comma in this position may rest in part on the other punctuation in the vicinity. In a comma-heavy context you would not want to add more punctuation than strictly necessary:

> By 1952 the disillusioned, impoverished young writer,
> having completed two novels and fifteen short stories that
> no one wanted to publish, was ready to forsake the literary
> life for a steady job.

Around Transitional Adverbs and Similar Interpolations
While words like *therefore, accordingly, indeed, certainly, of course,* and *perhaps* sometimes interrupt the sentence flow and require surrounding commas, they often fit snugly into the text, causing no disruption and needing no punctuation—usually because they occupy conventional adverbial positions. In these circumstances, though, you may add commas if you want to call attention to the adverb. In the first sentences of the following pairs you would use commas only if you chose this emphasis; in the contrasting sentences you would have to

add commas because the adverbs break the continuity, separating verbs from objects:

> I should(,) perhaps(,) add that we have no investments in that country.
> I should add, perhaps, that we have no investments in that country.
> We knew who was responsible. Consequently(,) we refused to take any action.
> We knew who was responsible. We refused, consequently, to take any action.
> You would(,) therefore(,) have a stake in the outcome.
> You would have, therefore, a stake in the outcome.

It is always necessary, incidentally, to set off the conjunctive adverb *however*, lest readers momentarily mistake it for the adverb *however* (cf. *However, John feels we should take the risk* and *However John feels, we should take the risk*).

Before a Conjunction Joining Short, Closely Related Independent Clauses

The comma is optional in sentences like these unless it prevents misreading:

> The sun is up(,) and the birds are singing.
>
> Orchids are more exotic(,) but I prefer roses.
>
> The staff writers met with the editor, and the two photographers took notes. (The comma prevents *photographers* from being misread as the second object of *with*.)

Before a Conjunction Joining Words, Phrases, or Subordinate Clauses That Differ in Form or Emphasis

If the units joined by a conjunction are not strictly parallel, if there is a marked break in thought or a difference in form or emphasis, you can punctuate to indicate the change of pace:

> If you're invited to the dean's reception, wear a simple black dress, or whatever you have that's dark and decorous.
>
> He was staring at her intently, but turned away quickly when she winked at him.
>
> Please bring your partner, and your secretary, too, if you like.

Between a Conjunction and an Introductory Modifier

When an adverbial modifier or a participial phrase follows a conjunction joining independent clauses, a comma after the conjunction is not so much optional as controversial. Few style and usage manuals offer guidance here, and practice differs even among knowledgeable writers. Probably, however, a comma is more often absent than present in these circumstances. For example:

> The senator agreed to support the project, but if he had
> known that most of his constituents were opposed, he might
> have decided otherwise.

A comma is conventional after any long clause that precedes the subject in a conventional sentence, but if that comma is really "the second of a pair," as Follett says, then there's reason to question the decision to leave out the first comma when there's room to put it in. A parenthetical or out-of-order modifier in the middle of a sentence ordinarily requires punctuation at both ends. While Follett does not discuss any exceptions to this practice, he himself omits the first comma when the parenthetical element follows a conjunction (e.g., "For despite all its deviations and excrescences, English does have a structure . . ." and "But even more important, we should remember that many seemingly single commas stand for a pair"). The *Chicago Manual of Style* says, also without giving any explanation, that the comma is usually omitted in this situation, and Strunk and White's *Elements of Style* merely says that it is not needed.

In *The King's English* the Fowlers do devote some space to this issue. Although they argue against using a comma after a conjunction followed by an adverbial modifier, they call the omission an offense against logic. "But," they go on, "the injury to meaning is so infinitesimal and the benefit to sound so considerable, that we do well to offend." Readers "will be grateful." The Fowlers base their advice on euphony—the absence of a natural pause after the conjunction. Others may argue that commas both before and after a conjunction seem to set it off from the rest of the sentence, thus doing more harm than good. Perhaps the conjunction is as valid a substitute for the first comma in the pair as a capital letter is when an adverbial modifier begins a sentence.

But not all writers who can accept a single comma with an introductory modifier in this context would allow only one when the modifier is clearly nonrestrictive:

> We can speed up the schedule, but, as I explained at the
> outset, a rush job will increase your costs.

In such sentences a pause after the conjunction seems natural enough, and the omission of the comma becomes less defensible. If you still object to enclosing a conjunction in commas, look for a way out of the dilemma. In the last example you could omit the comma before *but,* since the short independent clauses do not need the intervening comma for clarity. Or you could replace the comma before the conjunction with a dash or semicolon, substitute a pair of dashes for the commas enclosing the modifier, or transpose the modifier:

> We can speed up the schedule, but a rush job will increase
> your costs, as I explained at the outset.

When a participial or other adjective phrase follows the conjunction in a compound sentence, it is more likely than an adverbial modifier to need punctuation at both ends. While you may not pause before an adverbial element in that position, you usually do before an adjective phrase. Without a preceding comma, moreover, a present participle might be momentarily mistaken for a gerund—the *ing* form used as a noun—and be misread as the subject of the second independent clause:

> Injured at the starting gate, the black stallion falls behind
> the other horses, but making a tremendous effort at the end,
> he predictably wins the race.

Adding a comma after *but* in that sentence would be helpful, and you could then delete the comma after *horses* to avoid setting off the conjunction. The next two sentences illustrate the same situation: a comma belongs before the nonrestrictive participial phrase, but adding it would hem in the conjunction (the revisions evade the issue):

> Shakespeare often focuses on father-daughter relationships,
> and though varying in submissiveness, all the daughters in
> the plays seek patriarchal blessings before they marry.
>
> ■ . . . , and though the daughters in his plays vary in
> submissiveness, each seeks a patriarchal blessing before she
> marries.
>
> *Silas Marner* has a secure place in the Eliot canon, and while
> ranking below *Middlemarch* and *Adam Bede* in critical esteem,
> it remains a favorite for high school English courses.
>
> ■ While ranking below *Middlemarch* and *Adam Bede* in critical
> esteem, *Silas Marner* has a secure place in the Eliot canon
> and remains a favorite for high school English courses.

Before an Interrupting Modifier Following the Conjunction *that*

How to punctuate an opening modifier in a *that* clause is another question that authorities on usage largely ignore, but in their own writing some of them use a comma only after such a modifier, not before. Here, for example, is one of Follett's sentences:

> The drive toward a lean punctuation is such that even if we
> still wrote the complex, periodic sentences of Johnson or of
> Macaulay, we should punctuate them much less heavily.

Perhaps Follett does not consider the restrictive *even if* clause paren-thetical and uses the comma after *Macaulay* simply as a rhetorical device, not as the second of an implicit pair. When the adverbial element is clearly nonrestrictive, it should, of course, be punctuated at both ends:

> The teacher explained that, though he himself prefers a
> closed style of punctuation, a comma is not mandatory after
> a short introductory phrase.

Some writers use two commas even with a restrictive modifier that intervenes between *that* and the subject of the clause:

> The teacher told the students that, if they failed to complete
> any of the three major assignments, they would fail the
> course.

Those who prefer this punctuation might argue that enclosing com-mas are appropriate for any modifier out of its normal order and that a single comma groups the wrong words, separating *that* from the subject of the clause. But it is not usual to pause before a restrictive introductory modifier, and a pair of commas can also mislead, mak-ing an essential element seem expendable. Both arguments have merit, and one or the other may seem the more persuasive for a particular sentence. Since the rules here are obviously not clear-cut, reading aloud and noting pauses may be as valid an approach as any other.

Summary

The following outline summarizes the foregoing discussion of the uses and abuses of commas.

I. Use commas:

    A. Before conjunctions joining independent clauses (for an exception see III.C).

    B. Between adjacent parallel elements (coordinate adjectives and items in series) and before conjunctions preceding the final items in series in which commas separate the other items.

    C. Before and after parenthetical units (nonessential or dis-ruptive elements or out-of-place modifiers).

        1. Nonrestrictive (or nondefining) adjective, adverbial, or appositive phrases or clauses.

        2. Any other units not essential to the basic sentence structure: interjections, nouns of direct address, in-terpolated asides, qualifying or contrasting phrases, or absolute expressions.

   3. Interrupters: units, essential or not, that intervene between structurally related sentence elements and disrupt the continuity.
   4. Introductory modifiers in conventionally ordered sentences (for exceptions see III.A. below).
   D. Between adjacent elements that must be separated to prevent misreading.
   E. In special contexts.
      1. After the day and year in dates given in month-day-year order.
      2. In addresses incorporated into the text, after the addressee, street, town, and state or Zip Code (no comma between state and Zip); in block-style addresses, no commas at the ends of lines.
      3. Between consecutive uses of the same word if clarity requires.
      4. Where needed to mark ellipses.
      5. Before and after titles or affiliations following proper names.
      6. In all but short and verbless *the more . . . the merrier* constructions.
      7. Between direct quotations and the tags that introduce or follow them.
      8. Before direct but unquoted questions incorporated within sentences.

II. Do not use commas:
   A. Between structurally related elements, such as subjects and verbs, verbs and objects or complements, adjectives and nouns, and prepositions and objects.
   B. Before coordinating conjunctions joining parallel words, phrases, or subordinate clauses—unless you want rhetorical pauses at these points (see III.D.) or the conjunctions precede the final items in series in which the other items are separated by commas.
   C. Between the matching parts of correlative pairs—unless the parts are independent clauses.
   D. After adjective phrases that come first in inverted sentences.
   E. Before and after restrictive modifiers.

III. You may generally use or omit commas:
   A. After short adverbial phrases or clauses preceding the subjects of conventionally ordered sentences.

B. Before and after conventionally placed transitional adverbs and similar words that can blend unobtrusively into their sentences.

C. Before coordinating conjunctions joining short, closely related independent clauses.

D. Before coordinating conjunctions joining subordinate sentence elements that differ in form or emphasis or that involve decided breaks in thought.

E. Before parenthetical adverbial modifiers that follow coordinating conjunctions joining independent clauses.

F. Before restrictive adverbial modifiers that interrupt *that* clauses, separating the conjunctions from the subjects.

SEMICOLONS, COLONS, AND DASHES AND PARENTHESES

Semicolons

Semicolons have essentially only two functions: (1) to separate closely related independent clauses that are not connected by conjunctions and (2) to replace commas when the items to be kept apart have internal commas. The celebrated "comma fault," or "comma splice," is the use of the comma between independent clauses not connected by *and, but, for, nor, or, yet,* or *so.* (The last two connectives are fairly recent additions to this list; formerly, neither *yet* nor *so* could form a compound sentence without the aid of a semicolon, but a comma is now generally accepted, and even preferred in informal writing.) The following sentences illustrate the comma fault; if not recast, each would require a semicolon (or a period) instead of the comma:

> Students exhaust themselves during exam week, many of them stay up for days.
>
> They considered taking the product off the market, its prospects looked bleak.
>
> I would probably not find any useful evidence, still I had to go through all those files.

But the proscription of the comma splice has some legitimate loopholes. Commas are conventional between independent clauses in a series of three or more and in certain idiomatic constructions in which the second of two technically independent clauses completes the thought begun in the first:

> Mary claimed that she had been reading in her room, the vicar said that he had been working in his study, and John refused to account for his whereabouts.

> They saw it, they liked it, they bought it.
>
> The bigger they are, the harder they fall.
>
> It's not only a pity, it's a crime.
>
> It is true, isn't it?

In sentences like these you can use commas with impunity; in similar but not identical circumstances you might be faulted for not using semicolons. Borderline contexts leave room for disagreement and require some thought. When adjacent independent clauses work closely together, even if they do not quite fit the pattern of the preceding examples, the comma comes naturally. Semicolons seem too stiff and formal for sentences of this sort:

> We present food as it is; we don't cover it up.
>
> They had to stop finally; they were exhausted.
>
> The air was stifling; we could hardly breathe.

The semicolon appears infrequently in popular writing. It suggests the sort of complicated sentence that slows down readers, and most magazine editors, for example, would substitute a comma, a dash, or a period. Perrin and Ebbitt condone using a comma between "contact" clauses if your voice doesn't drop at that point when you read the sentence aloud, but other guides are more conservative. If you're unsure about the propriety of separating independent clauses with only a comma, it's safer to do something else. Once you start to play fast and loose with the rule against the comma fault, you open the way to imprecise punctuation or the endless weighing of whether or not particular violations are justified. Still, you don't have to settle for semicolons in sentences like those in the last set of examples. You can substitute a comma and a conjunction or subordinate one of the clauses:

> We present food as it is, instead of covering it up.
>
> They were so exhausted that they finally had to stop.
>
> The air was stifling, and we could hardly breathe.

Admittedly, these alternatives slacken the pace a bit and subtly change the tone. Your decision will have to rest on the context, your purpose, and your audience.

When a coordinating conjunction connects long independent clauses, especially if they have internal commas, clarity often requires a semicolon rather than a comma before the conjunction:

> Since she had two college degrees, good skills, and excellent references, she fully expected to find a job easily, despite the high rate of unemployment; but what she did not expect,

until she started looking, was the stiff competition for the positions available.

Although the café specializes in vegetarian dishes, it offers a few fish entrées, including lemon sole, smoked eel, and scampi; and these three, some food critics claim, rival comparable dishes at the best seafood restaurants.

A mere comma won't do to mark a break that's more emphatic than any other in the sentence. If the semicolon seems too formal for the context, either substitute a period or revise. In the last example, for instance, a pair of dashes could replace the comma after _entrées_ and the semicolon after _scampi_.

Although you can avoid semicolons in compound sentences, you have no choice in most series in which the items themselves contain commas. Without semicolons sentences like these would be rough going:

The consultants attributed the failure to increased costs, especially for fuel; the hostility of environmentalists, local residents, and the unions; abyssmal public relations, due in part to company policies; and shortsighted managerial decisions.

We get to eavesdrop on the thoughts and perceptions of Joan, Greg's first wife; Larry, Brenda's first husband and Greg's older son; Carol, Greg's twenty-six-year-old daughter; and Richie, his twelve-year-old son.

If you object to semicolons, you had better avoid complicated series.

Colons

In general use, a colon introduces a formal statement or quotation, an example, or an explanation of what has just been said. While the semicolon indicates a greater separation between sentence elements than the comma does, the colon serves more as a connective. Not all careful writers observe this distinction; some follow the older practice of using a colon as a stronger semicolon. While few experts consider this practice wrong, most use the colon primarily as a mark of anticipation. Here are some examples:

The diet was spartan: steamed fish, raw or steamed vegetables without butter or dressing, half a grapefruit, four ounces of skimmed milk, and unsweetened tea or coffee.

The families interviewed gave two reasons for moving: they needed more room, and the neighborhood was deteriorating.

> To solve the problem, use the Pythagorean theorem: The
> square of the hypotenuse is equal to the sum of the squares
> of the other two sides.

You should ordinarily lower-case the first letter after a colon, unless the material that follows is set off from the introductory text, but a formal statement after a colon should begin with a capital letter. A capital is also required if the colon introduces more than one sentence; in that case, however, you may have to make some adjustment, lest readers think that the colon applies to only the first of the following sentences. When the sentences are fairly short, you can change them to a series of independent clauses separated by semicolons. Sometimes you can use parenthetical numbers before the sentences governed by a colon. If neither of these devices seems appropriate and the context permits some question about how many sentences the colon governs, try rewording to eliminate the need for a colon.

Unless the colon precedes material set off from the text—say, a list or a long quotation—it should follow only a complete sentence; it should not come between verb and complement or between verb and object. It would be wrong, for example, to add colons after the verbs in these sentences:

> My courses this semester are History of the Renaissance,
> Introduction to Anthropology, Intermediate French, and
> Shakespeare.
>
> The reading list includes Richardson's *Pamela*, Fielding's
> *Joseph Andrews*, and Sterne's *Tristram Shandy*.

Dashes and Parentheses

Like pairs of commas, pairs of dashes and parentheses enclose parenthetical sentence elements. Dashes mark a sharper break in the continuity of the sentence than the commas do, and parentheses mark a still sharper one:

> My old dog—the whole neighborhood remembers him—
> always whined outside a closed door.
>
> The feeling in the audience—if it's fair to generalize—was a
> vague uneasiness.
>
> If you practice diligently (teachers recommend at least four
> hours a day), you can be giving recitals within a year.

Often there is no clear-cut basis for choosing commas, dashes, or parentheses to set off disruptive sentence elements. In some contexts any of these would be acceptable, and you need only select the type that best reflects your intention. In each of the following sentences, for example, no one could fault you if you substituted dashes or parentheses for the pair of commas—or, for that matter, if you used no punctuation—but your decisions would affect the way the statements are read:

> Use commas, or dashes or parentheses, to set off a
> qualifying phrase from the rest of the sentence.

> Whenever my mother invited anyone to spend the weekend,
> she would fill the good crystal vase with daisies, or whatever
> other flowers she could buy cheap, and place it on the
> bureau in the guest room.

If a parenthetical element contains internal commas, however, you have to set it off with dashes or parentheses:

> Beginning students may dream of interpreting a poem
> automatically—without the confusion, hesitancy, and
> uncertainty of guessing—but the more experienced students
> know better.

> For approaches of this kind (psychoanalysis, Marxism,
> structuralism, and the like), meaning is never on the surface.

For the sake of clarity, avoid writing sentences that need more than one set of dashes. Sometimes, to guide readers through a sentence, you have to use three levels of punctuation to designate parenthetical elements:

> For lunch try a fruit salad—say, cottage cheese, grapes,
> bananas, orange sections, and strawberries (you can
> substitute melon balls if you're prone to hives)—and see
> how satisfying it can be.

In the last example, which permits some difference of opinion about where the stronger marks of punctuation belong, the parentheses and dashes could change places; but you would then use only one dash after *strawberries*, since a dash can follow but not precede a closing parenthesis. The point is that the three degrees of punctuation make the sentence structure far easier to follow than it would be with only one.

Whereas pairs of dashes serve to set off parenthetical elements, single dashes introduce terms that summarize preceding series:

> Skill, courage, stamina, and heart—all these qualities are
> essential if the team is going to finish on top.

> Kennedy, Johnson, Nixon—our presidents during the
> Vietnam years still await the definitive judgment of history.

In informal writing a dash can also take the place of a colon and introduce an explanation or an example. It then has the sense of *namely* or *that is* and sometimes precedes one of these terms:

Paul stressed three virtues—faith, hope, and charity.

I hate turkey and most of the conventional trimmings—namely, chestnut stuffing, giblet gravy, baked yams, creamed onions, and cranberry relish.

Be careful to restrict the dash to its legitimate uses. Some writers are overfond of this mark, pressing it into service where the context requires a comma, a semicolon, or a period. Unwarranted dashes, the lazy author's when-in-doubt expedient, typify the gushy, immature, breathless style associated with adolescents' diaries.

Afterword

Many seem to believe that what matters is what you say, not how you say it, and they're half right. Thoughts that are trite or shallow or poorly reasoned do not, when felicitously expressed, turn into penetrating insights. An embroidered sow's ear remains a sow's ear, and style is no substitute for substance. But substance buried in an unreadable presentation isn't worth much either. Polishing can enhance a diamond in the rough, and if you have the right stuff, editing can vastly increase its value.

Throughout this book I have explained that editing is largely a matter of applying standard remedies to common faults, but it's now time to confess that the process is sometimes more complicated than I may have made it seem. Although most problems do yield to routine solutions, you can go wrong in so many ways that you're not likely to detect every flaw in one reading. Sometimes you have to remove one layer of errors before others become visible, and new mistakes may slip in as you eliminate the original ones. Professional editors read their manuscripts as often as the deadlines allow, making changes each time through, and these editors are working on material that authors have turned in as finished. In editing my own writing, I cover a freshly typed page with scribbled corrections, retype to see what I've wrought, then sharpen my pencil and attack again. The vicious circle stops only when I find myself restoring the earlier version of a sentence I "improved" last time around. I've reached the point of diminishing returns.

In reviewing your work, first tighten the wording. Then make separate checks for the errors you're prone to. Skim your draft for opening danglers; test all subjects and verbs for agreement; trace every pronoun to its antecedent; look for unbalanced pairs and series. This process gives you the best chance of catching oversights. While you can correct most mistakes quickly, the others can take considerable time. Those involving faulty word order, ambiguous pronouns, and lack of parallel structure can all be tricky to straighten out, and you'll probably be working under some pressure. If you get stuck, flag the trouble spot for later attention and go on. Sometimes you'll hit on an inspired solution after you've given the problem a rest. When you think you're done, go over the manuscript once more, looking for passages that fall short of clarity or grace. You may find that you've been overfond of some words or that your sentence structure needs varying. Try to put yourself in your reader's place and look at your writing with a stranger's eyes. No aspect of revising is more difficult or more important than developing critical detachment.

Editing can be hard work, but it's fun to work hard at what you like doing—whether it's playing tennis or chess or the guitar. Some writers find considerable pleasure in playing with sentences, and if you've read this far, you're likely to be among them. Enjoy yourself.

The Parts of a Sentence

A The body of this book explains how trained editors correct faulty sentences and how you can apply their methods to your own work. To learn these procedures, however, you need some understanding of syntax, the principles governing the ways words fit together. The short review of pertinent terms presented in the Introduction may be enough to jog the memories of those who've merely forgotten the grammar they once knew. But if you have never been exposed to the subject, which was in something of an educational eclipse during the sixties and seventies, or if—for whatever reason—you simply tuned out whenever the subject came up, a more expansive summary may be helpful. This appendix takes a more detailed look at the two interconnected ways of classifying the components of a sentence, first as the various structural elements that make up the whole and then as the parts of a speech that compose each element.

I describe sentence structure in the timeworn terms of traditional grammar, which are more widely known than the newer vocabularies and more suited to my purpose. While linguistic scholars have good reasons for finding fault with these concepts for in-depth analyses of the language, their alternative structural and transformational grammars do not seem appropriate here. To make sure that my terminology was not obsolete, I consulted several current handbooks of English, listed in the Selected Bibliography, and they reassure me that the old ways of looking at sentences remain alive and well. Watkins and Dillingham, for example, begin their discussion with this observation: "Although many methods have been devised for studying the fundamental elements of English, nothing has worked better and more consistently than the traditional approach."

139

STRUCTURAL ELEMENTS

Subjects and Predicates

The conventional sentence, the age-old definition goes, is a group of words that includes a subject and a predicate and expresses a complete thought. While not all formulations that begin with capital letters and end with periods meet these requirements, the few exceptions have little relevance to this discussion.

The word *predicate* tends to disconcert twelve-year-olds, but it's less daunting when you look at it from your full height. Basically, the predicate is the verb, the component that makes the statement (the predication) about the someone or something that is its subject. Because a verb is technically a part of speech, we should probably call it the simple predicate in its avatar as a sentence element, but for now we can adopt the common expedient of letting *verb* mean "predicate." Verbs are the words you ordinarily use when you order someone to do something—*Stop! Run! Slide! Write! Hush!*—though in some commands the verb is only implicit: [*Be*] *Quiet!* [*Talk*] *Louder!*

In such commands the subject, the one who will perform the ordered action, is understood to be *you*, the person addressed. But the typical sentence begins with an explicit subject, the person or thing or idea that is acting, being acted on, or simply existing in the state the predicate describes. When we talk about the subject of a sentence, we really mean the subject of the verb. This grammatical subject is not necessarily what the sentence is about. The sentence *I found the presentation dull and lifeless* concerns a boring presentation, but the subject is *I.* You can identify the subject of a sentence by answering the question formed by putting *What* or *Who* in front of the verb.

In skeletal sentences, of course, it's easy to distinguish subjects from verbs:

Elephants trumpet.	Dinner is served.
I type.	They have gone.
You did.	Objections have been raised.
Flowers smell.	We were talking.
Children play.	Talking may help.

In these examples, as in most other English sentences, the subjects precede the verbs, and the word order alone can show how elements function: *talking* is part of the verb in the penultimate sentence, but it's the subject in the last one. When a verb consists of more than one word, you can call it a verb phrase, since a phrase is any group of grammatically related words that you read as a unit but that does not include both a subject and a verb.

All the foregoing examples meet the traditional definition of a sentence: a group of words that includes a subject and a predicate and expresses a complete thought. If any of the examples began with a word like *although* or *when* or *since*, you would no longer read it as a sentence, with your voice falling at the end. You would read it as a condition or a qualification of something else and wait for the resolution that would complete the thought. Putting a period after such a word group would be like ending "The Star Spangled Banner" after "and the home." *Although objections have been raised*, what nonetheless has happened? *When I type*, what happens? *Since they have gone*, what has happened? Words like *although, when*, and *since* connect and subordinate the following subject and verb to another group of words that does make a statement that can stand alone. Any group of words containing both a subject and a verb is called a clause—as opposed to a phrase, a group of related words that lacks these elements. A clause that makes sense all by itself is called independent. If a sentence contains only one clause, this distinguishing term is unnecessary. The simple sentence and the independent clause are coextensive.

Objects and Complements

While you can often express a complete thought with only two elements—a subject and a verb—a sentence may need a third element to round out its meaning, most commonly a direct object or a complement. In the following sentences the verbs lead to direct objects:

Analysts study trends.	Executives want results.
Children love clowns.	I see friends.

A direct object, as these examples make clear, receives the mental or physical action conveyed by the verb and performed by the subject. What do analysts study? Trends. Whom do children love? Clowns. What do executives want? Results. Whom do I see? Friends. In other words, asking *What?* or *Whom?* after such a subject-verb combination, one in which the subject does what the verb indicates, yields the direct object—the person, thing, or idea that the verb acts on.

A verb that carries its action across to a recipient is described as transitive (the prefix *trans* means "across," as in *transcontinental* and *transatlantic*). That term may be another bugbear for grammarphobes, but the concept is simplicity itself. If a verb has a receiver for its action, it is transitive; if it does not, it is intransitive. Some verbs are usually transitive, others are usually intransitive, and still others can be either (cf. *They run the store* and *He runs fast, She smokes cigarettes* and *The fire smokes*).

And while we're confronting bugbears, you should also know that a transitive verb is in the active voice when its subject is acting (*Dogs chase cats*) and in the passive voice when its subject is acted on (*Cats are chased by dogs*)—that is, when the subject, not a direct object, receives the action. Once again, the only thing difficult about the distinction is the terminology. A verb in the active voice does not necessarily express more action than one in the passive does. The verb is passive, for example, in *The blow was struck with force*, active in *We considered the alternatives*. The word *voice* designates the verb form that indicates whether the subject is acting or acted on. It's the subject that's active or passive, that's doing or being done to.

A sentence may have not only a direct object, which receives the action of a transitive verb, but also an indirect object, which receives the direct object or the effect of the direct object:

Teachers give students   Leave me room.
guidance.

Send them telegrams.   They save you money.

Caterers served us dinner.   We awarded them prizes.

In each of these sentences the word directly after the verb is the indirect object. If the order of the objects were reversed, the indirect object would turn into a phrase beginning with *to* or *for*—*gives guidance to students, send telegrams to them, served dinner to us, leave room for me, save money for you, awarded prizes to them*. Usually the term *indirect object* applies only in the first circumstance, when the word is not embedded in a phrase. Incidentally, if you converted the verb in any of the above examples to the passive voice and made the indirect object the subject (*students are given guidance, they are sent telegrams*, and so on), the passive form of the verb would retain the direct object. It is only in this special case that the passive voice takes an object, which grammarians call a retained object. Here the subject of the passive verb receives not the action of the verb but the object of the action. In most passive constructions, the subject is acted on directly, so that there is no direct object.

The only other primary sentence element left to discuss is the complement, but to understand this term you first have to recognize a category of verbs that differ from those we have been discussing. While most verbs tell what is done by or to the subject, some express no action at all. They simply affirm the "being" of their subjects and lead to words indicating the condition or quality of that being. Having little meaning of their own, these linking, or copulative, verbs function essentially like equal signs: they connect the subjects on their left with the words on their right that either describe the subjects or serve as synonyms:

Circumstances are right.	You should be president.
Adjectives are modifiers.	We will be free.
I am optimistic.	I was being facetious.
It might have been you.	They were children.

The right-hand elements, called complements here, are often termed predicate complements and are sometimes subdivided into predicate nouns, predicate pronouns, and predicate adjectives. These names suggest that a complement belongs to the verb portion of the sentence (i.e., to the predicate, the part that makes the statement about the subject) and completes the meaning of the linking verb. It is also possible, however, to think of a complement as completing the meaning of the subject, and some grammar books call this element a subjective complement. (An objective complement, in contrast, is a word that follows and identifies or describes the direct object of a verb like *name, appoint, call,* or *make;* e.g., in *We named Jones chairman, chairman* is the objective complement of *Jones.*) Still others use complement as a blanket term for any word that completes the meaning of a subject-verb combination—an object as well as a predicate, or subjective, complement—so that *birds* would be a complement in both *Cardinals watch birds* and *Cardinals are birds.* But in this book the word *complement* alone means only a predicate, or subjective, complement.

The last set of examples all use the most common linking verb, *to be.* An irregular verb (one whose pattern of variations differs from that of most other verbs), it has many forms—*am, are, is, was, were,* and numerous phrases involving *be, being,* or *been.* But *to be* is not invariably a linking verb. When it does not lead to a complement, it usually either precedes a word or phrase that tells where the subject is, as in *We are here* or *The theater is on the left,* or serves as part of another verb. A combination like *might have been done, is walking,* or *will be finished* is a form not of the verb *to be* but of the final verb in the phrase.

There are, of course, many linking verbs other than *to be*—for example, *appear, seem, become,* and *remain*—and some verbs can be either linking or transitive:

Linking	**Transitive**
He felt feverish.	He felt the cloth.
Roses smell wonderful.	I smell perfume.
It is turning colder.	We are turning pages.
She got sick.	She got results.
Lemons taste bitter.	I tasted the cookies.

The subjects in the left-hand column aren't doing anything, and nothing is being done to them. They simply exist in the state indicated by the complements.

Word Groups as Sentence Elements

The primary sentence elements, then, are the subject, the verb, and the objects or complements. Every conventional sentence has at least one subject-verb combination, and it may or may not have other main elements—objects or complements. Though illustrated so far with one-word examples, the various elements are sometimes groups of words—phrases or clauses—that function as single units. In the next two sentences all the main elements except the verbs are clauses:

> Whoever reads this wonders who wrote it.
>
> What matters is that they gave us the contract.

The word combinations to the right and left of the verbs in these examples are not complete in themselves (unless, of course, you let the left-hand clauses stand alone and put question marks after them). Each functions as the subject, object, or complement of the sentence in which it appears. In the following examples all the elements except the verbs are phrases:

> Buying on margin involves taking risks.
>
> To capture an audience is to hold it enthralled.

If you have trouble identifying the main elements in a sentence, start with the verb, the heart of the sentence. The subject will be the word or group of words that answers the question formed by putting *What* or *Who* in front of the verb. In the last set of examples, asking *What involves?* and *What is?* yields the responses *Buying on margin* and *To capture an audience*. Putting *What?* after the verb—*Involves what? Means what?*—yields the direct object if the verb is transitive (*taking risks*) and the complement if the verb is linking (*to hold enthralled*).

A verb, of course, may have more than one subject or more than one object or complement, and a subject may govern more than one verb. Some sentences, in other words, have compound subjects, compound verbs, and so on. For example:

Compound subjects

> Plagues and wars controlled the population.
>
> What they promise and what they deliver are different.

Compound verbs

> They loved, honored, and obeyed.
> Consultants analyze problems and suggest solutions.

Compound objects

> She trades stocks and bonds.
> I said that I disapproved and that I would not cooperate.

Compound indirect objects

> They feed woodpeckers and starlings suet.
> We sent senators and representatives letters.

Compound complements

> They were gentlemen and scholars.
> They seemed willing and capable.

Modifiers

Nearly all the illustrative sentences used so far have had only primary elements, but most sentences also have secondary elements called modifiers—words, phrases, or clauses that describe or define main elements or that qualify other modifiers. Although a modifier that functions as a complement constitutes a main element, since it stands alone and completes the meaning of the sentence, other modifiers are subordinate parts of main elements.

In the example below, the main sentence elements are labeled S for subject, V for verb, and O for object. An m before any of these letters denotes a modifier of the designated element, and mm marks a modifier of a modifier. A phrase or clause that functions as a unit is treated as a single word. The first of the following examples has only primary elements; the successive ones add modifiers:

```
         S        V        O
     |Workers |demand |raises. |
```

```
       mS      S        V       mO     O
     |Factory |workers |demand |sizable |raises. |
```

```
      mS      S              mS              mV
  |Factory|workers|in the automobile industry|usually|

      V       mm     mO     O
  |demand|fairly|sizable|raises|

                              mV
  |whenever it is time for a new contract.|
```

In the last sentence the phrase *in the automobile industry* functions as a unit to modify the subject, limiting *workers* to a specific group, and the clause *whenever it is time for a new contract* works as a unit to modify the verb *demand*, indicating the time of the action.

Equipped with no more information about sentence structure than this discussion provides, you probably could not identify all the elements in every sentence you read. Outside the isolated world of controlled examples some components you encounter might seem to be anomalies. These pages merely provide a common basis for discussing ways of improving sentences, and that goal does not require a complete course in parsing.

Types of Sentences

The number and types of clauses in a sentence determine its grammatical classification as simple, complex, compound, or compound-complex. A sentence containing only one subject-verb pair is simple, no matter how heavily weighted with compound main elements and long modifying phrases. A complex sentence, which also includes only one independent clause, has in addition at least one dependent clause. The first two sentences in this paragraph are simple, but the third one is complex. A compound sentence, like the preceding one, lacks a dependent clause but has at least two independent clauses, usually joined by a comma and an appropriate connective (*and, but, or, nor, for, yet, so*) or by a semicolon. In other words, it has two subject-verb pairs, each capable of standing alone as a sentence; a group of words that has only one subject for two or more verbs—that is, a compound verb—does not qualify. The last sentence is compound-complex because it has a dependent clause (*that has only . . . verbs*) in addition to the two independent ones.

We occasionally treat a word or a group of words like a sentence even if there is no verb. Some locutions manage to convey a complete thought without predicates. "The verbs are not 'left out,'" Perrin says, "they are not thought, spoken, or written." This category includes exclamations like *What a great idea! Over my dead body!* and

Wow! and responses like *Yes, No,* and *Maybe.* While acknowledging the rightful existence of these atypical sentences—verbless constructions that can stand alone—we can continue to focus on the conventional sentence.

PARTS OF SPEECH

So far we have been looking at the conventional sentence as an assemblage of interlocking structural components, but we can also view it as a grouping of words with distinctive characteristics. The parts of speech, the eight types of words that make up the various sentence elements, constitute the second basic set of terms that you need in analyzing your writing.

Verbs

The predicate of a clause is that portion which says something about the subject. It comprises an action verb or a linking verb and the verb's objects or complements, along with any modifiers of these elements. Properly speaking, then, the term *verb* designates the part of speech that serves as the crucial ingredient in a predicate, though in common usage it also means the simple predicate, the role the verb plays. Since the normal order for English sentences is subject-verb-object/complement, the predicate of a clause usually consists of the verb and what follows, but there are many exceptions. In the last clause, for example, the subject *exceptions* follows the verb *are.* Sentences with this pattern are called inverted.

You might have trouble picking out the verb in a sentence if all you had to go on was its conventional definition as a word that expresses action or state of being. "State of being" is a nebulous phrase at best, and the "action" words in sentences are not always verbs. In *Exercise seems like work* and *Play is beneficial,* for example, the verbs are *seems* and *is.* You can sometimes recognize a verb by where it falls in a sentence, but its flexibility provides a more reliable test. You can change a verb to convey action or existence at an earlier or later time (*moved, will move*), as ongoing or completed or customary (*is moving, has moved, will move*), as conditional or imperative or emphatic (*if I were moving, Move! I do move*), as performed by the subject (*I moved*), or as happening to the subject (*I was moved*).

The verb in a clause is a word that you can leave in place and change in form without destroying the sentence structure and often without making any other adjustment. In *Exercise seems like work,* for example, you can substitute *will seem* or *seemed* for *seems* and keep the sentence intact. But you can't say *Exercised seems like work* or *Exercise seems like will work* or *Exercise seems will like work,* because *exercise* and *work* and *like* are not verbs here—though each could be a verb in a different sentence (*I exercise, I work, and I like these activities*). If you have trouble identifying the verb in a sentence, try moving the statement forward or backward in time. The word you change will be the verb.

Talking about verb forms can involve intimidating grammatical terms, some of which we've already defined, but fortunately verbs are more complicated to talk about than to use. You might not be able to say what the third-person singular present progressive passive form of the verb *to do* is, but you would have no trouble using *is being done* in a sentence.

A verb has four basic forms, or principal parts, from which you can construct all its variations by adding helping verbs, or auxiliaries (chiefly, *be, do, have, can, could, shall, will, should, would, may, might,* and *must*). The principal parts are the infinitive, the past tense, the present participle, and the past participle. The infinitive, usually signaled by a preceding *to,* is the root form of the verb—the form you look up in the dictionary and, with the exception of the verb *to be,* the form you use with the subject *I* in the present tense—for example, *to consider, to play, to work.* (Properly speaking, these examples are present active infinitives; there are other types—*to be considered, to have considered, to have been considered*—but for the moment we can disregard them.) Adding *ing* to a verb root usually produces the present participle, and adding *ed* ordinarily creates the past tense and the past participle.

The root serves as the present tense, typically acquiring a final *s* when the subject is a singular word other than *I* or *you* (i.e., when the subject is in the third person singular), and follows *shall* or *will* to form the future tense. The present participle after the auxiliary verb *to be* indicates action in progress in the present, past, or future: *is playing, was playing, will be playing, has been playing, had been playing,* or *will have been playing.* The past participle after the auxiliary verb *to have* expresses action completed before some other understood or stated time: *At this point we have considered the first two suggestions; We had considered others before we heard about this one; By the time we announce our decisions, we shall have considered all possibilities.* The past participle after the verb *to be* forms the passive voice: *is considered, was considered, will be considered, will have been considered,* and so on.

Some verbs have irregular principal parts, but if standard English is your first language, you almost always instinctively use the appropriate forms; that is, you say *I thought,* not *I thinked; I drank,* not *I drinked; I have seen*, not *I have seed*. Most irregular verbs form the past tense and the past participle by changing the vowel sound of the root instead of adding *ed*, and many have past forms ending in *t* or *en* instead of *ed*. Dictionaries show irregular verb forms, so that you have somewhere to turn if you do find yourself hesitating over, say, *She has swam* or *has swum the English Channel* or *He had drunk* or *had drank too much*.

Nouns

As traditionally defined, a noun is the name of a person, place, thing, quality, or feeling. It is the only part of speech that you can particularize with *a, an,* or *the*. A common noun, which you do not capitalize, designates any member of the category named (*a woman, a river, an organization, a war*); a proper noun, which you do capitalize, names a specific member (*Edna Browne, the Mississippi River, the United Nations, World War I*). Concrete nouns name material things; abstract nouns intangibles—concepts, feelings, and qualities. Collective nouns designate groups (*team, band, committee, family*); singular in form, they may be singular or plural in meaning, depending on whether you are referring to the group as a unit or to its members (*The team has won five games, The team of all-stars play well together*).

Nouns function primarily as the subjects, objects, or complements of verbs or as the objects of prepositions—a class of words, discussed below, that includes *as, of,* and *in* in this sentence. A clause that serves in any of these ways is called a noun clause. In the sentence *What I want to know is how many shares are outstanding*, both the subject (*What I want to know*) and the complement (*how many shares are outstanding*) are noun clauses.

Unlike verbs, nouns undergo few changes in form. Ordinarily the base form becomes plural when you add *s* or *es* and possessive when you add an apostrophe plus *s*; the apostrophe alone usually makes a plural noun possessive. Irregular plurals, such as *children, mice,* and *geese*, appear in the dictionary entries for the singular forms. Some words adopted from Latin and Greek retain the original plurals; others do not. (When you are unsure whether to write, say, *formulas* or *formulae, criterions* or *criteria*, check the dictionary; if it shows both forms and gives no further guidance, use the one shown first.) A few nouns have masculine and feminine forms—notably, *actor* and *actress*, royal couples like *prince* and *princess*, and foreign-language pairs that have entered English unchanged, such as *alumnus* and *alumna, fiancé* and *fiancée*, and *masseur* and *masseuse*. But most feminine forms—including *authoress, stewardess, aviatrix,* and *executrix*—have fallen into disfavor, along with the feminine mystique. Others, like *waitress, host-*

ess, and *heroine*, are under attack but, so far at least, seem somewhat more tenacious.

Pronouns

Pronouns substitute for nouns; they, too, refer to persons, places, things, feelings, and qualities—though not by name—and function as subjects, objects, or complements of verbs and as objects of prepositions. Without them prose would bog down in repetition. Consider what would happen, for example, if you had to do without *it* in a sentence like this: *Our year-round presence in the toy market has several advantages: it permits the product diversity that makes us a household word, it builds customer loyalty, and it provides early indications of what items to produce in volume for the Christmas peak.*

Although pronouns subdivide into several varieties, those that probably come immediately to mind are the so-called personal pronouns—the first person, which you use to refer to yourself (*I, my, mine, me; we, our, ours, us*); the second person, which you use to refer to those you're talking with (*you, your, yours*); and the third person, which you use for whomever or whatever you're talking about (*he, she, it; his, her, hers, its; him, her, it; they, their, theirs, them*). These words have more forms than nouns do. The first- and third-person pronouns have distinctive plurals, all three have possessive forms, most have different forms as subjects and objects, and the third-person singular pronoun has masculine, feminine, and neuter forms.

The possessive forms of personal pronouns, unlike those of nouns, do not have apostrophes. Among the alternative possessive forms (*my, mine; our, ours; your, yours; her, hers; their, theirs*), *mine* and the words ending in *s* can function as subjects or objects or complements—in other words, like nouns (*I prefer yours, but hers is also good, though she says that the best one is mine*). The other forms cannot; they serve only as modifiers (*my book, your word, her position, our goal, their responsibility*). Theoretically, *his* and *its* can work in both ways, though *its* on its own is unlikely (*That typewriter is even worse than his machine because his still has a shift key and its doesn't work*).

While the pronouns *I* and *you* can be replaced by nouns—say, the *writer* and the *readers*—the context ordinarily need not include those nouns to make clear which persons *I* and *you* refer to. But the third-person pronouns almost always derive their meaning from their antecedents—the words they stand for. In the last sentence *pronouns* is the antecedent of *their* and *they*. Nouns are also known as substantives, because they have substance in themselves; but most pronouns depend on substantives for substance. A sentence like *It is a common problem* communicates nothing unless you know what *It* refers to. (A few idiomatic uses of *it* are exceptions; in expressions like *it's raining* and *to put it mildly*, the pronoun requires no antecedent.)

The relative pronouns—primarily *who, which,* and *that*—also stand for nouns, or for other types of pronouns, but they appear in modifying clauses, called relative clauses, that they relate to other sentence elements. The antecedent of a relative pronoun is the word that the clause modifies. In the last sentence the antecedent of *that* is *word*. *Who* refers to a person, *which* to a thing, and *that* to either.

Of the three principal relative pronouns, only *who* varies in form: *who* is the subjective case (*one who is wiser*); *whose* is the possessive (*a person whose conscience is clear, a house whose foundation is sound*), and *whom* is the objective (*the person on whom the decision depends*). Relative pronouns do not have distinctive plural forms, but they are plural in meaning when their antecedents are plural.

Also antecedent-dependent are the demonstrative pronouns *this* and *that* and their plural forms *these* and *those*. These do not introduce clauses, but they do point to earlier words—as you might point when you tell the person behind the cookie counter that you would like some of these and some of those. Since you obviously cannot depend on digital demonstration when you write, the demonstrative pronouns you use must refer clearly to substantive words (as the opening *These* does in the last sentence). The antecedents for *this* and *these* should be nearer at hand than those for *that* and *those*. You might introduce your brother to your companion by saying, "This is my brother," but if your brother waved to you from across the street, you would be more likely to say, "That's my brother." You usually choose the appropriate pronoun automatically, and when you do have to think about which form to use, the distinction may be not only unclear but unimportant. (A *this, that, these,* or *those* that identifies a noun it directly precedes functions as a modifier. In *I like that approach* or *We chose these letters,* for example, the *that* and *these* are classified not as demonstrative pronouns but as demonstrative adjectives.)

Pronouns in the final class that concerns us differ from the others in not requiring antecedents. Words like *anything, each, either, everyone, neither, nobody, none, somebody,* and *something* are called indefinite pronouns—indefinite because they do not depend on antecedents, pronouns because they play the roles of nouns but do not name anything. Pronouns in this category use apostrophes for their possessive forms, as nouns do. Incidentally, when *that* or *those* directly precedes a relative clause, it constitutes an indefinite pronoun, not a demonstrative pronoun, and needs no antecedent. In a sentence like *Let those who share our belief join in our fight, those* means "the ones"; and in a sentence like *That which is true is also beautiful, that* has the sense of "anything."

In some circumstances, *who* and *which* are also indefinite pronouns. When they head noun clauses, not modifying clauses, they require no antecedents: *I told them who would be there* and *Which you choose depends on your taste.* (Curme would classify *who* and *which* here as "indefinite relative pronouns"—a category that also includes *what, whichever,* and *whoever*—but in this book the term *relative pronoun* applies to *who* and *which* only when they refer to antecedents and appear in modifying clauses.) Interrogative pronouns—*who, which,* and *what* used to introduce direct or indirect questions—also have no antecedents and thus qualify as a species of indefinite pronoun.

The few remaining types of pronouns rarely figure in the revision process. A pronoun with the suffix *self* or *selves*—attached, inconsistently, to the possessive form of a first- or second-person pronoun (*myself, yourselves*) but to the objective form of a third-person pronoun (*itself, himself, themselves*)—is called a reflexive pronoun when it serves as an object designating the same person or thing as the subject (*He asked himself . . . , I was talking to myself*); but it is called an intensive pronoun when it is used for emphasis (*I myself saw it happen; The president herself favors our plan*). Finally, *each other* and *one another* are reciprocal pronouns.

Adjectives and Adverbs

Adjectives and adverbs serve as modifiers, the secondary elements that describe or limit the basic structural units. Like the main elements, the modifiers can be either single words or groups of words (phrases or clauses) containing assorted other parts of speech, including nouns, pronouns, and verbs.

Adjectives are the parts of speech that modify—that is, describe or qualify—nouns and pronouns. Some denote a quality (*blue, tall, old, significant, remarkable, slight*) or indicate quantity, number, or order (*all, some, three, tenth*), and others simply single out or limit, as the articles and pronoun-derived adjectives do (*a, the, his, each other's, other, such, this, those*). A group of words that functions in any of these ways is called an adjective phrase or clause.

According to the dictionary, to modify a word is to restrict its meaning, but as grammarians use the term, it can also mean to describe a word without narrowing its denotation. In *Only a man who can swing through the trees like an ape could manage that stunt,* the adjective clause clearly plays a defining role, making the subject not any adult human male but one with a specific skill. But in *Only Tarzan, who can swing through the trees like an ape, could manage that stunt,* the *who* clause in no way limits the identity of the subject; Tarzan would still be Tarzan if the clause were omitted. Such a modifier is called nonrestrictive or nondefining, in contrast to the one in the first version, which is called restrictive or defining. Here's another example: *One undertaking that is proving successful is our Wheeling coal project, which we launched just two years ago.* Here the *that* clause is restrictive; the sentence concerns not just an undertaking but a successful one. The *which* clause, however, is nonrestrictive; it gives additional information about the Wheeling coal project but does not define it. In *Errors and Expectations* Mina Shaughnessy proposes replacing the term *nonrestrictive* with *extra*, which suggests the extra commas needed to mark nondefining modifiers as nonessential elements—as frills, not nuts and bolts. Some might find *extra* a less forbidding word and a useful mnemonic, but this book retains the traditional terminology, since many readers are familiar with it.

Another easy-to-understand pair of terms that may nonetheless sound intimidating are *attributive* and *predicative*. Attributive adjectives are adjacent to the words they modify; in contrast, predicative adjectives—or predicate adjectives, one type of complement—follow linking verbs and modify subjects. In the last sentence, *attributive, predicative, predicate, one,* and *linking* are attributive and *adjacent* is predicative.

Adjectives change in form only to show comparative degrees, as *good* does in the old autograph-book verse "Good, better, best / Never let it rest / 'Til your good is better / and your better best." The comparative forms of *good* are irregular in not retaining the base form, called the positive degree, but they do have the standard endings: *er* for the comparative degree, used in judging one thing against another, and *est* for the superlative degree, used in ranking at least three things. These endings leave most one- and two-syllable adjectives otherwise unchanged, except for the standard orthographical adjustments that suffixes require (*high, higher, highest; quick, quicker, quickest; big, bigger, biggest; lively, livelier, liveliest*). Many dictionaries include the *er* and *est* forms in the entries for adjectives, so that you can look up any that you are uncertain about. Long adjectives and others that would sound awkward with these suffixes use *more* and *most* to form their comparative and superlative degrees, and the dictionaries show no *er* and *est* forms for them (*more beautiful, most significant, more splendid, most fickle, more winning*). You sometimes have the option of using *more* or *most* even with adjectives that usually take the suffixes. For example, you may say either *I have never known a fairer judge* or *I have never known a judge more fair*—whichever provides the rhythm or emphasis you want in a particular context. Lesser, rather than greater, degrees require *less* and *least* regardless of the adjective's length (*less risky, least risky*). Of course, only descriptive adjectives have degrees. Pronoun-related adjectives and those that denote quantity or number do not.

In this book the term *adjective* applies to any word or group of words that modifies a noun or pronoun. This category frequently includes, for example, infinitives and participles, like the italicized words in the following sentence: *Alerted* to the *growing* dissatisfaction of women *denied* fair compensation, management set up a committee *to study* pay-scale inequities. Nouns, too, can serve as adjectives (*an army officer, an honor student, home rule, rice pudding*); for that matter, adjectives can act as nouns, as in *The rich get richer and the poor get poorer.* Function is the overriding consideration in classifying words as one part of speech or another.

Adverbs, the second type of modifier, do for other parts of speech what adjectives do for nouns and pronouns. Their principal job, as their name implies, is to qualify verbs, as in *completely failed* and *sincerely believed*, but they also qualify other modifiers, as in *extremely valuable* and *quite sincerely*, and entire sentences, as *unfortunately* does in this example: *Unfortunately the suspect completely failed to convince the jury that he had taken his employers' extremely valuable jewelry into his protective custody during the party because he quite sincerely believed that it might be stolen.* Typically, an adverbial element—whether a word, a phrase, or a clause—answers a question about the word or words modified: *How? Where? When? Why?* or *To what extent?* In the last example, *completely* tells how or to what extent the suspect failed, *sincerely* tells how he believed, *extremely* indicates the extent to which the jewelry was valuable and *quite* the degree of his sincerity, the adverbial *into* phrase tells where he took the jewelry, the *during* phrase tells when, and the *because* clause tells why.

Most single-word adverbs, but not all, end in *ly*, a suffix tacked onto the corresponding adjective without otherwise altering it, except that a final *y* preceded by a consonant becomes *i* (*strongly, publicly, whimsically, coyly, happily*). Not all words ending in *ly* are adverbs, however. Occasionally that suffix turns an adjective not into an adverb but into another adjective (*lively, deadly, sickly*), and *ly* attached to a noun usually produces an adjective (*earthly, friendly, homely, hourly, lovely, manly, mannerly, saintly, worldly*). Certain adverbs, moreover, have the same forms as the corresponding adjectives (*early, fast, first, hard, high, late, right, straight, wrong*). While some of these words also come in *ly* varieties, you can usually rely on your ear to tell you which form to use in any given sentence. You would not say that you *threw a ball highly into the air* or speak of your *high esteemed colleague*, nor would you be likely to get the adverbs mixed up in *Lately I have been working late in the office.* Another sizable group of adverbs that lack the characteristic *ly* endings also lack comparative degrees (*almost, here, now, once, quite, rather, since, sometimes, then, there, today, tomorrow, too, very, yesterday*). *Often* and *soon* are two atypical non-*ly* adverbs that can be compared but that do not also function as adjectives. Non-*ly* adverbs that have comparative degrees form them in the same way that adjectives do. Adverbs that end in *ly* invariably use *more* and *most*, *less* and *least*.

Prepositions and Conjunctions

The parts of speech discussed in the preceding section can serve as primary or secondary sentence elements—verbs as predicates; nouns and pronouns as subjects, objects, and complements; adjectives and adverbs as modifiers. Those we turn to now can only be parts of those components, and unlike the words in the other categories they never change in form. More functional than substantive, prepositions and conjunctions simply tie other parts of speech together.

A preposition forms a phrase with a noun, a pronoun, or a noun equivalent—called its object—that it links to another word in the sentence. The object may have modifiers (*about all things bright and beautiful*), or it may itself be a phrase or a clause (*in offering suggestions to whoever is in charge*). A prepositional phrase functions as a unit, usually as an adjective (*the end of the book, the store on the corner*) or an adverb (*left after the meeting, drove over the bridge*).

The words, or word groups, commonly used as prepositions include *about, above, according to, across, after, below, beside, beyond, by, concerning, despite, during, for, from, in, inside, into, like, near, of, on, out, outside, over, through, to, toward, under, up, within,* and *without.* But there is no need to memorize them. You can recognize prepositions, as you can other parts of speech, by what they do in a sentence. (To see what they do, try reading the last sentence without *of, by,* and *in.*) Besides, not all the words listed are invariably prepositions. While the word *up,* for example, is a preposition in *went up the hill,* it is an adverb in *look up* and an adjective in *walked down the up escalator; before* is a preposition in *darkest before the dawn,* an adverb in *as I said before,* and a conjunction in *look before you leap; down* is a preposition in *walked down the road,* an adverb in *all fall down,* a verb in *they down a beer or two,* and a noun in *a first down.*

While a preposition always takes an object—though occasionally only an implicit one—the object sometimes begins the clause that the preposition ends. While such constructions are the exception to the rule (a preposition normally occupies the "pre-position" relative to its object), virtually no one still argues that a sentence should never end with a preposition. Questions like *What was the memorandum about?* and *What audience are you aiming at?* are quite acceptable, as are the relative clauses in *The dealer that you bought it from will provide this service* and *The person that I wrote to is the assistant sales manager.* Ordinarily, however, you would omit the relative pronoun in sentences like the last two and let readers "understand" it as the object of the preposition: *The dealer you bought it from . . .* and *The person I wrote to. . . .*

In turning to conjunctions, the second type of connectives, we have to distinguish first of all between two main types, coordinating and subordinating. The principal coordinating conjunctions—*and, but, for, nor,* and *or*—join sentence elements of equal weight and of the same grammatical species, linking pairs and series of words, phrases, or clauses, as *and* and *or* do in this sentence. *But,* however, is not invariably a conjunction; it is sometimes a preposition meaning "except," as in *We have met all but one of their demands. For,* too, is often a preposition; in fact, unlike the other coordinating conjunctions, the conjunction *for* can only connect independent clauses; used in any other way, *for* is a preposition. In *They left no margin for error, for they were sure there would be none,* the first *for* is a preposition, the second a conjunction. In some constructions the conjunction that connects two subjects, verbs, objects, modifiers, or independent clauses works with a correlative that precedes the first of the paired elements. The correlative conjunctions—*both . . . and, neither . . . nor, not . . . but, not only . . . but also,* and *whether . . . or*—heighten the parallelism of the units they join, which should match in both form and function (the last four words are an example).

Unlike coordinating conjunctions, subordinating conjunctions do not join coequal words, phrases, or clauses; they invariably head dependent clauses and show how the words that follow relate to other sentence elements. Typically, they introduce adverbial clauses that modify either entire main clauses or the principal verbs and that state a contrast or a condition or answer one of the questions that adverbs usually do. In the following examples *unless, where,* and *if* are subordinating conjunctions: *Unless you agree, we will not proceed. Move where you please. Please pay within ten days if you want prompt delivery.* Sometimes the clauses are elliptical; that is, their subjects and verbs are implicit rather than stated. If we read *When only five, Mill knew Greek* or *Your story, though true, seems incredible,* we readily understand the missing "he was" or "it is," and *when* and *though* still qualify as subordinating conjunctions. Other common subordinating conjunctions are *after, although, as, as if, as long as, because, before, since, so that, until,* and *while.*

Some of these words—for example, *after, as,* and *before*—can also be prepositions, and it is important to recognize their distinctive functions. Both a preposition and a subordinating conjunction show how the words that follow fit into the sentence, and each forms a unit with the words it introduces. The essential difference is that the conjunction precedes a subject-verb combination, stated or implicit, and a preposition introduces a noun or a noun equivalent. While the object of a preposition may be a noun clause (*to whoever wants it*) or be modified by an adjective clause (*for students who hate grammar*), the preposition is not part of the following clause. It is part of the phrase that includes its object and the modifiers; it is not part of a clause that constitutes its object or a modifier. In contrast, a subordinating conjunction is always part of the clause it introduces. *After* is a preposition in *after the ball*, a conjunction in *after the ball is over*; *as* is a conjunction in *as I was saying*, a preposition in *as a writer who cares about her work*; *before* is a conjunction in *before I leave*, a preposition in *before the year that I spent in France*.

Although most subordinating conjunctions introduce adverbial clauses, the conjunction *that*, which introduces a noun clause (not to be confused with the relative pronoun *that*, which introduces an adjective clause), is a prominent exception (*That they refused to testify suggests that they do not wish to be implicated*). Other words that introduce noun clauses are not usually classed as subordinating conjunctions. Curme mentions, for example, interrogative pronouns (*I asked who did it*), interrogative adverbs (*I wonder why they did it*), and indefinite relative pronouns (*I do not know whom they invited*). These fine distinctions need not concern us here. The point to note is that not all words introducing subordinate clauses are subordinating conjunctions.

Interjections

Last and least of the parts of speech are the interjections—a category of virtually no concern in this book. These are words or groups of words that disrupt the flow of coherent discourse to express some feeling such as pleasure, pain, surprise, dismay, embarrassment, annoyance, or anger. Expressions like *Ah! Ouch! Shucks! Pshaw!* and *Balderdash!*—not to mention all the more currently popular outbursts— often function alone as sentences. (Curme comments, in fact, that they "belong to the oldest forms of speech. . . . Thus they are not words but sentences. Sentences are older than words.") When introduced into a sentence, an interjection has no grammatical relation to the other components and requires commas or dashes to set it off: *Oh bother, I forgot my keys; We'll do it, by George, if it takes all year; I tried again but—blast it!—this time I didn't even hit the target.*

Converts and Hybrids

As this discussion has emphasized repeatedly, many words usually classified as one part of speech sometimes function as another. "To find out what class a word belongs to," Jespersen says, "it is not enough to consider its form in itself; what is decisive is the way in which the word in connected speech 'behaves' towards other words and in which other words behave towards it." The nouns *house* and *dog*, for example, turn into adjectives in the terms *house arrest* and *dog collar*; they modify nouns and show no change for the plural (*house arrests, dog collars*). Such combinations are so common, in fact, that they often develop into single words (*cornerstone, doorknob, figurehead, fishbowl, houseboat, warmonger*). Similarly, adjectives readily become nouns (*the underprivileged, the disadvantaged, the wealthy, the superrich, the beautiful, the damned*). Even verbs are occasionally pressed into service as nouns (*the haves and the have nots*).

Although function is the essential consideration in assigning part-of-speech labels, a word that undergoes a grammatical shift does not necessarily exhibit all the characteristics of its adopted class. It remains, in a sense, a hybrid. Nouns used as adjectives, for example, differ from pure descriptive adjectives in not having comparative and superlative forms; for this reason some grammarians call them attributive nouns. The reasoning of grammarians, however, does not always seem consistent. Sometimes they insist on logic, as when they argue that the pronoun *he*, since it must stand for a noun or pronoun, has no antecedent in *The manager's directive explains why he objects to the proposal*. Because the possessive form *manager's* plays an adjective's role, it cannot also function as a noun and serve as an antecedent for a pronoun—except, of course, for a possessive pronoun. (To eliminate the error, you could say either *The manager explains in his directive why he objects* . . . or *The manager's directive explains his objections.* . . .)

But grammarians can also explain seeming violations of logic or accept them as idiomatic exceptions. For example, though adjectives do not modify other adjectives, *best* seems to be doing exactly that in *my best friend's dog*, where *friend's*, a noun in the possessive case, must be considered an adjective. Well, here, the argument runs, the possessive really belongs to the whole phrase *my best friend*. In a sentence like *It is worth the effort* some would call *worth* an adjective that atypically takes an object; others would say that, since adjectives do not take objects, *worth* is a preposition in that construction. Similarly, grammarians who list *like* as an adjective that takes an object use examples that look suspiciously like prepositional phrases (e.g., Jesperson's "He looks like an actor").

One class of hybrids that all grammarians accept as having characteristics of two parts of speech are the so-called verbals—infinitives, participles, and gerunds. Infinitives, the *to* forms of verbs, can function as nouns, that is, as subjects, objects, or complements (*To err is human; I asked to be excused*; and *To understand is to forgive*). They can also act as adjectives (*I have money to spend; Let's have something to eat; To succeed in this business, you need connections*) or as adverbs (*I come to bury*

Caesar, not to praise him; I am happy to accept; I went to meet them). But used in any of these ways, the infinitive retains some of the characteristics of a verb: it can have a subject, a complement or an object, and adverbial modifiers (*I believe them to be intruders, They agreed to investigate the matter thoroughly*). Incidentally, the discussion of infinitives here and elsewhere includes those that appear without an identifying *to*, which idiomatically disappears when the infinitive follows verbs like *make, help,* and *dare* (*You made me love you, I helped him build it,* and *I wouldn't dare contradict her*).

The present and past participles of verbs, the *ing* and *ed* forms used with auxiliary verbs in various inflections, function on their own as adjectives. Sometimes it makes little difference whether you construe a participle following the verb *to be* as part of the verb phrase or as a predicate adjective. In *We are impressed*, for example, you may either consider *are impressed* the first-person plural present passive form of *impress* or regard *impressed* as an adjective modifying *We*. But even when participles appear without auxiliaries and clearly serve as adjectives, they—like infinitives—still act in some ways like verbs, taking objects or complements (*Choosing my words carefully, I told them the whole story; This procedure, once considered daring, has become commonplace*). The participle, the words it governs, and any modifiers of these elements constitute a participial phrase.

A gerund, the *ing* form of the verb used as a noun, differs from the present participle only in function, not in form. But it is important to recognize the distinction. There's nothing wrong with *Concentrating on my work made the hours fly*, where the first word is a gerund, the subject of the verb *made*. But in *Concentrating on my work, the hours flew by*, you have the notorious dangling participle, an adjective form with nothing to modify. (To repair the sentence, you could match participle and subject: *Concentrating on my work, I made the hours fly by*).

The last example illustrates how a knowledge of syntax comes into play in correcting faulty sentences. "To revise a sentence," Mina Shaughnessy says, you "must have . . . a strategy for breaking into it," a way of seeing its "seams" and "joints" and "points of intersection." Knowing its components gives you the access you need.

A Glossary of Questionable Usage

B While the preceding chapters focus on general problems that keep sentences from working smoothly, this appendix deals with specific words and phrases that some critics find fault with. These fine points of usage have to do less with the sense and readability of sentences than with the sensibilities of readers. *Between you and I* is no less clear and graceful than *between you and me*, nor is *apples are different from oranges* obviously superior to *apples are different than oranges*—unless, of course, one or the other wording grates on your ear as wrong. If so, the "error" distracts you from the substance of what you are reading. As a writer, you should avoid putting such obstacles in your readers' path.

Virtually no one disputes the practicality of using standard English—the dialect of the educated—for reasonably formal, public exposition. But more is at issue here. Even usages common in reputable published writing are sometimes criticized as pompous, inexact, redundant, or ugly. Although objectionable diction may well be the least serious problem I discuss, writers probably crave guidance in this area more than in any other. In *Grammar and Good Taste*, Dennis E. Baron stresses the country's prevailing linguistic insecurity, attested by the popularity of books and newspaper columns on language abuse, and attributes it in part to "an educational system based on a doctrine of correctness and purity in language that invariably conflicts with the observable facts of English usage."

Critical of the traditional concept of "correct English," linguistic scholars like Baron are interested in scientifically describing language as it is spoken, by high-school dropouts as well as college graduates, and they do not judge one variety inferior to another (though they recognize that "standard English" is appropriate for formal discourse). They question whether native speakers of the language can make mistakes. Objectively studying how the language functions, how it develops and changes, they would not impose rules to inhibit its growth.

Baron reports a long history of conflict between language scholars and the word watchers who decry faulty usage. And "the cold war," Geoffrey Nunberg observes, "endures to this day." While the linguists have convinced "most of the educational establishment" that their views are correct, they have not swayed "the body of educated public opinion."

Thus the public still asks not what the language is but what it should be. And the language scholars, by and large, refuse to address the question. It would "involve value judgments," the linguist Samuel R. Levin comments, "which the linguist, as structuralist, does not reckon himself qualified to make." Observing that "[w]e should not ask linguistic scientists to tell us what sounds best," Nunberg finds them "no more sensitive to nuances of usage than mathematicians and chemists; they tend to regard prose as a necessary evil that serves only to smooth the transition from one formalism to the next."

With language scholars unwilling to pontificate about proper usage, many practical stylists have volunteered for the job. Most of these self-appointed authorities—after all, as Bernstein points out, they had no way of getting official appointments—are writers, journalists, editors, or teachers without formal training in linguistics. But these amateurs in the study of language are professionals in its use. Words are the tools of their trade, and they care about them in a way quite different from the linguists'. Instead of emphasizing patterns of speech, they stress written usage, which can reflect careful choices. For literary purposes some words are arguably better than others, and value judgments are in order.

The best of the language critics have devoted conscientious and intelligent thought to what makes good usage good; and they defend their preferences, in a nonauthoritarian way, as logical, useful, or felicitous. Of course, they often disagree, and Baron finds them "invariably inconsistent." But despite their many disagreements and inconsistencies, they can help us formulate our own judgments. Some arguments will seem more cogent than others or will have more adherents or will rest on stronger evidence.

In focusing attention on usages that these critics dislike, I am not rejecting the position of the language scholars. Though I would, in fact, argue for the peaceful coexistence of the two groups, for literary sensitivity informed by linguistic scholarship, my purpose here is not ideological but pragmatic. I want to alert you to wording that puts you at some risk and that you may therefore wish to avoid, whether or not you agree with the objections advanced. In editing for the Modern Language Association, I suggest alternatives to such wording because the MLA has unusually strong reasons for wanting its language to be above reproach (not that it has always achieved this end). Even opponents of traditional standards usually find it tactful to follow the precepts they disparage. Many who don't mind *like* as a conjunction or *hopefully* in the sense of "it is hoped" avoid these usages to forestall attack. No one likes to be thought ignorant, and the guardians of the language can be vicious. Baron reports that writers asked to comment on disputed diction have recommended fines, jail sentences, and even lynching for those guilty of certain errors. If you would not bow to the vigilantes out of cowardice, you may choose to respect the feelings of the less vindictive cherishers of proprieties. Some writers whom Baron quotes claim to be sickened or disgusted when they find words misused, and it is only civil to spare them distress.

Many suspect usages, I am well aware, have impressive literary precedents, especially in works written before the eighteenth-century grammarians attempted to impose order on the language. Only since about 1920 has *infer* been condemned in the sense of "imply," *lie* and *lay* have long been confused, as have *affect* and *effect*; Shakespeare was comfortable with double superlatives like "the most boldest . . . hearts of Rome"; and *disinterested* meant "uninterested," a usage currently criticized, before it came to mean "unbiased."

For our purposes, however, such historical evidence is of little importance. Linguists may argue that changes in the way a word has been used prove that its structure permits different interpretations and that objections to one or the other are mere prejudices. But while a perusal of the multivolume *Oxford English Dictionary* should discourage self-righteousness and dogmatism among the language critics, its citations do not necessarily refute the arguments of modern arbiters. Whatever was true in the past, certain usages are suspect today, and if you do not avoid them, you may be thought careless or uninformed. From the practical point of view adopted here, the record of the centuries is beside the point. I mention a few historical odds and ends for their inherent interest, but I emphasize the discriminations important to our contemporaries.

A glossary of usage confined to an appendix must obviously be selective about its entries, and I have given priority to questionable wording that occurs fairly often in manuscripts accepted for publication by the MLA. While I also include some usages that seem troublesome in the nation at large, though perhaps not to sophisticated authors, there are few, if any, of the sort considered nonstandard, such as *it don't* or *them things.* I have also generally excluded topics discussed in the body of the book—nouns misconstrued as singular or plural, for example, and jargon that contributes to wordiness. If you do not find what you are looking for here, consult the Index. Those interested in a more extensive treatment of usage can choose from several book-length glossaries. Of these I would single out Bernstein's *Careful Writer,* which is both amusing and helpful, and Copperud's comprehensive *American Usage and Style: The Consensus,* which takes into account opinions expressed in several leading dictionaries and usage guides.

The recommendations presented here are offered not as cast-iron rules but, in Nunberg's words, as "the tentative conclusions of thoughtful argument." In the end you must decide for yourself which advice seems worth taking, or at least not worth disregarding. If your usage is unexceptionable when judged by the most scrupulous standards, you offend no one. If it is not, you may handicap your writing.

a, an The choice of *a* or *an* before a word depends, of course, on the sound—not the letter—that follows: *a ukulele* but *an uncle; an $8 check* but *a $10 check.* We say *an heirloom, an honor,* and *an hour* because the initial consonants are silent; each word begins with a vowel sound. In the past, especially in England, the *h* was also virtually inaudible in words like *history* and *hotel,* so that the preceding article was *an.* But today the *h* is generally pronounced in these words, and the appropriate article is *a.* Some critics claim, however, that it is natural to use *an* when the first syllable of the *h* word is not stressed: *A history book lists as an historical fact that. . . .* The 1983 edition of *Webster's Collegiate,* while noting that both *a* and *an* occur before such words in print, claims that *an* is more common in speech; but the 1982 edition of the *American Heritage Dictionary* reports that an unpronounced *h* in words like *historical* and *hysterical* is "now uncommon in American speech." Though the appropriate article in that context may be a matter of opinion, or of varying pronunciation, *an* should clearly not precede a word that starts with an *h* you hear. Read a phrase aloud if you don't know which article to use. Would an hypocrite pretend to an humble heart?

absolute modifiers Strictly construed, expressions like *most unique, more complete,* and *more perfect* seem illogical. If *unique* means "only one," how can a circus act, say, be the most unique ever presented? If *complete* means "missing nothing," how can one list be more complete than another? And if *perfect* means "without a flaw," how can one gem be more perfect than the next? At this point, some style guides recall "the more perfect union" of the Constitution and, sooner than question the diction of the founding fathers, argue that everyone realistically takes *perfect* to mean "approximating perfection." Reasoning in a similar way, Curme exonerates comparative forms like *deader* and *more unique* from the charge of pleonasm.

But many language critics disagree. The *American Heritage Dictionary* reports, for example, that the "vast majority" of its usage panel objects to *most unique*. In speech illogical comparisons slip by unremarked, but writing gives readers a chance to notice and criticize. Think twice about assigning degrees to obvious incomparables like *mortal, endless, total, wholly, final, absolute, peerless, equal, devoid,* and *essential.* Qualifying such words is like putting *most* before adjectives ending in *est.* Shakespeare could use double comparative forms emphatically—Antony says, for example, that Brutus gave Caesar "the most unkindest cut of all"—but today no one over the age of six can get away with an expression like *the most biggest man.* Absolutes are superlatives in themselves; they cannot be intensified. If you preface them with *more* or *most,* you diminish their meaning. But you can approach these extremes more or less closely. A project can be less nearly complete than another, a record the most nearly perfect in the class.

affect, effect To affect is to influence, to effect is to bring about: *The new wage offer affected our willingness to compromise on the other issues, and we were able to effect a settlement within a few hours.* Perhaps some writers confuse the two verbs because the noun *effect* corresponds to both; it can mean either "influence," as in *The report concerned the effect of gamma rays on man-in-the-moon marigolds,* or "result," as in *This approach had the desired effect.* The noun *affect,* defined as "the subjective aspect of an emotion," exists only as a technical term in psychology.

all of In a phrase like *all of the people, all of my friends,* or *all of the time,* the *of* is expendable. It's not incorrect, just needless, and you may as well eliminate it. Prepositional phrases have a way of running to excess, and it's good to have one you can jettison automatically. But you have to keep the *of,* of course, when a personal pronoun follows: *all of us, all of them.*

alternate, alternative With increasing frequency, *alternate* and *alternately* are replacing *alternative* and *alternatively. Webster's Ninth,* which features usage notes not included in earlier editions, lists the two adjective forms as synonyms and reports no objections. Most other guides, however, argue for preserving a distinction. *Alternate* and *alternately* mean "in turn," "first one and then the other," whereas *alternative* means "available as another possibility" and *alternatively* means "or." Traditionalists would find no fault with the following examples: *New York City allows parking on alternate sides of the street. The editor visits the Washington and Boston bureaus alternately. We could lease more space elsewhere; alternatively, we could remodel and enlarge our present offices. Many college language teachers have had to find alternative careers.* In sentences like the last, however, *alternate* is probably more common than *alternative.* Theaters ask us to list alternate dates when we order tickets; book clubs offer alternate selections; and attorneys choose alternate jurors. Highway signs use *alternate* in two senses—*Use alternate merge* and *Take alternate route*—and drivers can understand both. But in some contexts failure to observe the distinction can lead to ambiguity: *We have alternate vacation plans; Alternately, we could go to Spain and Italy.* Why not maintain a distinction that enriches the language? What do you gain by relinquishing it?

alternative The Latin base *alter* means "other of two," and some language critics have argued that the noun *alternative* denotes one or the other of two possibilities, not one of three or more. In discussing the word as a synonym for *choice*, *Webster's Ninth* explains that it "implies a necessity to choose one and reject another possibility." Offered a choice—say, coffee or tea—you can refuse both. Presented with alternatives—for example, a fine or a jail sentence—you have to take one or the other. Accordingly, when there's no escaping one of even several possibilities, *alternatives* is a handy word, *choices* a less precise substitute. Perhaps for this reason, the rule restricting *alternative* to *either–or* contexts no longer has many adherents. Copperud reports that it is "discountenanced by no fewer than nine authorities."

among See **between, among.**

an See **a, an.**

and/or In legal and commercial writing *and/or* may be a useful device, but elsewhere it seems heavy-handed. Usually just *or* or *and* will do, but if you must give a choice, *one or the other or both* conveys the notion more gracefully.

anticipate, expect *Anticipate* means "to foresee and prepare for." If you anticipate higher interest rates, you may want to add to your bank account. And if you anticipate losing your lease, you may start looking for new quarters. *Expect* simply means "to look forward to" or "to consider probable." You may expect to sign a contract, to complete a project on time, or to make a profit. In some contexts either word will fit—dictionaries, in fact, list the two as synonyms—but *anticipate* may sound stilted where *expect* will do.

anxious, eager When you await something with pleasant expectations—say, your vacation—you're eager for it. When you're worried about something—say, a visit to the dentist—you're anxious about it. The usage mavens argue that *anxious* should retain the notion of anxiety. If you simply use it to mean "eager," you're not getting your word's worth. Admittedly, though, this usage prevails colloquially, and the historical record shows *anxious* in both senses. Bernstein notes that *eager* is rare in speech and that *anxious* is the usual substitute, but he advocates honoring the distinction in writing, where both words are common.

apt, liable, likely Though often used interchangeably before infinitives, these words differ in connotation. *Apt* implies a natural inclination (the word *aptitude* may provide a mnemonic): *Studies show that men are more apt to interrupt a conversation than women are.* *Likely* suggests simple probability: *The bill is likely to pass.* *Liable* involves vulnerability to something undesirable: *If you drink the local water, you're liable to get sick.* Most experts discriminate between *liable* and *likely* or *apt*; fewer insist on the *likely–apt* distinction.

as—missing or superfluous The second *as* required in a comparison like *as rich as Midas* tends to drop out in constructions complicated by an alternative comparison—for example, *as rich if not richer than Midas.* To correct the problem, you can simply add the missing *as* and put commas around the interrupting *if . . . than* phrase. Or, to avoid a break between the related words, you can complete the first comparison before making the next: *as rich as*

Midas, if not richer. Though this solution is usually the easiest and best, it isn't always. In a sentence like *He was as frightened by this threat, if not even more frightened, than I had been as a child*, the standard maneuver produces a rather long-winded revision: *He was as frightened by this threat as I had been when I was a child, if not even more frightened.* Adding *at least* offers a way out, but you have to juggle the wording as well: *This threat frightened him at least as much as it had me when I was a child.*

Sometimes an *as* drops out because a sentence needs more *ases* than it can comfortably accommodate. Most commonly the missing *as* is the one that idiom requires in constructions like *depicted her as aggressive* or *portrayed him as a martinet.* For example, in *Future historians will regard these developments as significant as those of the Industrial Revolution,* the first *as* of the pair making the comparison can't do double duty as the preposition that should follow *regard.* Since the sentence won't tolerate a third *as* (*as as significant as* is impossible), try to eliminate the need for at least one of them. Often you can replace a verb like *regard* with a synonym that doesn't take *as*—here, *consider* or *judge.* In other types of *as*-heavy sentences, too, you have to edit out one kind of *as* construction to leave room for the other. In *He wanted to be remembered as much as a poet as a statesman,* the *as* after *much* cannot serve both to complete the comparison and to parallel the *as* before *statesman.* Since you can't have a second *as* after *much,* you have to reword: *He wanted to be remembered as much for his poetry as for his statesmanship.*

Occasionally writers use one *as* where logic requires two. In *Her load suddenly felt light as a feather,* for example, the sense is not "light like a feather" but "as light as a feather," and the second *as* before *light* makes the comparison clear. Curme traces the single *as* in such constructions to older English and notes that it lingers on. Scrooge's partner, you may remember, was "dead as a doornail," and even today the first *as* is unlikely in some informal contexts: *Quick as a flash, I saw my chance.*

In contrast, a construction may attract a superfluous *as.* The first *as* does not belong in *As light as it was, the load seemed heavy after a while.* The sentence is not making a comparison; the conjunction after *light* has the force of "though." Follett comments that "*though,* slipping less readily off the tongue, is more emphatic," and he speculates that writers may be trying "to give *as* the same degree of emphasis [when they] begin with an unidiomatic *as* that, once standard, has long been obsolete."

A superfluous *as* may also attach itself to a verb like *consider, judge, deem, name, appoint,* or *designate.* When the verb is in the active voice, the *as* intervenes between the object and the objective complement; when the verb is in the passive voice, the *as* falls between the past participle and the following complement. Idiomatically, you consider, judge, or deem something important, not as important; and someone is named, appointed, or designated your successor, not as your successor. Not every verb in this category attracts an inappropriate *as* (*as* would be unthinkable in *thought him stupid, called her wrong,* or *found me innocent*), and when *as* is appropriate in similar structures, it's almost inevitable—unless its omission is overlooked because an *as* required for another purpose seems to do the job. In a straightforward context like *He viewed him as a father figure* or *She regarded her job as dull,* no one forgets the *as.* Writers are far less likely to omit *as* after a verb that requires it than to use *as* with a verb that can function on its own. Curme, in fact, reports a growing tendency to use *as* with words like *consider* and *judge.* If you're uncertain about the need for *as,* leave it out. A verb that does take *as* leaves no room for doubt.

as, because Though some experts accept *as* in the sense of "because" or "since," most consider this usage ambiguous, since *as* more usually means "while." Either interpretation is possible, for example, in *As I was planning a trip to Paris, I took a crash course in French.* To some ears *as* for "since" also sounds affected: *Please give this proposal your immediate attention, as the deadline for recommendations is 15 March* or *As I shall need the report by 15 March, please attend to it promptly.* Fowler doesn't object to beginning a sentence with a causal *as,* but Copperud comments that this practice is more British than American.

as, like The adverse response to the old advertising slogan *Winston tastes good like a cigarette should* gave grammar more publicity than it had had in years. Though *as* can serve as either a conjunction or a preposition, traditional grammarians allow *like* in comparisons only as a preposition. Even Curme, who notes that the colloquial conjunction *like* has been "gaining ground" for the past four hundred years, acknowledges that "our literary language still requires the colorless, less expressive *as.*" While he defends the conjunction *like* as a natural outgrowth of the adverb *like* once common in clauses beginning with *like as,* his argument does not sway the opposition. "The status of *like* is a topic of historical linguists, not a problem of usage," Follett says. "[I]n workmanlike modern writing, there is no such conjunction." To be on the safe side, then, don't use *like* to introduce a clause. Substitute *as* or *as if* in a sentence like *On our farm we live like people did a hundred years ago* or *They act like they expect to take over the market.*

The usage critics have made some writers so uneasy about *like* that *as* even turns up where *like* would be both natural and correct. In a letter to students' parents a college president writes, "We, as you, are concerned about rising costs." One could argue that in this sentence *as* introduces an elliptical clause, as it does in *I am as concerned as you,* in which *are* is implicit after *you.* But that interpretation seems strained, and an *as* used in place of a correct *like* almost certainly reflects a rule misunderstood. Besides, it can result in ambiguity. In *Her colleagues, as her friends, remarked on the change in her appearance,* for example, are the commenting acquaintances the same group or separate groups? The difficulty arises because the preposition *as* can mean either "in the capacity of" or "like." Substitute *like* for *as,* and there's no problem. In some contexts, however, either connective is possible. *A noun can function like an adjective* likens a noun to an adjective; *a noun can function as an adjective* indicates that a noun plays an adjective's role. Both statements are true, both prepositions defensible.

assure, ensure, insure You can insure your possessions against fire and theft, you can assure a prospective customer that no salesman will call, and you can ensure or insure prompt delivery. *Insure* is the only proper verb when you mean "to protect against loss." *Assure,* defined as "to give a guarantee to," needs a person or persons as its object—or, in the passive voice, as its subject—and the thing assured appears after *of* or *that: They assured us that they would cooperate* or *We were assured of their cooperation.* Although either *ensure* or *insure* can mean "to make certain of," use one or the other consistently. Some guides claim that *insure* is the more usual choice, but others would restrict *insure* to its narrow meaning, thus ensuring *ensure* the right to exist.

as to Imprecise and often superfluous, *as to* borders on uselessness. You can usually delete it before an indirect question, as in *There is some doubt as to whether they will comply,* and in other contexts you can substitute a more precise preposition—usually *about, of,* or *on: We do not share your opinion as to [of] your staff's efficiency, I have doubts as to [about] the outcome, The lawyer advised us as to [on] how to conduct ourselves at the hearing.* Only one use of *as to* escapes criticism. At the beginning of a sentence, the preposition can sometimes help to make a transition or to highlight a subject that would otherwise appear in a later and weaker position: *As to tax shelters, our advice is not to invest more than you can afford to lose.*

author In the opinion of five authorities surveyed by Copperud, authors may write books, but writers shouldn't author them. Although the verb *author,* the *OED* reports, appeared as early as 1596 (in the sense "to originate," not "to write"), its critics are not impressed. They see no value in resurrecting an antique usage that serves no purpose; Follett includes the verb in his short list of needless words. But presumably some authors are finding it a handy synonym for *write* when they need some variety, and it may yet return to full respectability. While the 1969 *American Heritage Dictionary* notes considerable opposition to *author* as a verb, the 1982 edition makes no comment.

awhile, a while You can linger awhile or for a while but not for awhile. In other words, use the article and noun, not the adverb, after a preposition. But you can also use the article and noun adverbially: *A while later I left the house.* Use *awhile* only where you can substitute the synonymous phrase *for a time.*

because See **as, because** and **for, because, since.**

beside, besides The two words have had a tangled history, but in current usage *besides* means "in addition to," and *beside* means "next to," as in *No one besides your witness noticed the person sitting beside her.*

between, among Whether you choose between evils or among them depends in part on how many there are. You wouldn't choose among the devil and the deep blue sea, though you might among the Four Horsemen of the Apocalypse. But while *between* is the proper and natural choice when the object of the preposition consists of only two, *among* is not invariably required for three or more, despite a widespread belief to the contrary. Although derived from the Old English word for two, "*between* has been, from its earliest appearance, extended to more than two" (*OED*). Restricting it to two can result in some rather odd sentences: *They constantly travel among Athens, Rome, and Paris.* You use *among* when you're singling out a member of a group (*the best among the eight candidates*) or referring to something distributed throughout a group or held in common (*the esprit de corps among the players*). But if the members of a group interact two at a time, *between* is still appropriate (*the exchanges between the five panelists*). *Between* applies to a one-on-one situation and usually connotes a more specific relation than *among* does: *Differing ideologies have caused wars between nations, but a common enemy may yet bring peace among them.* The *OED* comments that *between* "is still the only word available to express the relation of a thing to many surrounding things severally and individually, *among* expressing a relation to them collectively and vaguely."

between each, between every Although *between* obviously needs a plural or compound object, illogical phrases like *between each one* and *between every one* are common: *I ate the scrapple slowly, grimacing between each bite; Between every inning the fans went wild.* Jespersen explains such constructions as elliptical, with *and the next* understood after the object of *between*; but other commentators, including Curme, find the wording self-contradictory. To revise, you need only make the object plural (*between bites*) or change the preposition (*after each inning*).

born, borne *Borne*, the past participle of *bear*, means "carried" or "endured": *The queen was borne on a litter, He has borne his burden patiently.* When used in the active voice of the perfect tenses or when followed by a *by* phrase, *borne* can also mean "given birth to": *She has borne three children, He disinherited the children borne by his first wife.* Other references to birth call for the adjective *born*: *She was a woman born to rule, A child is born, Revolution is born of social inequities.*

both—redundant *Both*, which means "two jointly," serves no purpose in sentences that convey this information with other words (shown in roman type in the following examples): *Both James as well as John made that recommendation, They both agree on its importance, The brothers both resemble each other, They both have the same habits.* In each of these examples *both* is redundant. You can eliminate it and leave the meaning of the sentence intact. But if *both* provides the emphasis you want, you can often get rid of the competing words instead: *They both think that it's important, They both have those habits.*

bring, take You bring something here and take something there. *Bring* indicates movement toward the speaker, *take* movement away from the speaker. Whether you took your umbrella to the office and forgot to bring it home or brought your umbrella to the office and forgot to take it home depends on where you are when it starts to rain.

but he, but him In the famous line about the boy standing on the burning deck "whence all but he had fled," the pronoun after *but* seems suspect. *But*, meaning "except," certainly looks like a preposition, and the object of a preposition, of course, belongs in the objective case—*him*, not *he*. Yet critics who prefer *he* in that context justify the usage by arguing that *but* is a coordinating conjunction introducing an "unexpanded clause"—presumably an "understood" clause—whose subject is *he*. Curme, Jespersen, and the *OED* all give some support to this interpretation. *Webster's Third* illustrates the preposition *but* with "no one left but me" and the conjunction *but* with "whence all but he had fled." Follett, however, views the distinction as "invisible to anyone but a lexicographer who wants to illustrate the historical confusion between the preposition and the conjunction, and who is ready by twists of interpretation to demonstrate that the first is the second." Bernstein, perhaps trying to make some sense of the dictionary's examples, likes to think of *but* as a conjunction when it falls early in the sentence, where it naturally assumes the case of the subject (*Everyone but she approved the proposal*), but as a preposition when it falls near the end, where the objective case is idiomatic (*Everyone approved the proposal but her*). This reasoning seems to me a specious juggling of syntax to rationalize what sounds right. My own ear is not offended by "whence all but him had fled"—the line even appears that way in some editions, Copperud says—and I'm much more comfortable with the grammar. If *Everyone but her approved the proposal* seemed to ring false, I'd move *but her* to the end of the sentence before I'd substitute *she*. (Of course, if *but* introduces an exception to an object, the pronoun that follows must be in the objective case whether you construe *but* as a preposition or as a conjunction: *The proposal was approved by everyone but her*.)

can, may Using *may* rather than *can* when you ask for something is almost a point of etiquette, like saying "please" and "thank you." In formal contexts, the rule goes, *may* refers to permission, *can* to ability: *May I leave now? Can she bake a cherry pie?* But no one will hold you to the distinction in informal writing, and it's sometimes impossible to maintain. *Why may I not?* and *Because you mayn't* are too artificial for anyone to advocate. Besides, *may* is sometimes ambiguous. In *You may use* can *for* may, for example, does *may use* mean "have the right to use" or "will perhaps use"? In short, have the courtesy to use *may* if you can do so appropriately, naturally, and clearly.

cannot help but Some grammarians object to this sequence, contending that *but* has the force of "nothing but" and that "cannot help nothing but" is nonsense. Curme, however, says that the construction is still used by "good authors." In view of the controversy, the safe course is to delete the *but* and change the following verb to a gerund. *I cannot help but feel sorry* is dubious; *I cannot help feeling sorry* is unexceptionable and, Curme says, becoming more popular. According to Follett, the most vehement opponent of *cannot help but*, you can also substitute *cannot but feel* (meaning "cannot feel otherwise") or *can but feel* (meaning "can only feel"), but these choices strike others as bookish.

case of pronouns See I, me and who, whom.

center around *Webster's Ninth* calls this expression "standard idiom" but admits that it is often criticized as illogical. The critics have a point. Where *center* means "to focus" or "to zero in on," *center on* is the logical choice: *The discussion centered on the need to improve the faculty-student ratio.* If you prefer *around*, change *center* to *revolve*.

certain *Certain* lends itself to ambiguity. In *Certain truths are self-evident*, for example, the truths might be either unquestionable or specific but unspecified. *We cannot make certain remodeling plans* and *Certain eventualities, like death* *and taxes, require resignation* also permit two interpretations. Usually the context prevents misunderstanding, but be alert to the possibility and reword if you find an uncertain *certain.*

circumstances, in the or **under the** *Under the circumstances* has been attacked from time to time on the grounds that *circumstances* means "surroundings" and that things exist or act in surroundings, not under them. Fowler dismisses this argument as "puerile," and the consensus now is that both phrases are in good repute. But Follett and Bernstein, drawing support from the *OED,* suggest that *in the circumstances* is the appropriate phrase when you refer to existing conditions that exert no pressure for action: *Gasoline was cheap and plentiful in those days, and in the circumstances the big-car market flourished.* They restrict *under the circumstances* to situations—usually temporary rather than ongoing—that require some response: *As we started to climb over the fence, the bull charged; and under the circumstances we decided not to trespass.*

compare to, compare with You can compare a gadabout to a butterfly or life to a river journeying to the sea, but you would compare Bach with Mozart or bluefish with mackerel. You use *to,* in other words, when you are making an analogy, pointing out a likeness between disparate things, and you use *with* when you are evaluating things in the same category, putting them side by side to show similarities, dissimilarities, or both.

comparisons See **absolute modifiers; as—missing or superfluous; as, like; of any;** and **than.**

comprise To comprise is to include, contain, enclose, or take in; it is not to compose, make up, or constitute: *The bride's bouquet comprises roses, lilies, and forget-me-nots; Three kinds of flowers are comprised in the bouquet.* But *The bouquet is composed* [not *comprised*] *of three kinds of flowers; Roses, lilies, and forget-me-nots make up* [not *comprise*] *the bouquet.* If you are not sure that you have used *comprise* correctly, try substituting the corresponding form of *include.* If it fits, you have the right word. If it doesn't, try *compose.*

connive The verb used to mean—and, according to the dictionaries, still does—"to close one's eyes to, look the other way while some improper behavior goes on": *The residents complain that the police connive at drug peddling* or *The authorities connive at the black market.* But perhaps through confusion with *contrive, connive* came to mean "to conspire," and this sense now prevails, though some critics continue to call it an error. The preposition that follows *connive—at* or *with* or *in*—signals the meaning intended. Of course, a sentence like *The proctor connived at the cheating that went on during the examination* may seem odd to readers unfamiliar with the older usage. Some may think that the writer blundered; others may check their dictionaries and learn something. Used "properly," the forms *connivance* and *conniving* are especially liable to misinterpretation, since there's often no preposition to suggest that the words mean other than what they normally do. A report alleging that a prison break occurred with the guards' connivance may be charging that the conniving guards ignored what was happening, but it's likely to suggest that they helped plan the escape. If it is essential that readers understand *connive* as "to wink at" rather than "to scheme," the context must make that meaning clear: *They accused the inspector of taking bribes to connive at violations of the building code.*

connote, denote What a word connotes is what it suggests—its overtones and associations. What it denotes is its objective, factual content. Words that dictionaries define as synonyms have the same denotation—or "shared meaning element"—but usually differ in connotation. Both *childlike* and *childish* denote "resembling a child," but the one connotes appealing qualities like trust and openness and the other suggests unattractive characteristics like impatience and fretfulness. Though *kill, execute, murder, assassinate, slay,* and *slaughter* all mean "to deprive of life," their distinctive associations keep them from being interchangeable. No one would say that meat packers execute thousands of animals a day, and a newspaper would be accused of editorializing if it reported that the state murdered the condemned man in the gas chamber.

consist in, consist of To consist in is to lie in or to inhere in—that is, to have as a defining attribute: *Happiness consists in choosing the inevitable, The proof of the pudding consists in the eating, The actor's charm consists in his relaxed manner.* To consist of is to be composed of: *My staff consists of my assistant, two secretaries, and a receptionist; Breakfast consists of half a grapefruit, dry toast, and coffee with skimmed milk.*

contact Because *contact* started out as a noun meaning "a physical coming together, a touching," some defenders of tradition—a majority of the *American Heritage Dictionary*'s usage panel, for example—object to its use as a verb meaning "to communicate with." Follett associates the resistance with a diminishing few who remember the verb as a neologism. The figurative sense of the noun *contact,* as in *come in contact with,* is much older and generally accepted. As a verb, *contact* is a handy replacement for *call, write, or come in* or *get in touch with,* and its full acceptance may not be far off. But as objections fade to the word as a converted noun, its all-occasion popularity may keep it under a small cloud as jargon. Bernstein comments that *contact* is "seized upon by those lovers of the fad word who would rather be up to the minute than specific." If "phone or write" is all you mean, it's better to say so, and certainly there's no excuse for sentences like *For further information contact 555-8609, Contact me by mail at this address,* and *The detective contacted the suspect telephonically and ordered him to come out with his hands up.*

contemporary Since *contemporary* means "of the same time," it often amounts to "current" or "modern," that is, "of our time." Usually the context makes this sense clear, as in *I prefer antiques to contemporary furniture,* but sometimes the word is ambiguous. In *Judged by contemporary standards, Dickens's sentimentality does not seem extreme,* the standards may be understood as present or Victorian, and substituting the appropriate adjective—here *Victorian*—clears up the confusion. In *Dickens's popularity with contemporary readers stems from several qualities,* you could use *modern* instead of *contemporary,* or you could delete the *with* phrase and add *current* before popularity or *today* after *readers.*

continual, continuous Although for centuries these words were apparently interchangeable, at some point careful writers began to define *continual* as "constantly recurrent" and to reserve *continuous* for "uninterrupted." But this valuable distinction has blurred in general use, and dictionaries treat the words as synonyms. If a nightclub advertises continuous entertainment from nine to two, do you expect no intermissions? If the writer discriminates but the reader doesn't, precise usage won't aid communication. To make clear that something goes on without a break, rather than over and over again, you may have to define *continuous* or use an equivalent that readers understand. But the strict sense of the term is not entirely lost to us. A residual tendency to distinguish *continuous* from *continual* occasionally surfaces. *Continuous* seems almost inevitable, for example, in phrases like *a continuous stream of traffic, a continuous flow of water over the dam,* and *the continuous hum of machinery.* It also survives in some technical phrases that depend on its narrow meaning— *continuous radio waves,* which do not change in intensity; *continuous casting* in steel production; and *continuous process manufacturing,* which designates a round-the-clock operation, like oil refining.

convince, persuade *Convince* means "to induce belief through argument," *persuade* "to induce mental or physical action through argument." Accordingly, *persuade,* not *convince,* should precede an infinitive. You convince someone of a truth or that something is true, but you persuade someone to accept a statement as true.

could care less This expression—a puzzling corruption of the faddish *couldn't care less*—says exactly what it doesn't mean. Anyone who stops to think realizes that only one who cares could care less. Someone who doesn't care at all couldn't care less. There's no logic in a sentence like *Blue-collar workers could care less about expense-account cutbacks.* It is true that idioms are not necessarily logical, but since both the logical and the illogical versions are idiomatic, why not make sense?

critique The verb *critique* has not yet won full acceptance. Although the *OED* traces the usage to 1751, the *American Heritage Dictionary* did not acknowledge its existence in 1969 and added the entry in 1982 with the note that many consider the verb "pretentious jargon." (Copperud reports that three arbiters object to the noun for the same reason, though he dismisses this judgment as "dated and pedantic.") Since neither *criticize* nor *review* invariably suggests, as *critique* does, "to give a critical examination of," the verb is tempting as a convenient way of avoiding the wordy "give a critique of." It's foolish, of course, to resort to *critique* where *review* works just as well. To some sensitive ears *to critique a play* still sounds like a fingernail on a blackboard.

denote See **connote, denote.**

different A needless *different* commonly appears between a quantitative adjective and the noun it modifies: *I read three different newspapers every day, Many different cities report similar problems. Different* belongs in such sentences only if you want to stress the dissimilarity of the units that make up the plural noun, as in *On three quite different occasions the same question arose;* in the first two examples *three newspapers* and *many cities* are as discrete as they would be without the *different.* Some usage critics also object to *different* where *various* will do, where you mean only "a number of" things, not "a number of dissimilar" things: *Various* [not *Different*] *books have dealt with the subject. Various* [not *Different*] *women's colleges reported declining enrollments.*

different from, different than In educated American usage, one thing is different from another, not different than another. (The argument on our side of the Atlantic is that the prefix *dif,* or *dis,* calls for *from,* as in *differs from* and *distinct from,* whereas the English prefer *different to,* by analogy with *similar to.*) But when a clause, or an elliptical clause, follows *different,* some careful writers resort to *than* rather than use the cumbersome construction that *from* would require. *We use a slightly different method than they do* seems preferable, for example, to *We use a slightly different method from the one they use.* Again, *The poem affected me differently than it ever had before* compares favorably with *The poem affected me differently from the way it ever had before.* Still, it seems unprincipled to cast aside the *different from* rule whenever it becomes inconvenient. If *different than* is sometimes acceptable, why object to it at all? Why indeed? the linguists might echo. But those, like Follett, who believe in the traditional concept of correct usage argue that you need not choose between awkwardness and error. Rewording usually provides a means of avoiding both. You can revise the first of the preceding examples to read *Our method differs slightly from theirs* and the second to read *Never before had the poem affected me that way.*

dilemma Though loosely applied to any difficult problem, *dilemma* has a Greek root meaning "two assumptions" and, strictly construed, denotes a predicament that presents two equally unpleasant alternatives. A dilemma involves a damned-if-you-do, damned-if-you-don't choice; it's a no-win situation. The horns of a dilemma might be Scylla and Charybdis, the devil and the deep blue sea, the frying pan and the fire, or a rock and a hard place.

discreet, discrete *Discreet* means "circumspect, or prudent, especially in speech"; *discrete* means "separate or distinct": *Discreet investors keep their eggs in discrete baskets and their business to themselves.* (The word that means "separate," incidentally, is the one in which *t* separates the two *es.*)

disinterested, uninterested Careful writers still distinguish between *disinterested,* meaning "unbiased or impartial, with no thought of personal advantage," and *uninterested,* meaning "lacking interest or indifferent." You can be interested in a controversy in which you are disinterested. Geoffrey Nunberg suggests, however, that it is difficult to preserve *disinterested* in the sense of "impartial" because in current usage *interested* rarely means "biased." The distinction is so commonly disregarded that you may have to substitute a synonym for *disinterested* if the context leaves room for misinterpretation.

double prepositions When two words that can serve as prepositions occur together, one is often superfluous. Although *Webster's* lists combinations like *outside of* and *off of* as prepositions, the *OED* and some other dictionaries still consider them adverbs and prepositions, which they certainly were originally. In any event the preposition *outside* means the same thing as *outside of,* and in the interests of economy you should write *keep that talk outside the office,* not *outside of the office.* Some similar-looking combinations, however, involve an adverb followed by an essential preposition. You cannot say, for example, *keep that talk out the office;* it has to be *out of the office.* Always check what appear to be double prepositions to make sure that you need both. Your ear should tell you whether or not one is expendable. *See also* **from among; inside of; of from;** and **off of.**

doubt that, doubt whether, doubt if We often use *doubt*—politely or modestly, perhaps—to express not uncertainty but conviction. When the clause after *doubt* states something thought to be true or untrue, not merely possible, it logically begins with *that*: *I do not doubt that he means what he says, I doubt that the Yankees can win the pennant this year.* But if the doubt is genuine, the clause should begin with *whether* or, more casually, *if*: *There's some doubt whether we can equal last year's sales, I doubt if they can get past the first round of the play-offs.* Although some object to *if* before a noun clause, most critics cite ancient precedent for this usage and condone *if* provided that it is not ambiguous. It might be misinterpreted, for example, in *We have reason to doubt if they are telling the truth* (If they're telling the truth, we have reason to doubt?). Though the context usually makes the meaning clear, *whether* is the safer choice in formal writing.

due to In traditional usage *due to* is considered not a preposition but an adjective followed by the preposition *to*. Thus the phrase must modify a noun or pronoun. A sentence containing *due to,* in other words, must name the thing that is due to something. You can write *The accident was due to the icy road* but not *The car skidded due to the icy road.* In the first example *due to* follows a linking verb and attaches to the subject—an accident due to the icy road. The second example has no grammatically suitable word for *due to* to modify (the car was not due to the icy road); such a construction, strict grammarians contend, calls for an adverbial modifier—usually *because of.*

Though usage critics may honor this distinction themselves, few still insist on it or even defend it. Most say that *due to* has evolved into a legitimate preposition, like *owing to* before it, and can modify either a verb or a noun. Why allow *owing to* as a preposition and not grant *due to* the same status? Bernstein offers this speculation about the use of the two phrases: "It seems likely that for every *owing to,* five *due to's* are written or spoken. . . . Probably the same quality that accounts for the relatively infrequent use of *owing to* explains its readier acceptance: it has a more dignified, a faintly stilted, sound to it." What currency *owing to* has may reflect copy editors' efforts to avoid the adverbial *due to.*

For more than fifty years the adverbial *due to* has been judged almost fully respectable, but current style guides are still telling writers to expect criticism if they use it. Those who have mastered a grammar rule, especially those indoctrinated at an early age, are loath to relinquish it, and an endangered few still complain when games are canceled due to rain.

each other, one another Some usage critics argue that *each other* applies to two, *one another* to three or more. They point out that logically *the other* makes sense only in reference to a pair. One twin helps the other; one triplet helps another. Hence the twins help each other; the triplets help one another. Few critics insist on the distinction, however, and many reputable writers apparently regard the reciprocal pronouns as interchangeable.

eager See **anxious, eager.**

effect See **affect, effect.**

either of the three *Webster's Ninth* defines *either* as "one or the other" and gives no other meaning. Using it to refer to three or more, making it mean "one or another," is questionable usage at best, according to Bernstein, Fowler, and the *American Heritage Dictionary.* You can stay out of trouble by substituting *any* or *any one* for *either* in a phrase like *either of these three choices.*

employ See **use, utilize, employ.**

ensure See **assure, ensure, insure.**

enthuse This widely criticized verb may never gain full acceptance. It's been around since 1869, according to the *OED,* which labels it "*U.S. (colloq. or humorous.)* [An ignorant back-formation from *enthusiasm*]." A back-formation, when not facetiously intended, is "ignorant" because it is a coinage from a word that is mistakenly thought to be its derivative, not its source. But several words that got their start in this way have no stigma attached to them—*resurrect* from *resurrection,* for example, and *edit* from *editor* (at least according to most dictionaries). Such words often lack approval in their youth but gain respectability with age, after everyone forgets their ancestry. *Donate,* from *donation,* was once as suspect as *enthuse*—the *OED* defines it as "vulgarly (in U.S.), to give, bestow, grant." Presumably only useful back-formations exhibit this upward mobility, but the variables that determine a word's fate resist analysis. Do we need *donate* when we have *give, bestow,* and *grant?* Can *rave* always replace *enthuse?* Can you think of any other one-word equivalent?

equally as The phrase is redundant. You can say that one film is as good as another or that the two are equally good, but to say that one is equally as good as another is to indulge in verbal featherbedding.

everyday, every day The solid form is an adjective, the two-word form an adverb. Everyday events are ordinary occurrences, not necessarily events that occur every day.

everyone, every one *Everyone* is a pronoun. *Every one* is a phrase made up of the adjective *every* and the pronoun *one.* The one- and two-word forms are not interchangeable. Use *everyone* only where you can substitute *everybody: Everyone who answers the questionnaire will receive a prize,* but *We will award a prize to every one of the respondents.*

expect See **anticipate, expect.**

faculty In referring to the teaching staff of an institution, you can confidently use *faculty* as an adjective or as a collective noun but not as the plural of *faculty member.* It is inappropriate in a sentence like *Both students and faculty served on the committee,* since it designates an aggregate group, not several individuals. The term needed is *faculty members*—or *teachers.*

farther, further *Farther* means "more distant," usually in a measurable sense, as in *Is Washington or Boston farther from New York?,* but sometimes in a figurative sense, as in *My sister and I were growing farther apart.* The more abstract term *further*, meaning "more" or "additional," has a much wider application—*a further complication, develops further, pursuing the topic further.* No one misuses *farther* for *further*, and you're safe with *further* provided that you don't apply it to distance. Several usage critics have even predicted that *further* will eventually absorb the meaning "more distant," driving *farther* into extinction. Some already advocate using *further* for figurative distance—as in *further along the road of life.* Curiously enough, however, *Webster's Ninth* reports that the two words, though "used more or less interchangeably throughout most of their history . . . are showing signs of diverging."

feel bad or **badly** If you regret something—say, an accident in which someone was hurt badly—you may say that you feel bad about it. Some writers reverse the adverb and the adjective in these contexts, but if you substitute a synonym for *bad* or *badly*, you can usually tell immediately which word to use. You wouldn't say that you felt sadly about something or that someone was hurt severe. When *feel* means "to be conscious of" or "to give a sensation of," it leads to an adjective that modifies the subject: *We feel responsible, The air feels cool.* If *feel* means "to touch" or "to believe," an adverb is appropriate to describe the action of the verb: *She carefully felt her way down the dark hall, I feel strongly that he should resign.*

fewer, less *Fewer* applies to units, *less* to quantity. With rare exceptions, *fewer* modifies a plural noun (*fewer persons, things,* or *ideas*), *less* a singular noun (*less joy, anger,* or *money*): *If you take fewer risks you may realize less profit, though less risk may also mean fewer losses.* But *less* is appropriate before a plural regarded as a single entity, not as a number of units: *I wrote fewer than ten checks this month, but I now have less than a hundred dollars in my account; The road frontage is less than 450 feet; We ran the 10K race in less than 40 minutes.* If you can't decide between *fewer* and *less* with this sort of figure, make the sum the subject of a clause and see whether you naturally choose a singular or a plural verb: *One hundred dollars (are, is) all you need, Four hundred and fifty feet (are, is) the required road frontage, Forty minutes (are, is) a good time for that race.* If you make the verb *is*, make the adjective *less*.

finalize Newly coined *ize* words often have a hard time winning respectability. While no one objects to established words like *realize, idolize,* and *harmonize*—verbs created long ago through the union of that suffix and a noun or an adjective—neologisms like *prioritize* and *verticalize* tend to provoke shudders and grimaces. *Finalize* is probably the most common and the most commonly attacked of these words. Who needs it, the argument runs, when the language already offers *close, complete, conclude, end, finish, perfect,* and *terminate*? But not everyone finds *finalize* unnecessary, and those who attack it as a neologism are on shaky ground, since the *OED* has citations dating back to 1922. If *finalize* means "to put in final form," does it have a synonym? What word would you substitute, for example, in *The committee finalized its recommendations*? While *perfected* may come closest in meaning, it seems pretentious in that sentence, and neither *finished* nor *completed* would have quite the same sense of "put the finishing touches on."

Perhaps *finalize* has been somewhat maligned, stigmatized by its association with bureaucratic jargon; it sometimes seems the only word for "finish" in the lexicon of officialdom, and its faddish overuse has made it anathema to many careful writers. Certainly avoid it if you can find a fully established equivalent to replace it. There seems no reason, for example, to write *finalized the preparations for the reception* when you mean only "completed the preparations." If you choose *finalize* simply to avoid repeating a synonym, you can usually find a better alternative.

first, firstly Either *first* or *firstly* is an acceptable sentence modifier, but if you begin with *first*, don't continue with *secondly*; and if you start with *firstly*, don't move on to *second*. All things being equal, why not adopt the shorter forms? Noting that commentators sanction *secondly, thirdly*, and "what is almost invariably designated as *etc.*," Bernstein wonders whether "*etc.* covers *forty-thirdly* or *eight-hundred-seventeenthly*." If you adopt the non-*ly* forms consistently, you can move up to forty-third with no trouble.

flaunt, flout To flaunt is to show off, to display ostentatiously or boastfully; to flout is to treat contemptuously or mockingly. Writers commonly use *flaunt* when they mean *flout*, but not vice versa. The following sentences flaunt both words correctly: *Flouting ancient laws, some young Iranian women at the marketplace flaunted Western dress. Imposing a heavy fine, the judge told them, "You cannot flout the law and flaunt your contempt for the authorities."* Anyone who flouts the law, says Bernstein, flaunting his love of puns and mnemonics, is a "floutlaw."

for, because, since As a coordinating conjunction, *for* sounds rather stilted and old-fashioned these days, and writers usually choose *since* or *because* instead. No one objects, but there is a shade of difference. *For* joins clauses that are less closely related than those connected by the subordinating conjunctions. It often introduces an explanation, rather than a cause, of the statement that precedes: *I wanted to see this production because the reviews were excellent. It moved me more than it did my friends, for I had never seen the play before.* You are unlikely to use *for* if the context requires *because*. If you are uncomfortable with *for* even though it fits the sense, you can usually substitute *since*, which tends to mean not so much "for the cause that" as "for the reason that." These distinctions need rarely concern you, since the correct choices are usually automatic.

free gift Since a gift is inherently free, this phrase is redundant. Something you pay for is no gift.

from among Rather than choose from among three possibilities, choose from them or among them. You don't need two prepositions to do the work of one.

further See **farther, further.**

fused participle See **possessives and gerunds.**

gender The usage manuals that discuss this word dismiss it as an erroneous or facetious substitute for *sex*, as in *persons of the female gender. Gender*, they say, applies exclusively to the grammatical classification of words as masculine, feminine, or neuter—labels more important in foreign languages than in English, where they apply only to the personal pronouns. Since the seventies, however, *gender* has been increasingly pressed into service in a new sense—or, if we take the evidence of the *OED*, in the sense it had in late Middle English. With the growing focus on sexual inequalities in society, many have felt the need for a word less loaded than *sexual* to refer to various forms of discrimination based on femaleness. Thus the MLA's Commission on the Status of Women in the Profession uses the term *gender harassment* to designate the disparagement of women as a cultural group, as opposed to the mistreatment of women as sex objects. The media refer to the difference in men's and women's earning power as "the gender gap." And some universities offer courses in "gender studies." Whether or not this political usage is justified, it's clearly in effect. There's so little call for *gender* in the grammatical sense that the revived connotation has apparently evoked little protest. *Gender*, then, relates to men and women as groups within society considered apart from any sexual activity.

general consensus Since *consensus* means "general agreement," the expression *general consensus* is redundant.

gerunds See **possessives and gerunds.**

get, got, gotten While *get* serves in many established idioms (*get up, get going, get ahead*), it is sometimes imprecise or redundant or too informal for its context. You might want to consider replacing some *gets* in your writing. The following examples show alternatives in brackets: *The teller got [became] suspicious. We've got to [must] act fast. Employees did not get [receive] raises. I've gotten [persuaded] them to approve.*

Dictionaries give both *got* and *gotten* as standard forms of the past participle of *get.* But Albert H. Marckwardt points out that in American speech the difference between *I've got* and *I've gotten* is that between "I have" and "I have obtained." The British, who do not use *gotten,* make do with *obtained* or some other synonym.

graduate In the context of formal education, the verb *graduate* was once restricted to the passive voice; it meant, in other words, "to be granted a diploma or a degree": *My grandfather said he was graduated from high school in 1920.* Today, however, the preferred and more common meaning is "to receive a diploma or a degree": *My mother graduated from high school in 1945.* But the definition does not include the preposition *from,* which must appear before the degree- or diploma-granting institution. So far at least, *She graduated high school* remains objectionable.

hanged, hung Executions and suicides provide the only occasions for the *ed* forms of the past tense and the past participle of *hang. Hung* is the appropriate form in every other sense of the verb. *At the end of the hall they hung a portrait of Nathan Hale, whom the British hanged as a spy in 1776.*

he, her, him See **I, me.**

historic, historical A historic event is a memorable one, worthy of a place in history. A historical event is simply one that took place in the past. A historical study concerns history; a historic one makes history. Often *historical* simply means "actual" as opposed to "literary," "mythic," or "figurative": *The* *historical king was less bloodthirsty than Shakespeare's character.* Bernstein suggests that among *ic/ical* pairs with different meanings the longer forms often have the more specific or down-to-earth connotations. *Webster's Ninth,* discussing synonyms for *laughable,* suggests that *comic* means eliciting "thoughtful amusement," while *comical* means arousing "spontaneous hilarity." Thus a squirrel's antics at the bird feeder are more likely to be comical than comic, and a novel is more likely to have a comic theme than a comical one. Similarly, reusing jars is economical ("thrifty"), not economic ("pertaining to economics or the economy"), and a classical scholar studies the works of ancient Greece and Rome, whereas a classic work may be a fundamental study in any field. If you're unsure about the connotations of such words, it's a good idea to check dictionary definitions before deciding on one form or the other. In discussing *ic/ical* words with the same meaning—like *ironic* and *ironical, bibliographic* and *bibliographical,* and *satiric* and *satirical*—Fowler argues that the language would be better off with only one, and he urges that we hasten the obsolescence of the less common form by not using it. If the shorter of the synonymous terms sometimes functions as a noun, he would disqualify it as an adjective; thus, a zealot, being a fanatic, could have only fanatical, not fanatic, beliefs. Of course, poets—as well as writers who take care with their prose rhythms—would doubtless dispute this view and find the language diminished by Fowler's restriction.

hopefully Word watchers who wince at what some call a "dangling hopefully" have much to endure these days. *Hopefully* sometimes seems to begin every third sentence, but only rarely does the sentence indicate who is full of hope. The adverb is unexceptionable when it means "in a hopeful manner," as in *The candidates are hopefully awaiting the election results,* but it's suspect in *Hopefully the results will be favorable,* where no one is behaving hopefully. Some critics maintain that you cannot make *hopefully* mean "it is hoped that." If that's the sense you intend, that's the wording you should use—or, less formally, *I hope that* or *let's hope that.*

While you still risk criticism if you use a dangling *hopefully,* many commentators seem resigned to this usage, bowing to its wide popularity. In *Dos, Don'ts & Maybes of English Usage* Bernstein confesses that he has changed his mind on this point and now accepts an unattached *hopefully* as "somewhat analogous" to *fortunately* and *luckily.* Having been converted himself, he finds it odd that "opposition continues to grow." Apparently the pundits have done some effective proselytizing, despite the defectors among their ranks. A note in the 1982 edition of the *American Heritage Dictionary,* while not condemning the secondary sense of *hopefully* as incorrect, concludes that it has become "such a bugbear to traditionalists that it is best avoided on grounds of civility."

You might decide to forgo the controversial *hopefully* simply because it's overworked, but if you object to it as ungrammatical, you should recognize that certain other adverbs are in the same category. Any adverb describing a mental attitude is inappropriate, by strict standards, in a sentence that does not indicate who has that attitude. If *hopefully* is incorrect in *Hopefully it is not true,* words like *sorrowfully* and *regretfully* would also be wrong. But adverbs like *fortunately* and *regrettably,* which do not describe states of mind, are acceptable sentence modifiers; they mean "it is fortunate that" and "it is regrettable that." *Regrettably* can safely replace the objectionable *regretfully* in a sentence like *Regretfully, the trains don't leave at convenient times.* Unfortunately, English does not have a *hopably* to replace the questionable *hopefully* in *Hopefully, the trains will run on time.*

human Adjectives commonly evolve into nouns, but for some reason *human* has met resistance. While not all critics object to *human* for *human being,* the usage still faces strong opposition. Follett admits that it has "historical precedent as well as logical parallel and the support of some dictionaries," but he still considers it a stylistic blunder, like "calling a horse an *equine* or a woman a *female*—usages that have also had their day." Copperud says that *human* "may sound quaint or technical in ordinary contexts" and concludes that, although it "is acceptable as a noun, there is still objection to it."

hung See **hanged, hung.**

I, me No one fluent in English would say *Me will be there.* But when the first-person singular pronoun is part of a compound subject, careless speakers sometimes shift to the objective case: *John and me will be there.* A far more common fault, however, is the use of the subjective case in compound objects. Those who would never say *She gave I a present* or *She spoke with I* may be quite capable of saying *She gave John and I presents* or *She spoke with John and I.* The most popular error of this sort is probably *between you and I.* Children who were taught not to say *You and me are best friends* may have picked up the notion that *you and I* is invariably correct. If you have trouble with *I* and *me* in such contexts, reading the questionable pronoun without the other member of the pair should immediately indicate the proper form.

But your ear may not be a reliable guide when a pronoun falls after some form of the linking verb *to be* (*am, are, is, was, were, being, been*). Since this verb functions only as an equal sign, a pronoun that follows should logically be in the same case as its equivalent on the other side of the equation. Ordinarily, then, the pronoun to the right of *be* belongs in the subjective case. The following sentences are grammatically correct: *It will be you and I who suffer the consequences. It is they who are responsible.* In informal contexts, though, the grammatical rule is often set aside. Most usage guides, in fact, consider *It's me* and *That's him* acceptable and even preferable in general use, where the strictly correct alternatives would seem stilted.

After the infinitive *to be,* the objective case is usually both idiomatic and technically accurate. *They expected me to be the winner* and *They expected the winner to be me* are both good grammar, since the subject of an infinitive must be in the objective case and a subject and complement should match. If the infinitive does not have a subject, however, the complement is in the subjective case, matching the subject of the main verb: *She wished to be I.* That sentence, of course, suggests greater formality than anyone recommends for ordinary purposes. "I'm so lucky to be me" goes the song from *On the Town,* and no one faults the lyricist.

The rules governing *I* and *me* also apply to the other personal pronouns with distinctive subjective and objective cases: *he, him; she, her; we, us;* and *they, them.*

ic, ical See **historic, historical.**

impact A word fit to describe the crash of a wrecker's ball against its target, *impact* has become a substitute for *bearing, influence, significance,* and *effect.* It's so overworked in officialese and journalese that the more appropriate terms are falling into disuse. Both Follett and Bernstein have harsh words for this "faddish" abasement of the noun. How much more horrified they might have been had they lived to see the current vogue of the verb *impact* in the sense of "to have an impact" or "to have an impact on" (*Loose usage adversely impacts the language*). The 1982 edition of the *American Heritage Dictionary,* which does not stigmatize *impact* for *bearing,* reports that a "large majority" of its usage panelists disapprove of the corresponding use of *impact* as a verb.

imply, infer If you hint that something is true, without saying so directly, you imply what you mean, and the person who catches your drift, by reading between the lines or interpreting your expression, correctly infers your meaning. Only the one making the veiled suggestion implies, and only the one drawing the conclusion infers. Almost all careful modern writers observe this distinction and regard *infer* for *imply* as a solecism. *Imply* should replace *infer,* for example, in *I did not mean to infer that the witness is lying.*

in, into, in to If you walk in a room, you move around within it; if you walk into a room, you enter it. *In* generally means "within"; *into* implies movement from one place to another. But *in* often appears in place of *into,* and it is probably pedantic to correct this usage, especially in informal contexts, if it sounds idiomatic. No one is likely to complain about *Go jump in the lake* or *Put the bonds in the safe.* Idiom also calls for *in* after the verb *place* even where the sense calls for *into.* You could put bonds into a safe if you wanted to, but you'd have to place them in a safe.

Write *in* and *to* as separate words when only the *to* is a preposition and the *in* is an adverb closely tied to the preceding verb: *Don't give in to temptation, I turned my report in to the inspector, I told the messenger to take the package in to the receptionist.* Sometimes, though, as in the last example, the *in* is superfluous in such constructions. Always consider this possibility when you revise.

infer See **imply, infer.**

inside of The *of* in this phrase is usually expendable. When the preposition *inside* means "in the interior of" or "on the inner side of," does *inside of* mean anything else? *Of* is generally also superfluous with *outside* or *alongside.* The following sentence could be *of*-less: *The show was soon to begin inside of the theater, and a long line had formed outside of the building, stretching alongside of the armory on South Street. Inside of* seems least objectionable, if objectionable at all, when it means "in the space of" or "in the period of," as in *The runners tired inside of the first three miles* or *The factory must be completed inside of five years.* In such contexts, however, *within* can often replace *inside of* if *inside* alone seems unidiomatic.

insure See **assure, ensure, insure.**

interface As an intransitive verb, *interface* means to become connected at a common point between distinct systems and to interact harmoniously. When a computer and a machine interface, they coordinate smoothly. The growing influence of the new technology has so popularized this term that it has passed rapidly into general use. Such interactants as authors and editors, actors and directors, and teachers and students now tend to interface more than they talk, confer, meet, or work together. Although this extended use of the word does not seem inherently wrong, it's fairly new, not clearly needed, and greatly abused. In any event it still makes the sensitive wince.

in the light of Many writers omit *the* before *light* in this expression, but the *of* phrase makes the light specific and mandates the definite article. The reference is to a particular light, the light shed by the object of the following phrase. In contrast, the *of* phrase in the expression *in view of* doesn't particularize *view* when it tells what is viewed, not who or what is viewing. The difference becomes clear if you compare *in view of the committee's decision* with *in the view of the committee.*

into, in to See **in, into, in to.**

its, it's Writers commonly confuse these two words, but the error is inexcusable. *Its* is the possessive case of *it* (the possessive forms of personal pronouns do not have apostrophes), and *it's* is the contraction of *it is: When the salt has lost its savor, the Bible tells us, it's good for nothing.*

join together This combination strikes modern critics as redundant, despite the rhetoric of the marriage rite. *What God has joined, let no one part* would do as well—*pace* the poets. If you like your language lavish, make sure that its rhythm redeems it.

just exactly Where *just* means "exactly" (as in *Baby bear's chair was just right*), the *just–exactly* combination is redundant. *That's just exactly what will happen* means "That's exactly exactly what will happen."

kind of Since *kind of* introduces the name of a category, not a unit in that category, it cannot logically precede *a* or *an.* By current critical standards the articles are incorrect, for example, in *What kind of a person would accept that sort of an offer?* The rule applies as well to similar expressions, such as *sort of, type of,* and *manner of.*

lay, lie Writers who confuse these two verbs don't get no respect; violations of the standard usage, Bernstein says, "can only be classed as illiterate." *Lay* means "to place or put," *lie* "to rest or recline"; *lay* (unless you're talking about productive hens) takes a direct object, *lie* does not. If you are not sure which verb to use, try substituting the corresponding form of *place* or *rest,* or see whether the verb has an object. Either of these tests can keep you from going wrong, provided that you can recognize the distinctive forms of the two verbs: *lay* has *laying* as its present participle and *laid* as its past tense and past participle; *lie* has *lying* as its present participle, *lay* as its past tense (not to be confused with the present tense of the verb *lay*), and *lain* as its past participle. In the following sentences all the verbs are correct: *I thought I had* *left my reading glasses lying on the bedside table, where I had laid my book when I lay down for a nap yesterday, but I apparently mislaid them. The book has lain there unread ever since. I don't like to lie down for a nap without reading awhile first, and when I find my glasses, I won't lay them down again without paying attention to where I am laying them.*

leave, left If you read that artists usually work best when left alone, you might not know whether they are most creative when isolated from others or when not harassed with criticism and advice. Interpreted literally, the sentence could be arguing for the inspirational values of the solitary life. To leave is to go away from, to let is to permit. If you want others to stop bothering you, to grant you some peace, you should, properly speaking, ask them to let you alone—unless, of course, you're really saying that you want to be by yourself. Though widely tolerated, *leave me alone* for *let me alone* sacrifices a sometimes useful nuance. In other contexts, of course, *leave* for *let* is a classic blunder. You should let sleeping dogs lie, not leave them lay—though you should, perhaps, leave setting hens to their laying. *See also* **lay, lie.**

less See **fewer, less.**

let, let's "Let us go then, you and I," says T. S. Eliot's Prufrock, having the good sense to know when to disregard a grammatical rule. Since *you and I* is in apposition to *us*, all three pronouns logically belong in the same case; the *I*, in other words, should be *me* (*us* = *you and me*). The objective case—*us* in Eliot's line—follows *let* automatically when there is only one pronoun, but a second pronoun can slip inconsistently into the subjective case. *Let Bill and I share the responsibility* and *Let's you and I see what we can do* are both wrong by traditional standards. The pronouns look like subjects of the verbs that follow, and they are; but *share* and *see* are *to*-less infinitives, not ordinary verbs, and the subjects of infinitives belong in the objective case. The syntax is the same as it is in *Allow Bill and me to share* and *Allow us, you and me, to see.* But you don't have to know all that to choose the appropriate pronoun. The question only arises when the pronoun is one of a pair, and you'll get the right answer if you ask yourself what form you would use if the pronoun were on its own.

liable See **apt, liable, likely.**

lie See **lay, lie.**

like See **as, like.**

likely See **apt, liable, likely.**

literally As generally used, the adverb *literally*, like *actually*, doesn't mean much. It merely adds emphasis, often to a statement that doesn't need it. *Literally* should mean "in the strict sense" or "without exaggeration," but it usually means quite the opposite—"figuratively." Sentences like *I literally died laughing* or *I was literally walking on air* obviously shouldn't be taken at face value. If *literally* were always used precisely, it could have considerable force, showing that a seemingly hyperbolic or figurative statement is a matter of fact: *Her voice could literally shatter glass;* "*He can't come to the phone,*" Houdini's *secretary said. "He's literally all tied up."* Try to keep *literally* out of your writing unless you mean it literally. Abuses of the word can seem ludicrous, and those who recognize them enjoy pointing them out.

majority In general, avoid *majority* if you don't have precise numbers or percentages to support it—if you're not reporting, say, the results of a survey or an election. *Most* can generally replace *a majority of* and, for that matter, *few* can replace *a minority of.* You could say that the phrases are justified in only a minority of the cases in which they occur, that the majority of the time they are expendable. But you might better say that such phrases are rarely justified and usually expendable.

may See **can, may.**

may, might When used to express doubt or desire, *may* and *might* are present and past subjunctive forms, but both point to the future. Ordinarily the choice of *may* or *might* requires no thought. You automatically select the form that matches the tense of the governing verb: *We think that the market may improve in the fall, We thought that the market might improve in the fall.* Though you can also say *We think that the market might improve,* you cannot say *We thought that the market may improve.* When tense is not an issue—that is, when the subjunctive is not governed by a past indicative—you can express possibility with either *may* or *might.* But *may* suggests better odds than *might* does: *That horse may show, he might even place, but he certainly won't win.* Whether you say that you may be wrong or that you might be wrong depends on how confident you are that you're right. The greater uncertainty implicit in *might* makes that form suitable, Curme says, for stating "an opinion or a wish modestly, politely, or cautiously": *We might be able to help, You might try a different approach, That might satisfy them.*

may possibly, might possibly Since *may* and *might* express possibility as opposed to certainty, combining either with *possibly*—or with *perhaps* or *maybe*—is making the same point twice. Sentences like *That might possibly be true* or *Perhaps that may be true* are common enough in speech, where the intensifying adverbs may even help, but listening and reading audiences take in ideas differently. In writing you're safer with *Perhaps that is true* or *That may be true.*

me See **I, me.**

minority See **majority.**

myself In general, avoid *myself* where you can use *I* or *me.* The form is appropriate only when it refers to the subject of the sentence, as in *I take care of myself* and *I hurt myself,* or follows *I* as an intensive, as in *I myself would never do that* or *It was I myself who saw it happen. Myself* is objectionable in sentences like *They praised only Judy and myself* [me] and *The only members who plan to attend are Doyle and myself* [I]. The rules for *myself* apply as well to the other *self* forms—that is, the reflexive and intensive pronouns: *ourselves, yourself, yourselves, itself, herself, himself,* and *themselves.*

nauseous, nauseated Although the distinction between these words has all but vanished, those who know it continue to ridicule those who do not:

something that makes you sick to your stomach—a rocking ship, perhaps, or a rotting carcass—is nauseous; you are nauseated. "A person who feels sick," Bernstein says, "is no more *nauseous* than a person who has been poisoned is poisonous." Nonetheless, those who suffer queasiness are far more likely to call themselves nauseous than nauseated, and *nauseous* is extremely rare in the sense of "sickening." You may occasionally find it in the attributive position—for example, *nauseous odors* or *nauseous violence*—but the usual word for causing nausea is *nauseating*. Used strictly or loosely, *nauseous* can get you into trouble. You're better off limiting yourself to the participles.

nor, or Writers who pair *neither* with *or* or *either* with *nor* are merely careless; grammatically and idiomatically, the correlative conjunctions are *either . . . or* and *neither . . . nor*. When *or* and *nor* are on their own, however, the choice between them can be confusing, especially in negative statements. If a word like *no, not,* or *never* precedes the conjunction but clearly carries over to what follows, the *or* is appropriate; there's no need for a *nor* to repeat the negation for the second part. In the following sentences the *nor* is questionable at best, and *or* would be above reproach: *He said that he had no physical handicaps, harmful habits, nor antisocial tendencies. They did not report the incident to the manager nor confide in their coworkers. She has never explained her actions nor answered questions about her whereabouts.* Follett would find the *nor* in these sentences unequivocally wrong, but Bernstein would accept either *nor* or *or,* contending that the *nor* simply makes the negative more emphatic. Although the construction looks like a double negative, those who condone it may think of *nor* as introducing an elliptical clause: *nor [has she] answered questions about them.*

In contexts in which *nor* is mandatory, the negative idea would not otherwise extend beyond the conjunction. When, for example, the conjunction joins not two elements governed by the same negative modifier but two independent clauses, the second seems affirmative if *nor* does not replace *or*: *Jogging obviously has no appeal for the sedentary, or does it necessarily attract athletes who enjoy team sports.* Here are two more examples that require revision because the negation stops at the conjunction: *My friends gave me no advice or offered to help* [*. . . neither gave me advice nor offered to help* or *. . . did not give me advice or offer to help*]. *Morton had never objected to company policies or was willing to join a union* [*Morton had never objected to company policies nor was he willing . . .* or *. . . had never objected to company policies or been willing to join a union*]. In the last revision we readily "understand" *had never* before the participle *been,* but if *been* were *have been,* we would not supply the elliptical *never.* Fowler explains that since a negative adverb goes with the auxiliary verb it follows, it is not implicit if the auxiliary is repeated with a second verb. In other words, it's clear to say *had never thought or acted* but wrong to say *had never thought or had acted.*

of any Not all experts would fault a sentence like *Amalgamated offers the best car-loan rates of any bank in the city.* As a commercial message, it makes its point. But if the statement appeared in an objective comparative study of New York City banks, sticklers for logic could fault it on several counts: the statement compares Amalgamated with itself (Amalgamated, after all, is a bank in the city); calls something the best of one (*best of any* is a "blending" of *best of all* and *better than any other*—"a usage," Curme says, "which in general is now avoided in good English"); and contrasts Amalgamated's rates with any bank rather than with the rates of any other bank. To correct the sentence, you can substitute the comparative degree for the superlative: *Amalgamated's car-loan rates are better than those of any other bank in the city.* (Notice that *other* is necessary when you compare one thing with others in the same category.) Sometimes you need only delete *of any* to make a sentence acceptable, as in *Advanced calculus was the most demanding [of any] course I took* or *The fifth of July was the hottest day [of any] last summer.*

off of Confronted with an intruder, you can properly say *Get out of my house* but not *Get off of my land.* In the first example *out* and *of* are adverb and preposition, and the sentence needs both to make sense. *Off of* in the second example was once construed in the same way, but now *off* and *of* together are doing what *off* can do alone. *Get off of my land* means no more than *Get off my land.* Incidentally, *of* can be equally redundant after *out* in contexts where *out* can serve as a preposition. Though *Get out of my house* can't do without *of*, *Look out of the window* can. Some "double prepositions" may survive colloquially because they seem more emphatic in speech (just as double negatives do). Our ears and our eyes take in information in different ways. A grounds keeper might shout at thoughtless children "Keep off of the grass!" and point out a sign that reads "Keep Off the Grass."

of from A superfluous *from* often shows up in constructions like *The defendant was sentenced to from ten to fifteen years* and *The job requires a typing speed of from forty-five to fifty-five words per minute.* Two prepositions in a row are often one too many. *From among, inside of,* and *off of* are other combinations in which the second word is usually expendable.

on, onto, on to *On* relates to *onto* as *in* does to *into*: unlike *on*, which can mean "on top of," *onto*, meaning "to a position on," necessarily implies movement from one place to another. Walking onto the beach is not the same as walking on the beach. In many contexts, though, *on* or *to* can have the same meaning as *onto.* You might move books onto your desk, but you could also move them to your desk. And *on*, not *onto*, is idiomatic in sentences like *He placed his hand on the Bible* or *We put the plates on the table* or *She got on her horse.* *Onto* is the only correct form, however, when you mean "knowing about" or "aware of," as in *We're onto their game.* Where *on* and *to* are used together as separate words, *on* is an adverb closely associated with the preceding verb, while *to* alone is the preposition for the phrase that follows. You might move on to better things or ramble on to a tolerant listener or walk on to the end of the road. You might even continue on to the beach, then go onto the beach, and stay on the beach for an hour or two.

on, upon Don't use *upon* where *on* will do. Where the two are interchangeable, *upon* adds a bookish note. In some phrases, of course, it's idiomatic—*once upon a time*, for example, or *set upon by thieves* or *assumed a put-upon expression*—and you may occasionally want it in other contexts if the prose rhythm benefits from two syllables instead of one. But *on* should be the routine choice for phrases that follow verbs like *base, brood, comment, depend, hit, look, rely,* and *verge.*

one another See **each other, one another.**

onto, on to See **on, onto, on to.**

or See **nor, or.**

oral, verbal *Oral* means "spoken," as opposed to "written," and many writers use *verbal* as if it were synonymous. When they refer to verbal contracts they mean agreements not formalized in writing. But whereas *oral* derives from the Latin word for mouth, *verbal* comes from the Latin for word and, strictly construed, means only "in words," whether spoken or written.

passed, past Do not confuse *passed,* the past tense and the past participle of the verb *pass,* with *past,* which can be a noun, as in *from the past;* an adjective, as in *past hopes;* an adverb, as in *is past due;* or a preposition, as in *go past the barn.* The following sentences use *passed* and *past* correctly: *The president passed the buck. Two hours were passed in playing cards. The day of the five-cent cigar is long past. We passed the house. We drove past the house.*

past history Since *history* means "past events," *past history*—that is, "past past events"—is a redundancy. The adjective *past* is often expendable in other combinations too. Expressions like *past experience* and *past records* usually convey nothing more than the nouns would if left unqualified.

people, persons Strict usage requires the plural *persons* for small groups and restricts *people* to masses—*crowds of people, the American people, the people at the rock concert.* Observing this distinction calls for common sense. Usually we're as likely to use *people* after *three* as after *three thousand,* and substituting *persons* for countable numbers may do more harm than good. Where *people* is too informal for the context but *persons* sounds affected, you can usually find a more specific plural. Knighthood may be bestowed, for instance, on four distinguished British subjects instead of four distinguished persons. Persons invited for dinner can be guests, persons sitting on a panel can be participants, and persons waiting for a train can be commuters or travelers.

persuade See **convince, persuade.**

possessives after *of* Most grammarians refer to phrases like *a friend of Jane's* and *a relative of mine* as "double genitives," and some critics consider them redundant. Since both the *of* phrase and the possessive case can denote ownership, the objection may seem logical, but such constructions are unquestionably established idiom. Certainly no one suggests "correcting" *a play of his* to *a play of him.* Those who condemn the double genitive would have to change the construction to *one of his plays* or *a play by him.*

Some thoughtful commentators, however, take no exception to *of* followed by a possessive noun or pronoun. Follett, among others, regards *a friend of Jane's* as an elliptical way of saying "of Jane's friends" (i.e., "among Jane's friends") and therefore finds the possessive appropriate. In some contexts, in fact, it lends clarity, since without it the *of* phrase would be ambiguous: *an interpretation of Ruskin* is not necessarily equivalent to *an interpretation of Ruskin's.*

In such constructions, however, the possessive form of an inanimate object is neither idiomatic nor grammatical. We say *one leg of the table,* not *one leg of the table's.* No critic disputes the redundancy of a sentence like *Our school has an enrollment higher than that of any other's* (the correct alternatives are *higher than any other's* or *higher than that of any other*). But such lapses are rare. Where a possessive form comes naturally after *of*, you can generally use it in good conscience. All that you need absorb from this discussion is that informed critics condone constructions like *that attitude of Alice's* and that some contexts permit either the regular or the possessive form of a noun after *of*, with only a nuance of difference: *a responsibility of the manager* or *a responsibility of the manager's*.

possessives and gerunds Would you say *if you don't mind me asking* or *if you don't mind my asking*? If *my* sounds natural, you have a discerning ear. Since a gerund, by definition, is the *ing* verbal used as a noun, it needs a possessive modifier, just as any other noun does. *If you don't mind me asking*, at least in theory, is no better grammar than *if you don't mind me question*. Failure to use the possessive case before a gerund can create ambiguity, as in this sentence: *Harold did not approve of his daughter living in New York or of his grandchildren playing in the street.* Here *grandchildren* and *daughter* look like objects modified by restrictive particles, *ing* verbals used as adjectives. Using the possessive forms, *daughter's* and *grandchildren's*, would make clear that Harold disapproved not of his relatives but of their activities.

In 1906 Fowler coined the term *fused participle* for a gerund whose "subject" is not a possessive, and he denounced the construction as a grammarless atrocity. But most later experts have contested this blanket condemnation. They point out that the possessive case is not always feasible before a gerund and that the rule therefore needs qualification. When the subject of the verbal is heavily modified, compound, abstract, or incapable of showing possession, the possessive case is impossible. No one advocates adding *'s* in any of the following sentences: *He objects to the man who lives next door putting up a fence. What do you think about Russia and its satellites refusing to participate in the Olympics? She disapproved of pragmatism dominating all our decisions. The possibility of this occurring here is unthinkable.*

It's difficult, of course, to claim importance for a grammatical principle that you can disregard whenever it becomes impractical. Though one exception may prove a rule, many can discredit it. Here again, idiom would seem to triumph over logic. But experts determined to impose order on the language have tried to explain away the need for possessives in resistant constructions. Follett, for example, finds the fused participle acceptable where he can construe the *ing* phrase as a "heavy (long-drawn-out) apposition" to the preceding noun or pronoun. This reading is possible, he contends, whenever the stress is on the person or thing acting, not on the action, as in *We do not object to you and your partner sitting in on the meeting, but we cannot accommodate any additional visitors.* But one could more easily argue that in these circumstances the *ing* form becomes a clear-cut participle, with nothing fused about it: *It is unusual to see both labor and management adopting that position, and I was surprised to find the head of the company taking the initiative.*

Sometimes, though, there's no getting around the grammatical need for a possessive that idiom proscribes. Faced with this dilemma, many writers forgo grammar, but strict constructionalists avoid the issue by recasting the sentence. The necessary rewording can be quick and easy. Thus, *They were hardly prepared for the justice of the peace refusing to marry them* readily converts to *They were hardly prepared for a justice of the peace who would refuse to marry them* or *They never anticipated that the justice of the peace would refuse to marry them.*

Although the experts disagree about some aspects of the fused-participle issue, they all recommend using the possessive before a clear-cut gerund whenever this choice has no undesirable side effects. With the few exceptions already noted, a one-word subject of a gerund—especially a personal pronoun or a proper noun—belongs in the possessive case.

preparatory to, previous to, prior to Don't use any of these circumlocutions if *before* will do. Wordy at best, they often sound pretentious or introduce an inappropriate technical note. *Preparatory to* is all right if you want to stress the idea of "in preparation for," as in *Preparatory to the interview, I did some research on the company*; but there's no excuse for *Preparatory to going to the bank, I stopped at the post office,* where *before* is obviously the natural choice. *Prior to,* according to Follett, suggests "necessary precedence"—"from its origin in the law" and its extension to logic. Thus it's justifiable in *Fees must be paid sixty days prior to the start of the new term* but stilted in *She runs four miles prior to breakfast.* Dictionaries define the preposition *previous to* only as "prior to, before"; so unless you need it for variety or euphony, substitute *before.* Never use an elaborate word for a simple one merely to sound grander or more genteel.

presently Though many writers use *presently* in the sense of "at present," critics object to this practice and restrict the meaning to "in a short time." With alternatives like *now* and *currently,* there seems no reason to adopt the contested usage. Besides, *presently* for *at present* can be ambiguous. *You can presently see the film at the Broadway Theater,* for example, may be referring to a coming attraction, not a current one. If *presently* does mean "currently" there, it's superfluous as well as suspect. Unless you mean to emphasize *now* as opposed to *then* or *later,* the present tense is usually the only temporal indicator you need.

previous to See **preparatory to, previous to, prior to.**

principal, principle *Principal* is either an adjective meaning "main" or a noun meaning "the main thing" or "head person." *Principle* is always a noun meaning "rule." The two words are commonly confused. As a noun, *principal* is rarely appropriate in a general sense, but it has several specific denotations in various fields. It may refer, for example, to the chief administrator of a school, a person represented by an agent, a lead performer, one who commits a crime (a perpetrator as opposed to an accessory), the main body of an estate, or a noun represented by a pronoun (an antecedent).

prior to See **preparatory to, previous to, prior to.**

prone Used precisely, *prone* means "lying face down"—not just "lying flat"—and contrasts with *supine,* "lying face up."

proved, proven When you need the past participle of *prove* in a verb phrase, make it *proved: it has proved, it has been proved. Proven* is preferred only in certain legal phrases and as an adjective preceding the word it modifies:

proven ability, a proven fact. Perhaps the alternative participles once corresponded to the two meanings of *prove,* "to test" and "to provide convincing evidence of," but if so the distinction has long since been lost.

quite *Quite* can mean either "wholly" or, paradoxically, "to a considerable degree." Though the first is the older and stricter sense, the second prevails today and no longer provokes criticism, except perhaps in a highly formal context. In fact, if either meaning is possible, as in *The meeting was quite successful,* "to a considerable degree" is the more likely interpretation. Thus you're better off not using *quite* for "wholly" if you're not quite certain that the context makes that sense quite clear.

rather than Derived from the comparative degree of an Old English adverb meaning "quickly," *rather* is redundant when used with another comparative term that does the same job, as in the following sentences: *Eight out of ten dentists under forty prefer brushing with soap rather than with toothpaste. It would be better to improve our product rather than to lower the price. Caught outdoors in a lightning storm, you may be safer lying down rather than standing up.* To revise, you would edit out one or the other comparative term, either *rather* or its rival: *Eight out of ten . . . prefer soap to toothpaste for brushing their teeth; We should improve our product rather than lower the price; Caught outdoors in a lightning storm, you may be safer lying down than standing up.*

Unlike later dictionaries, the *OED* lists *than* only as a conjunction, not as a preposition, and critics who still hold this view contend that *rather than* must link grammatically comparable terms. They object, for example, when a gerund after *rather than* contrasts with an ordinary, or finite, verb. In the following sentences the approved choices appear in brackets: *We use a computing company for our payroll rather than handling [handle] it ourselves. I would accept that decision rather than prolonging [prolong] the controversy.* Sometimes, though, the force of idiom so strongly favors the *ing* form in such a context that the required verb sounds odd: *Rather than do the work yourself, delegate the responsibility to an assistant.* While many commentators would accept *rather than* as prepositional in that sentence and use *doing,* it's safer to substitute *instead of,* a clear-cut preposition, which makes the gerund unquestionably right: *Instead of doing the work yourself, delegate. . . .* Though *instead of,* "in place of," is not perfectly synonymous with *rather than,* "in preference to," the shade of difference rarely matters.

reaction This scientific term denotes an automatic response to a stimulus, as in *a knee-jerk reaction, a toxic reaction to a drug, a chemical reaction between substances,* and *a backlash reaction.* Though the word commonly substitutes for *response, opinion,* or *view* in general contexts, careful writers reserve it for its technical use. In each of the following examples the alternative shown in brackets is preferable: *The audience reaction [response] was enthusiastic. We asked the customers how they reacted to [what they thought of] several innovative proposals.*

reason—redundant While you can properly begin an explanation with *The reason is that* or *This occurs because,* several critics object to *The reason is because.* Since both *reason* and *because* indicate that an explanation will follow, you need only one or the other. *The reason why,* though less widely condemned, also has its opponents. If you recognize that *why* means "the reason for which," you can see the excess in *the reason why,* "the reason the reason for which." Instead of writing *That is the reason why the program failed,* you can say either *That is the reason the program failed* or *That is why the program failed.*

relationship Explaining that the suffix *ship* makes a concrete noun abstract, as in *friendship, showmanship,* and *sportsmanship,* Fowler objects to the inappropriate use of *relationship* for *relation.* Since *relation,* except when it refers to kin, is an abstract term in itself, adding *ship* is needless and illogical. According to Fowler, you "might as well make *connexionship, correspondenceship,* or *associationship,* as *relationship* from *relation* in abstract senses." Though other usage experts disregard this argument, perhaps because the cause seems lost, Fowler's reasoning does seem cogent, and *relation* usually can replace *relationship.* But not always. Rightly or wrongly, the relation of one person to another is called a relationship these days—even if it doesn't lead to betrothalship or marriageship. *Relations* won't do for *relationships* in a sentence like *I had better relationships with my professors than with the other students.*

respective, respectively When used to relate the members of one pair or series to those of another, these words can clarify what goes with what: *Jacques, Sean, and Enrico designed accessories—respectively, hats, jewelry, and shoes.* Here the adverb keeps readers from assuming that all three men specialized in all three types of accessories. But *respective* and *respectively* serve no purpose in sentences that do not follow this pattern. The following examples could do without them: *Three planes are scheduled to leave Chicago at 10 a.m.—bound, respectively, for New York, New Orleans, and Los Angeles. The two winners gave Cranford, New Jersey, and Schenectady, New York, as their respective birthplaces.* Even when a sentence relates two pairs or series the proper combinations may be obvious without *respective* or *respectively.* The modifiers are not misused in the following sentences, but they hardly seem necessary: *John, Bill, and Robert are married, respectively, to Judy, Beth, and Amy. This year Yale and Vassar held their graduation ceremonies on, respectively, 20 May and 27 May.* Since *respective* and *respectively* make readers stop to pair the right elements, you're better off constructing sentences that do not need these props. The *respectively* is essential in *Rural and urban areas tend to favor, respectively, potatoes and pasta* but not in *Rural areas tend to favor potatoes, urban areas pasta.*

restive Although dictionaries indicate that the original meaning of *restive*— "balky" or "resisting control"—still lives, the word more commonly serves as a synonym for "restless." Copperud says that "popular misuse has added another sense" to *restive,* but he probably thinks of a half-empty glass as half full. Less sanguine critics complain that popular misuse has destroyed a useful word and replaced it with an unneeded alternative for *restless.* A few loyal supporters of the older meaning consider the new usage incorrect, but even if they use *restive* right, readers are likely to understand it wrong. *Our guide tried to calm the restive donkey* probably suggests an uneasy animal, not a mulish one. Still, since the donkey was doubtless both uneasy and mulish, the misinterpretation is not serious. You have nothing to lose by keeping *restive* to its strict meaning, and you may be helping a valuable distinction stage a come-back.

sequence of tenses The managing of tenses is too large a subject for the scope of this glossary, but here's the tip of the iceberg. Ordinarily the tenses of verbs used in sequence reflect the chronology of the events reported: *I had planned to attend the opening, but I changed my mind; I still haven't seen the play, but I will soon.* Sometimes, though, you may indicate time relations with adverbs and subordinating conjunctions instead of shifts in tense: *She attended Bowdoin before she went to Yale; After they saw Paris, we couldn't keep them down on the farm; Last year we sold a million units, but this year we had a 50 per cent decline.*

The verb in the main clause normally determines the tense of a verb in a subordinate clause: *He says that good management will make a difference,* but *He said that good management would make a difference.* A related verbal is usually in the present tense if its action occurs at about the same time as that of the main verb and in the past tense if its action occurs earlier: *Mincing no words, he claimed that poor management had been responsible,* but *Having studied the record, I think that poor management was responsible.* If the main verb in the last example were *thought,* the verbal would remain unchanged; it's the only past form we have, and it would still designate an action preceding that of the main verb. Since such adjustments are usually automatic, there seems no need to discuss them in greater detail. When writers have trouble, it's generally with the exceptions.

Not all subordinate verbs change to match the main verb. Other considerations sometimes come into play. In *They say that an artist had owned the house my family bought,* a shift from *say* to *said* would not alter the tenses in the *that* clause. No other tenses would make clear that one past action occurred before the other. Another exception is the subordinate clause introduced by a verb in the past tense but stating an enduring truth—one that is as valid now as it was in the past: *They searched the suspect's house, which is located on Orchard and Vine; He said that lilacs bloom in May in this part of the country; She taught us that parallel lines never meet.* See also **may, might**.

The present tense is also appropriate when you report what appears in print. A book contains now exactly what it did earlier: *Hamlet condemns his mother's marriage.* By extension you can use the present tense to discuss what an author has written: *Shakespeare portrays Macbeth as superstitious, Marx advocates a classless society, Aristotle argues for a golden mean.* Of course, you can also use the past tense in such statements. While the work expresses itself in the permanent present, you can say that the author either described or describes in a work. But be consistent. If you write *Nietzsche claims* but *Kant argued,* readers may wonder why you are making a distinction. Even though you use the present tense in discussing what authors say in their works, you should ordinarily use the past in recounting what they were or did: *Emerson, who stresses the relation between nature and the soul, studied theology at Harvard.* An exception, of course, is "the historical present"—the present tense used to describe past events as if they were happening now: *It's Sunday afternoon, 7 December 1941. The radio is playing Christmas carols, and my eighteen-year-old brother and I are clearing the table after dinner, squabbling as usual about whose turn it is to wash. Paul gives in finally, cursing his rotten luck in having me for a sister. Then the music stops, right in the middle of "Silent Night," and an excited, incredulous voice announces the end of our world: "The Japanese have bombed Pearl Harbor!" Paul breaks a glass, and I rush to hug him.* If you adopt this device in the interest of vivid narration, make sure to stay with it. It's easy to lapse into the past.

shall, will; should, would The auxiliary verbs *shall* and *will*, of course, are used to form the future tenses, and *should* and *would* express—among other things—the future from the point of view of the past. Grammar books used to devote considerable space to the distinctive uses of these words, but today they tend to accept whichever comes naturally, tacitly acknowledging that proscription has made no headway against instinctive usage. The many complicated and conflicting sets of rules and descriptions that have been attempted over the last two hundred years or so have generally been too convoluted to help. Jespersen, the Fowlers, and Follett, for example, all devote twenty or more pages to the subject, but the Fowlers seem to acknowledge the futility of their endeavor: "It is unfortunate that the idiomatic use [of *shall* and *will*], while it comes by nature to the southern Englishman (who will find most of this section superfluous), is so complicated that those who are not to the manner born can hardly acquire it; and for them the section is in danger of being useless."

Among the authorities Copperud surveyed, only Follett insists on "a relatively small nucleus of orthodox principles" governing *shall* and *will*. If you have some knowledge of these rules, a brief review may be useful, if only to lay their ghost. "For a dialect that does distinguish *shall* and *will*," Julian and Zelda Boyd provide this succinct "summary of the handbooks . . . (ignoring the negative and subordinate occurrences)":

1. I shall—predicts, foretells, surmises, etc.
2. I will—promises, threatens, warns, etc.
3. You shall (he, she, it, they, etc.)—promises, etc.
4. You will (he, she, it, they, etc.)—predicts, etc.
5. Shall I (we)?—asks for orders
6. Will I (we)?—asks for a prediction
7. Shall you?—asks for a prediction (rare, British)
8. Will you?—makes a request
9. Shall he (she, it, they)?—asks for orders
10. Will he (she, it, they)?—asks for a prediction

In the same dialect *should* and *would*, when simply referring to the future, follow similar rules: *should* is reserved for the first person (*I said that I should like to apply, and they said that they would like an interview*). But both words have other standard uses that muddy the waters. For example, *should* can also mean "ought to" (*You should do as you please*) or express a condition (*If it should rain, the picnic will be canceled*); *would* can also express a condition (*If you would try, you might succeed*), as well as habitual past action (*Every night we would dine at eight*), contingency (*I would if I could*), desire (*Would that it were so*), and, along with *will*, capacity (*My old car would take five passengers; the new one will seat only two*). In these special senses *should* and *will* and *would* are appropriate with all persons.

In modern usage *should* survives primarily in statements of condition or obligation, and *shall* occurs mainly in questions such as *Shall we dance?* and *Shall I answer the door? Will* and *would* are usual in all other contexts. In the sentence *We will offer the successful candidate a competitive salary*, the *will* seems to modern readers simply a straightforward future, not an atypical usage denoting a pledge. But though the earlier conventions are rarely honored, neither are they proscribed. You can use *should* with *I* on occasions that call for formal politeness. If in applying for a job you write *I should like to be considered for the position you advertised*, a few potential employers might even be impressed. For the simple future, however, the first-person *shall* or *should* may sound stilted or quaint.

she See **I, me.**

since See **for, because, since.**

so, so that In formal writing *so* is not appropriate when used alone as an intensive, as in *That is so true.* When *so* precedes a modifier, except in comparisons, it means "to the extent" and needs a qualifying *that* clause to complete its meaning: *We were so concerned about the decline that we called in a consultant, We were so disappointed in the product that we discontinued it.*

Formal contexts also call for *so that*, rather than *so* alone, to introduce a clause expressing purpose or result: *They left before dawn so that they could avoid traveling during the hottest part of the day; She had practiced for weeks, so that the audition went well.*

In negative comparisons *so . . . as* sometimes seems more natural than *as . . . as*, to American ears at least, and grammar teachers used to insist on this usage: *I am not so sure as you that we have made the right decision.* Today, however, you have a choice; according to Copperud, *not so sure as* and *not as sure as* are "equally acceptable."

so-called Don't use *so-called* before a term enclosed in quotation marks. Both the adjective and the quotation marks call attention to a special usage, and one or the other can do the job alone.

so that See **so, so that.**

subjunctive mood The subjunctive mood is easier to use than to contemplate. Even grammarphobes terrorized by the term usually shift smoothly into the subjunctive whenever it's appropriate. In contrast to the indicative mood, which designates the ordinary verb forms used in factual statements, the subjunctive expresses certain conditions, wishes, demands, and resolves. But because most subjunctive forms are the same as the indicative ones, writers often use the subjunctive without recognizing it. In the past tense the only variation for the subjunctive is that *were* replaces *was*, but the past subjunctive refers, not to the past, but to the present or future. In *If you wanted better grades, you would work harder*, the verb in the *if* clause is the past subjunctive. In the present subjunctive the only differences are that *be* replaces *am, are,* and *is* and that the base form of any verb—the form that follows the infinitive sign *to*—replaces the third-person singular form, as in *Long live the queen* instead of *Long lives the queen.*

The *long live* formula, expressing a wish, is one of the many frozen phrases in which the subjunctive still appears. Others include *Thy will be done, Come hell or high water, If need be, Heaven help the working girl, The devil take the hindmost, God damn it,* and *So be it.* Such expressions are survivors from a time when the subjunctive was more common than it is now. Today we are more likely to express conditions, wishes, and resolves with the auxiliary verbs *may, might, should, would,* and *let: If the need should arise, May heaven help us, Let it be so.*

If clauses are the primary occasions for giving the subjunctive any thought. A condition that differs from the one known to exist—a condition contrary to fact, in other words—still requires the subjunctive: *If I were younger, I might consider the move; If she were a man, you would have behaved differently; If I were there, you would not have asked that question.* But writers with a vague notion about using *were* instead of *was* in an *if* clause sometimes resort to the subjunctive when the clause expresses a condition that may or may not exist, not one known to be contrary to fact. The *was* is appropriate, for example, in *If he was at the meeting, he has undoubtedly heard the news.* He may have been there—we don't know. Thus the clause states a possibility, not something obviously not true. Here are a few more *if* clauses in which the indicative verb form is correct: *If she was responsible, she should admit the fact; If you are correct, we still have a chance; If a customer fails to pay within two months, we extend no further credit.*

In addition to contrary-to-fact conditional clauses, some noun clauses require the subjunctive. Since wishes are often for contrary-to-fact conditions, it is not surprising that they are expressed in the subjunctive mood: *I wish you were here, I wish I were taller, She wished she were rich.* But you can also use auxiliary verbs to state wishes: *I wish that it would rain, I wish that I could be with you.* Finally, the subjunctive is appropriate in formal recommendations, resolutions, commands, and statements of necessity: *We recommend that the department institute scholarships for language study abroad and sponsor an exchange-student program.* The same *that* clause could also follow *Be it resolved, We demand,* or *It is essential.* But you would ordinarily use a less elevated formulation: *We asked the department to institute . . .* or *It is essential for the department to institute. . . .*

take See **bring, take.**

than If, as most modern dictionaries report, *than* can be a preposition, the *me* is legitimate as well as natural in a sentence like *My sister is older than me.* But the *OED* labels *than* incorrect as a preposition, and most careful writers would still say *My sister is older than I,* construing *than* as a conjunction introducing an elliptical clause. In such sentences the case of the pronoun that follows *than* depends on the role the pronoun plays in the implicit clause: *You helped Elizabeth more than I [did]* or *You helped Elizabeth more than [you helped] me.* If you mentally complete the clause after *than,* you can tell which case is appropriate. Or you can note the terms being compared, the terms that *than* links: the pronoun after *than* belongs in the subjective case if it contrasts with the subject or subjective complement of the preceding clause and in the objective case if it contrasts with an object. The compared terms are *you* and *I* in the first of the last two examples and *Elizabeth* and *me* in the second. (Those who consider *than* a preposition would use *me* in both examples, so that the comparison would be ambiguous.) Because *than* is commonly treated like a preposition colloquially, the subjective case may sound stilted when it is required after the conjunction. If so, Fowler suggests, add the appropriate verb after the pronoun: *My sister is older than I am.* But the phrase *than whom* lies outside these considerations. In constructions like *a politician than whom none has greater integrity* the *whom* is inviolable—a sacrosanct, idiomatic exception to the rules of grammar (at least for those who will not recognize *than* as a preposition). Nowhere is it written, though, that you have to resort to such awkward wording.

 Than, of course, does not always precede a pronoun that has distinctive subjective and objective forms to clarify what terms you are comparing. Sentences like the following are at least technically misleading, and an unintended comparison can be ludicrous: *I take better care of our pets than the children. Chimps resemble human beings more than other apes. In interpreting dreams, analysts reveal more about themselves than their patients.* Confronted with this sort of ambiguity, you should complete the implicit clause or at least add enough words to identify the contrasting terms: *I take better care of our pets than the children do; Chimps resemble human beings more than they do other apes; In interpreting dreams, analysts reveal more about themselves than about their patients.*

 Comparisons involving *than any* need special watching. In the following sentences they are illogical: *I like Sardi's better than any restaurant in the theater district. Jefferson is taller than anyone on the team. Mary Pickford was more popular than any young actress of her day.* If Sardi's is in the theater district and Jefferson is on the team and Mary Pickford was a young actress of her day, they are all being judged as superior in some way to themselves. To correct such slips, add *other* or *else: better than any other restaurant, taller than anyone else on the team, more popular than any other actress.*

that, which Relative clauses that modify inanimate nouns or pronouns usually begin with *that* or *which.* The force of idiom and the weight of critical opinion favor *that* for restrictive, or defining, clauses and *which* for nonrestrictive, or nondefining, clauses. A defining clause identifies the word it modifies, limiting it to a particular member of a group, as in *The novel that the instructor recommended depicts the Civil War period in the South.* It is essential to the meaning of the sentence. But a nondefining clause in no way restricts the sense of the word it describes; it simply provides supplementary information. In *The novel* Gone with the Wind, *which the instructor recommended, depicts the Civil War period in the South,* the relative clause is expendable, as the enclosing commas indicate. Since the title identifies the book, omitting the *which* clause would not alter the meaning of the sentence.

 The usage critics who recommend *that* for defining clauses argue not that *which* is incorrect but that restricting *which* to nondefining clauses helps convey necessary information. Although nondefining clauses are set off by commas and defining clauses are not, Follett, for one, considers the mere omission of commas an inadequate means of signaling a defining clause. In a sentence like *Banks which offer investment counseling are another possible source of help*, he argues, readers cannot be sure that the absence of punctuation is significant. Maybe the writer forgot to put in the commas, or maybe the typesetter overlooked them. Is the intended meaning "Banks, which offer investment counseling," or "Banks that offer investment counseling"? In other words, are all banks a source of help or only those that offer counseling? If the clause began with *that* instead of *which*, the question wouldn't arise.

And if *that*, not *which*, were mandated for restrictive clauses, a comma would not have proved so powerful a weapon for conservative Republicans in composing their party's 1984 platform. That policy statement, as originally drafted, took a position against "any attempts to increase taxes which would harm the recovery. . . ." In other words, the party opposed increasing taxes that would be harmful, thus implying that some tax increases might not be. But the right-wing faction succeeded in inserting a comma before *which*, thus making the clause nonrestrictive and expendable, putting the party on record as opposing all tax increases and explaining, parenthetically, that they would harm the recovery.

While *which* may not sound amiss in a restrictive clause, *that* is virtually impossible in a nonrestrictive clause. If you're not sure that you can distinguish between the two types, try substituting *that* whenever you write *which*. If it fits, chances are that the clause is restrictive and the *that* preferable. This test, incidentally, should also indicate whether or not the clause needs enclosing punctuation.

In two circumstances, however, restrictive clauses must begin with *which* instead of *that*. *Which* is necessary for a clause describing either the demonstrative pronoun *that* or, usually, a noun preceded by the demonstrative adjective *that*. *That that must be done should be done quickly* is clearly impossible; *which* must replace the second *that*. *That deed that must be done* is similarly objectionable, but in such sequences changing the second *that* to *which* is not always your only alternative. Instead, you can sometimes substitute an article for the first *that* and keep the second one: *A deed that must be done should be done quickly*. *That* is also impossible when the relative clause begins with a preposition. Whether or not the clause is restrictive, *which* is the only choice in such contexts; *the issue on which they disagree, the book from which we quoted, the events with which the report deals*. But *that* is all right—preferable, in fact—when the pronoun is the object of a preposition that it precedes: *the issue that they disagree on, the book that we quoted from, the events that the report deals with*.

If a sentence has more *that*s than it can handle, switching to *which* for a restrictive clause should be a last resort. You usually have options. You can sometimes leave *that* implicit at the head of a clause or reduce the clause to a word or phrase. The following sentence, with its five *that* clauses, poses an editing challenge: *He said that they realized that an institution that failed to comply with the law that bars discrimination in schools that receive federal funding might have to close.* But revising leaves only one: *They realized, he said, that an institution* *might have to close if it failed to comply with the law banning discrimination in federally funded schools.*

that, who Either *that* or *who* can refer to a person. Use whichever comes naturally or sounds better in a given context: *No one that the agency sent us is as qualified as Mary Johnson, who has exactly the sort of background we're looking for.* In modern expository prose *who* seems almost inevitable in a nonrestrictive clause, but there's nothing wrong with it in a restrictive clause either: *Anyone who takes on this project must be highly motivated.*

that of This phrase often appears where it doesn't belong and fails to show up when needed. It's excess baggage in *One popular sport in Michigan is that of figure skating*, but it's absent without leave in *The appeal of the country was stronger than the city*, where its omission after *than* results in an illogical comparison. Here are two more examples, the first with a superfluous *that of* and the second without a necessary one: *Often the earliest symptom is that of a sharp chest pain. But this pain is not like a heart attack.*

they, them See **I, me.**

too In the sense of "overly," *too* sometimes seems inappropriate when it precedes a modifier denoting a negative quality. Calling a plan *too prone to failure*, for example, may prompt the question "As opposed to *just prone enough?*" When *too* appears without any indication of the standard for judging a quality excessive, it implies "to a degree greater than desirable." Thus if you write *The candidate is too arrogant*, you suggest that there is a desirable degree of arrogance. To avoid this implication, either omit *too* or qualify it: *The candidate is too arrogant to have much chance at the polls.*

A more common stricture condemns the *not too* construction, as in *I am not too sure about that.* Barzun, for one, criticizes it as ambiguous and illogical. He considers it a corruption of a proper *none too* or *not any too* phrase, which he translates as "not overly in any degree" and sees as an "ironic rendering" of "not at all." Thus we understand *I am none too certain of that* to mean "I am not at all certain." But when *not* replaces *none*, the meaning can be either "I am not more certain than I can be" or "I am not very certain." Even though the second meaning is almost always what the writer intends and the reader understands, formal contexts call for greater precision. Besides, such statements are sometimes more than theoretically ambiguous. *I cannot be too optimistic about your chances*, for example, can mean either "your chances are so good that I can't feel more optimism than they warrant" or "your chances are so slight that I can't be very optimistic about them." *I cannot recommend him too highly* is similarly open to interpretation. To clarify such sentences, eliminate *too* if it means "very" (*I cannot recommend him highly*) and eliminate both *not* and *too* if it means "overly" (*I can recommend him highly*).

uninterested See **disinterested, uninterested.**

unique See **absolute modifiers.**

upon See **on, upon.**

us See **I, me.**

use, utilize, employ Discussing _utilize_ as a synonym for _use,_ the 1982 edition of the _American Heritage Dictionary_ finds the word "especially appropriate" in the sense "of making useful or productive what has been otherwise or of expanding productivity by finding new uses for the thing or person involved." While _use_ can have the same meaning, it has broader applications. _Use_ works wherever _utilize_ does, but _utilize_ cannot always replace _use._ Except when _employ_ "applies to the hiring of persons," it is broadly "interchangeable" with _use._ Both _employ_ and _utilize_ are overworked, pretentious substitutes for _use._ If you use them at all, be sure to restrict them to their narrow meanings. But while a sentence like _We employ 200 workers_ is unexceptionable, critics regard _utilize_ as pompous even when used as dictionaries define it: _Scouts learn to utilize two sticks of wood to start a fire._ Modern style guides all insist that plain is better than fancy, and you should always at least consider replacing _utilize_ and _employ_ with _use._ If you've used _use_ already and don't want to repeat it, you usually have other options. The scouts, for example, can _learn how to start a fire by rubbing two sticks of wood together._

verbal See **oral, verbal.**

very, very much When used as an adverb, _very_ intensifies other modifiers; in traditional grammar it cannot qualify a verb, since an action cannot be intensified, but it can qualify an adverb of manner or quantity that modifies a verb. Thus, while you can't talk very, you can talk very much. The problem of _very_ versus _very much_ arises with past participles—the verbals that characteristically end in _ed_—which both function as adjectives and combine with auxiliaries to form passive-voice and perfect-tense verb phrases. Since _very_ can modify an adjective, can it also modify a past participle? Or does the participle remain verb enough to require _very much_? Can we, for example, be very interested, or must we be very much interested?

Concern about this issue may be fading, but the use of _very_ with certain past participles is so strongly condemned by some critics—Follett, for example, finds it offensive to "finer ears"—that you may want to heed the proscription. While the _OED_ permits _very_ in the sense of "very much," illustrating the usage with quotations from writers like Joseph Addison and George Eliot, the 1982 _American Heritage Dictionary_ still warns against it.

A few past participles have developed into full-fledged adjectives with separate dictionary entries. You can, for instance, be very depressed about the economic outlook and very worried about your investments. But most _ed_ forms retain too strong a verbal identity to accept the intensive _very._ They require proper adverbial modifiers like _much, well,_ and _highly:_ A performance can be very much enjoyed but not very enjoyed; a proposal can be very well received but not very received; a book can be very highly praised but not very praised.

The participles that cause trouble are borderline forms like _encouraged, appalled,_ and _surprised._ Some critics sanction _very_ with such words, accepting them as adjectives; others insist on _very much._ And the dictionary may be no help on this issue. _Known_ and _chosen,_ for example, are labeled as adjectives, but celebrities are well known, not very known, and words are well chosen, not very chosen. The prudent course is to use an adverb like _much_ or _well_ whenever it sounds all right. Maybe you can get away with *I am very interested,* but you're clearly safe with *I am very much interested.* A participle that unquestionably qualifies as an adjective won't accept *very much* as a modifier. *I am very much tired,* for example, is impossible. Fowler suggests another consideration, pointing out that a participle is at its most adjectival when it directly precedes the word it modifies and at its most verbal when it follows an auxiliary verb and precedes a *by* phrase. Thus the context may influence your decision on *very* or *very much*: *One very surprised winner said that she had been very much surprised by the news.* The issue may seem complicated, but it should rarely arise. Intensives like *very* are usually unnecessary at best. If you choose the right words, your writing can be *very*-free.

via Though *via* is often treated as a synonym for *by, through,* or *by means of,* its strict meaning is "by way of," interpreted geographically, and careful writers use it only in describing travel routes. You can go via the Thruway or the Taconic Parkway if you're traveling to Albany from New York City, but you can't go via bus or car. You should avoid *via* in other senses where a precise and proper alternative sounds natural, but if you insist on sending letters via air, you might be accused of pedantry.

we See **I, me.**

which See **that, which.**

while Insisting that *while* means only "at the same time as," English teachers of the past did not allow it in the sense of "although" or "whereas." Though this restriction has been eased, *while* still seems ludicrous when it's used in a way that contradicts the notion of simultaneity: *While our ancestors took months to cross the continent, we do it in five hours.* But modern critics accept *while* for "although" or "whereas" if the temporal meaning fits as well: *While American women did not fight in World War II, they produced the weapons and supplies that ultimately brought victory.*

who See **that, who.**

who, whom In traditional grammar, the choice of *who* or *whom* depends on the same principles that govern *I* and *me.* But *who* and *whom* often occur in convoluted contexts that complicate this choice. You have to analyze the syntax before you can determine the proper pronoun. Since conversation offers no opportunity to formulate sentences in advance, no less to parse them, most critics condone "misuses" in speech. ("Who shall I make this check out to 'om?" asks a dowager in an old *New Yorker* cartoon.) In fact, even though writers have time to figure out the appropriate case, more and more commentators are questioning the value of bothering. In his 1975 essay "Whom's Doom," Theodore Bernstein forswore his allegiance to the old rules and proposed abolishing *whom* except directly after a preposition. When he presented this recommendation to twenty-five "experts" ("teachers, consultants on dictionaries, writers, and knowledgeable linguists"), he found fifteen who agreed with it, four who equivocated, and six who disagreed. But the 1983 edition of *Webster's New Collegiate Dictionary,* pointing out that language watchers have been predicting the "demise of *whom*" since at least 1870, reports that the word "shows every indication of persisting quite a while yet." Even some of Bernstein's supporters admitted that they probably wouldn't act on his proposition.

Using *whom* correctly—if you too want to be on the safe side—is not so difficult as all the fuss about the word suggests. You do have to analyze sentences now and again, but the process may be good for you. If you're concerned about the effect of Velcro, calculators, and digital clocks on today's children, you should be able to see the value in mastering *whom.* Lionel Trilling commented to Bernstein that the effort involved in figuring out the proper case "tends to build character," and Russell Baker said that "having to pause at the thorn patch of *whom* assists the cause [of] having less said better."

The proper use of *whom* involves determining what role the pronoun plays within its own clause. If you mentally isolate the clause from its context and then put it in normal subject-verb-object order, the structure becomes clear. Use *whom* if the pronoun is the object of a preposition, even one at the opposite end of the clause; the direct or indirect object of a verb; or the subject of an infinitive. Use *who* if the pronoun is the subject of a finite verb or the subject of a subjective complement. It may help to substitute a personal pronoun for a questionable *who* or *whom.* Use *who* where you would use *I, we, he, she,* or *they;* use *whom* where you would use *me, us, her, him,* or *them.*

The following sentences are correct:

1. *The police have captured the man who they think robbed the bank.* The pronoun is the subject of *robbed,* not the object of *think.* Always use *who* if you can delete the subject-verb combination immediately after the pronoun and still have a coherent statement. Try this test on the following sentences, all of whose *whom*s should be *who*s: *The customer summoned the waiter whom she remembered had served her. She asked him whom he thought had poured vinegar into her wine glass. He didn't know how to answer this woman, whom the manager had said spelled trouble.* In these examples, incidentally, *whom* is wrong in everybody's book. Neither natural nor correct, it's the conscious choice of those with "a little learning." They recognize that *whom* is appropriate for a direct object but fail to see that the pronoun is not the object of the verb that directly follows but the subject of the next verb. The *who* clause as a unit functions as a direct object or a modifier.

2. *The official whom they wanted to question would not cooperate.* Here omitting the subject-verb combination after the pronoun would not leave a sentence that makes sense. Isolating the clause *whom they wanted to question* and putting it in normal order, *they wanted to question whom,* shows that *whom* is correct. It can only be the object of *question.*

3. *Is there no one whom we can trust?* Rearranged in subject-first order, *whom we can trust* becomes *we can trust whom,* and the choice of *whom* becomes obvious—unless, of course, *trust who* sounds as right to you as *trust whom.* If so, try the personal-pronoun-equivalency test. If you would say *trust him* rather than *trust he,* you can be sure that *whom* is appropriate.

4. *The editor whom she had hoped to work with rejected the manuscript.* Without *she had hoped,* the sentence would be gibberish. The relative clause is *whom she had hoped to work with*—in normal order, *she had hoped to work with whom. Whom*

is the inevitable choice once you recognize the pronoun as the object of the preposition *with*.

5. *The prize goes to whoever finishes first.* The rules governing *who* and *whom* also apply, of course, to *whoever* and *whomever*. Here, since the subordinate clause is already in normal order, you should have no trouble recognizing *whoever* as its subject, provided that you identify the clause as *whoever finishes first*, not as *to whoever finishes first*. The preposition *to* belongs to the main clause; the *whoever* clause is its object. If you can't tell whether a pronoun alone or a whole clause is the object of a preposition, you can quickly find the answer by analyzing the clause. Ask how the pronoun relates to the verb. In the example *who* has to be the subject of *finishes*; thus it cannot also be the object of the preposition. The structure is different when a relative clause begins with a preposition. For example, in *The man to whom I was talking is my neighbor*, the clause *to whom I was talking* modifies *man*. Within the clause the subject and verb are *I was talking* and *whom* is the object of *to*. The preposition is clearly part of the clause; without it, *whom I was talking* makes no sense.

6. *He is not the person who I thought he was.* Without *I thought*, the sentence remains structurally sound (though the omission affects the meaning), and you can recognize *who* as a subjective complement if you begin the clause with the subject: *he was who*. *Was* serves only as an equal sign, linking the subject *he* with its complement *who*, and both sides of the equation belong in the same case. The grammar changes if you express the same idea in these words: *He is not the person whom I thought him to be.* Here the *I thought* is indispensable. In the rearranged clause, *I thought him to be whom*, the infinitive *to be*, like other forms of the verb, links grammatical equals, but since the subject of the infinitive (*him*) is in the objective case, the complement (*whom*) is also objective.

7. *Whom do you want to handle the deal?* When you begin the sentence with the subject, you get *You do want whom to handle the deal?* As the subject of the infinitive *to handle*—the person doing the handling—*whom* is correct. You wouldn't say *Do you want I to handle the deal?* would you?

The most common mistakes in the use of *who* and *whom* are *whom* as the subject of a verb that does not immediately follow the pronoun (*I did not see the dancer whom the critics said was the best*), *whomever* as the subject of a clause that functions as the object of a preposition (*He asked to speak to whomever is in charge*), and *who* as an object of a nonadjacent verb or preposition (*Who did she ask for? He invited someone who I considered rude*). Though an ungrammatical *whom* takes some effort, an ungrammatical *who* comes naturally, and it is the least objectionable of these errors—in speech, in fact, it is quite acceptable. But if a correct *whom* seems stilted in writing, revise the sentence to avoid the need for it. Don't simply substitute an ungrammatical *who*.

All this to-do over the letter *m* may seem foolish. The choice of *who* or *whom* rarely affects clarity, masterpieces of literature contain "mistakes," English has a long tradition of shedding case endings, and in many contexts the spoken *whom* is at least obsolescent. The arguments against maintaining a *who–whom* distinction are strong, and the experts willing to defend the old rules are dwindling. But, esteemed or not, the traditional usage remains dominant in literate writing. Few authors who know the rules are willing to flout them.

who am, who are, who is The verb that follows the subject *who* agrees with the word the pronoun stands for. Thus you would say *I who am; you, we,* or *they who are;* and *he* or *she who is.*

whom See **who, whom.**

whose, who's Like the personal pronouns, *who* has no apostrophe in the possessive case. The possessive form *whose* can mean either "of whom" or "of which." In other words, it can refer to either a thing or a person: *that book, whose jacket James designed* is as acceptable as *that woman, whose jacket James designed. Who's,* of course, is the contraction of *who is.* It's *Guess Who's Coming to Dinner,* not *Guess Whose.* . . .

will See **shall, will; should, would.**

wise The word *wise,* in the sense of "knowing," legitimately combines with nouns to form such adjectives as *streetwise,* "wise in the ways of the street," and *money-wise,* "knowledgeable about money." The suffix *wise* is also unexceptionable when it means "in the manner of," "in the direction of," or "in the position of," as in *crabwise, otherwise, clockwise,* and *edgewise.* But faddish compounds in which the *wise* suffix means "regarding" strike most language watchers as dubious at best. Critics denounce terms like *policywise, qualitywise,* and *decisionwise* not only as jargonistic and overworked but as cumbersome and needless. Though such words theoretically provide short and snappy alternatives to long-winded phrases like *from the standpoint of* and *with regard to,* they often do nothing of the sort. *Careerwise, he was going downhill,* for example, is hardly superior to *His career was going downhill;* nor is *Enrollmentwise, colleges are now healthier than they were a decade ago* better than *College enrollments are higher than they were a decade ago.*

would See **shall, will; should, would.**

Selected Bibliography

Primary References

Barzun, Jacques. *Simple and Direct: A Rhetoric for Writers.* New York: Harper and Row, 1975.

Bernstein, Theodore M. *The Careful Writer: A Modern Guide to English Usage.* New York: Atheneum, 1977.

Follett, Wilson. *Modern American Usage: A Guide.* Edited by Jacques Barzun. New York: Hill and Wang, 1966.

Fowler, H. W. *A Dictionary of Modern English Usage.* 2nd ed. Revised by Sir Ernest Gowers. New York: Oxford University Press, 1965.

Strunk, William, Jr., and E. B. White. *The Elements of Style.* 3rd ed. New York: Macmillan, 1979.

Other Works Cited

Baron, Dennis E. *Grammar and Good Taste: Reforming the American Language.* New Haven: Yale University Press, 1982.

Bernstein, Theodore M. "Whom's Doom" (1975). Reprinted in *Dos, Don'ts & Maybes of English Usage.* New York: Times Books, 1977.

Boyd, Julian, and Zelda Boyd. "Shall and Will." In *The State of the Language.* Edited by Leonard Michaels and Christopher Ricks. Berkeley: University of California Press, 1980.

The Chicago Manual of Style. 13th ed. Chicago: University of Chicago Press, 1982.

Copperud, Roy H. *American Usage and Style: The Consensus.* New York: Van Nostrand Reinhold, 1980.

Fowler, H. W., and F. G. Fowler. *The King's English.* 3rd ed. New York: Oxford University Press, 1931.

Levin, Samuel R. "Comparing Traditional and Structural Grammar." *College English* 21 (1960): 260–65.

Markwardt, Albert H. *American English.* New York: Oxford University Press, 1958.

Miller, Casey, and Kate Swift. *The Handbook of Nonsexist Writing.* New York: Lippincott & Crowell, 1980.

Nunberg, Geoffrey. "The Decline of Grammar." *Atlantic* (December, 1983): 31–46.

Shaugnessy, Mina P. *Errors and Expectations: A Guide for the Teacher of Basic Writing.* New York: Oxford University Press, 1977.

Simon, John. *Paradigms Lost.* New York: Clarkson N. Potter, 1976.

Zinsser, William. *On Writing Well: An Informal Guide to Writing Nonfiction.* 2nd rev. ed. New York: Harper and Row, 1980.

Handbooks of English

Crews, Frederick. *The Random House Handbook.* 2nd ed. New York: Random House, 1977.

Ebbitt, Wilma R., and David R. Ebbitt. *Writer's Guide and Index to English.* 7th ed. Glenview: Scott, Foresman, 1981.

Hodges, John C., and Mary E. Whitten. *Harbrace College Handbook.* 9th ed. New York: Harcourt Brace Jovanovich, 1982.

Kierzek, John M., and Walker Gibson. *The Macmillan Handbook of English.* 6th ed. Revised by Robert F. Willson, Jr. New York: Macmillan, 1977.

Perrin, Porter G. *Writer's Guide and Index to English.* 4th ed. Revised by Karl W. Dykema and Wilma R. Ebbitt. Glenview: Scott, Foresman, 1968.

Watkins, Floyd C., and William B. Dillingham. *Practical English Handbook.* 6th ed. Boston: Houghton Mifflin, 1982.

Intensive Grammars

Curme, George O. *English Grammar.* New York: Barnes and Noble Books, 1947.

Jesperson, Otto. *Essentials of English Grammar.* University: University of Alabama Press, 1964.

Dictionaries

The American Heritage Dictionary, Second College Edition. Boston: Houghton Mifflin, 1982.

The Oxford English Dictionary (OED). 13 vols. Oxford: Clarendon Press, 1888–1933.

Webster's Ninth New Collegiate Dictionary. Springfield: Merriam-Webster, 1983.

Webster's Third New International Dictionary. Springfield: G. & C. Merriam, 1961.

Webster's II: New Riverside University Dictionary. Boston: Houghton Mifflin, 1984.

Index

But he, but him, 170–71
By, placement problems and, 36–37

Can, may, 171
Cannot help but, 171
Center around, 171
Certain, 171–72
Circumlocution, 1, 13–14. *See also* Wordiness.
Circumstances, in the or *under the*, 172
Clarity. *See* Ambiguity.
Clauses, xvi, 141
   adjective, xviii, 40–41, 113–14, 152. *See also*
     Relative clauses.
   adverbial, xix, 41–42, 114–17, 154
   as complements, xvii, 144, 149
   conditional (*if*), 196–97
   dependent (subordinate), xvi, xix, 146, 156
   elliptical, 30, 70, 156
   independent. *See* Independent clauses.
   modifying, xvii, 146
   nonrestrictive (nondefining), 152–53,
     198–200. *See also* Nonrestrictive elements.
   noun, xviii, 149, 152
   as objects, xvii, 144
   parallelism and, 66
   position of, 40–43
   prepositions and, 155–56
   relative. *See* Relative clauses.
   restrictive (defining), 153, 198–200. *See also*
     Restrictive elements.
   short, 125, 126
   as subjects, xvii, 144
Collective nouns, 84–85, 94, 149
Colons, 133–34
   capitalization after, 134
   dashes vs., 135–36
Comic, comical, 181
Commands, 140
Commas, 109–31
   absolute construction and, 117
   addresses (street) and, 121
   adjective phrases and clauses and, 113–14
   adjectives separated by, 111
   adverbial phrases and clauses and, 114–17
   appositives and, 113–14
   complementary phrases and, 118
   compound objects separated by, 124
   compound subjects separated by, 124
   compound verbs separated by, 120
   conjunctions and, 110, 120, 122–23, 126–29
   conjunctions separated from independent
     clauses by, 126–28
   contrasting elements and, 117, 123
   dashes or parentheses vs., 134–35

   dates and, 121
   direct address and, 117
   discretionary (optional), 124–29
   ellipsis indicated by, 121
   emphasis and, 126
   exclamations and, 117
   "fault" or "splice," 131–32
   harmful, 122–24
   helpful, 110–21
   however and, 126
   idiomatic constructions and, 122
   independent clauses and, 110, 126
   interjections and, 117
   interpolations and, 117–19, 125–26
   interrupters and, 117–19, 128–29
   introductory modifiers and, 119–20, 125,
     126–28
   misreading prevented by, 120–21
   nonrestrictive modifers and, 112–19
   pairs of, 112, 122
   parallel items and, 110–11, 121, 124, 126
   parenthetical elements and, 111–20
   proper nouns and, 113–14
   quotations and, 122
   repeated words separated by, 121
   restrictive vs. nonrestrictive elements and,
     112–19, 124, 129, 199
   semicolons vs., 131–33
   serial, 110–11, 124
   short phrases or clauses and, 125, 126
   specialized functions of, 121–22
   summary of uses of, 129–31
   that and, 128–29
   titles of persons and, 122
   transitional words and, 117, 125–26
   verbs separated from objects by, 124
   verbs separated from subjects by, 123
Comparatives
   absolute modifiers and, 164–65
   adjective, 153
   adverbial, 154–55
Compare to, compare with, 172
Comparisons
   as and, 166–68
   elliptical clauses and, 70
   like and, 168
   of any and, 187–88
   parallelism and, 69–72
   possessives and, 70
   so . . . as and, 196
   than and, 197–98
Complementary phrases, commas and, 118
Complements, xvii, 142–44
   clauses as, 144, 149
   compound, 145